GW00711478

INSIGHT GUI

Barcelona

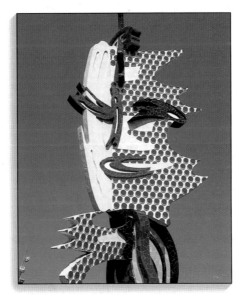

APA PUBLICATIONS

Part of the Langenscheidt Publishing Group

L

ABOUT THIS BOOK

Editorial
Project Editor
Pam Barrett
Managing Editor
Emily Hatchwell
Editorial Director
Brian Bell

Distribution

UK & Ireland
GeoCenter International Ltd
The Viables Centre, Harrow Way
Basingstoke, Hants RG22 4BJ
Fax: (44) 1256 817988

United States
Langenscheidt Publishers, Inc.
46–35 54th Road, Maspeth, NY 11378
Fax: (718) 784 0640

Canada
Thomas Allen & Son Ltd
390 Steelcase Road East
Markham, Ontario L3R 1G2
Fax: (1) 905 475 6747

Australia
Universal Press
1 Waterloo Road
Macquarie Park, NSW 2113
Fax: (61) 2 9888 9074

New Zealand
Hema Maps New Zealand Ltd (HNZ)
Unit D, 24 Ra ORA Drive
East Tamaki, Auckland
Fax: (64) 9 273 6479

Worldwide
**Apa Publications GmbH & Co.
Verlag KG (Singapore branch)**
38 Joo Koon Road, Singapore 628990
Tel: (65) 6865 1600. Fax: (65) 6861 6438

Printing

Insight Print Services (Pte) Ltd
38 Joo Koon Road, Singapore 628990
Tel: (65) 6865 1600. Fax: (65) 6861 6438

©2002 Apa Publications GmbH & Co.
Verlag KG (Singapore branch)
All Rights Reserved
First Edition 1990
Third Edition 2000
Updated 2002

CONTACTING THE EDITORS
We would appreciate it if readers
would alert us to errors or out-
dated information by writing to:
**Insight Guides, P.O. Box 7910,
London SE1 1WE, England.
Fax: (44) 20 7403 0290.**
insight@apaguide.demon.co.uk

www.insightguides.com

This guidebook combines the interests and enthusiasms of two of the world's best known information providers: Insight Guides, whose titles have set the standard for visual travel guides since 1970, and Discovery Channel, the world's premier source of nonfiction television programming.

The editors of Insight Guides provide both practical advice and general understanding about a destination's history and culture, about its institutions and people. Discovery Channel and its website, www.discovery.com, help millions of viewers to explore their world from the comfort of their own home and also encourage them to explore it first-hand.

This completely updated edition of *Insight: Barcelona* is carefully structured to convey an understanding of Barcelona and its culture as well as to guide readers through its sights and activities:

♦ The **Features** section, indicated by a yellow bar at the top of each page, covers the history and culture of the city and region in a series of informative essays.

♦ The main **Places** section, which is indicated by a blue bar, is a complete guide to all the sights and areas worth visiting. The places of special interest are coordinated by number with the maps.

♦ The **Travel Tips** listings section, with an orange bar, provides a handy point of reference for information on travel, shops, restaurants, accommodation and much more.

The contributors

This new edition of *Insight Guide: Barcelona*, based on an earlier version by Andrew Eames and Don Murray, was produced by **Pam Barrett**, a London-based editor who has lived in Barcelona. The book has been completely updated with the invaluable help of a number of Barcelona experts.

The history chapters are the work of **Dr Felipe Fernández-Armesto**, an eminent historian who has written his own book on the city: *Barcelona: A Thousand Years of the City's Past*.

The chapters on Language and Literature, and People, and the Cosmopolitan City feature, were the work of **Valerie Collins**, a Barcelona-based writer who also updated and revised the chapter on the Making of Modern Barcelona. For the Language chapter, Collins built on

foundations laid by Catalan novelist **Carme Riera**.

Ann Michie, another long-term Barcelona resident, wrote about Art and Inspiration. Architect **Jane Opher**, who has an insider's knowledge of the recent developments in the city, contributed the chapter on Architecture and Design. The essay on Gaudí and Modernism and the Sagrada Família feature, originally by **Don Murray**, were adapted for this edition by **Caroline Bugler**. The feature on football was written by **Lluís Permanyer**, a one-time staff writer for *La Vanguardia* newspaper.

The Places section was revised and thoroughly updated by **Judy Thomson**, who also wrote several brand new chapters, essential in a city that has changed so much in a few years. She was able to draw on earlier contributions from **Marcelo Aparicio**, **Xavier Martí** and **George Semler**. A writer and translator who has lived and worked in Barcelona for many years, Thomson contributed to the earlier edition of the guide, and also updated the entire book in 2002.

The Insight colour features on Festivals, Markets and the Parc de Collserolla were also Thomson's, as were the new chapters on Catalan food and wine.

The Travel Tips section was completely overhauled and updated by **Rachel Thalmann** and edited by **Nicholas Inman**.

Many of the stunning pictures included in the book were taken by a regular Insight photographer, **Bill Wassman**, but there are also valuable contributions from **J. D. Dallet**, who has appeared in many Insight Guides over the years, **Don Murray** and **Annabel Elston**.

Map Legend

▬▬ ▪ ▪	International Boundary
▬ ▪ ▬ ▪	National Park/Reserve
▬ ▬ ▬	Ferry Route
Ⓜ	Metro
▨	FGC Suburban Rail Line
✈ ✈	Airport: International/ Regional
🚌	Bus Station
Ⓟ	Parking
❶	Tourist Information
✉	Post Office
† ✝	Church/Ruins
†	Monastery
☾	Mosque
✡	Synagogue
🏰	Castle/Ruins
∴	Archaeological Site
∩	Cave
⚊	Statue/Monument
★	Place of Interest

The main places of interest in the Places section are coordinated by number with a full-colour map (e.g. ❶), and a symbol at the top of every right-hand page tells you where to find the map.

CONTENTS

The Casa Milà, Gaudí's massive apartment house.

Insight on ...

Information panels

Travel Tips

Places

AN INSISTENT CITY

Barcelona is a vibrant city, and proud of the characteristics

that make it so different from the rest of Spain

Barcelona is the heart, lungs and legs of Catalonia, Spain's leading economic region. Covering 6.3 per cent of the nation's land mass, Catalonia supports over 15 per cent of the Spanish population and produces 20 per cent of the country's gross domestic product. Well over two-thirds of the region's people live in the greater metropolitan area of Barcelona itself (5.1 million in total), jammed between the hills of Tibidabo, Montjuïc and the sea. Barcelona is the largest city on the Mediterranean seaboard.

Catalonia was once a state in its own right and regained a large measure of freedom under the Statute of Autonomy of 1978, although many Barcelonans still believe that the region deserves more autonomy than it currently has. Certainly, Barcelona is like no other Spanish city. It has its own language and its own culture and customs. The Barcelonans are unlike most other Spaniards; they are more introverted, more work-motivated, more self-conscious, more difficult to get to know.

Perhaps because of the Catalans' own insistence on separateness, their city has had a turbulent past, caught between the various powers of Europe in its allegiances against Madrid. Its growth reflects the eras of its greatest successes, from the Roman walls, through the Gothic Quarter to the palaces of the 17th century, right up to the 19th-century Eixample. In its latest phase, the city reflects the work done for the 1992 Olympic Games, acknowledged around the world as a triumph for Barcelona. It transformed the waterfront, created whole new districts, and was a catalyst for a series of building works and changes to prepare the city for the 21st century.

The Catalan character has had to go underground so often that it expresses itself in surprising ways. The Eixample is studded with the extrovert work of modernist architects, of whom Gaudí was one; the Barcelona football club – a sort of unofficial army – has a vociferous following which sees goals as assertions of the Catalan identity. At times the club has been virtually shut down by central government, or forced to share its best players with Madrid.

All in all, it is a city with a lot to offer, and one which has repeatedly and insistently thrust itself to the forefront of European cities. In *Don Quixote*, Miguel de Cervantes wrote: "Barcelona: innately courteous, offering shelter to the travel-weary, hospitals for the poor, home for the brave, revenge for the offended, reciprocating friendship and unique in situation and beauty." This insistent city is worth getting to know. ❏

PRECEDING PAGES: Barcelona's sparkling new harbour; the big dipper in Tibidabo park; sinuous windows of Gaudí's Casa Batlló; street performers. **LEFT:** *castellers*, human towers, celebrate the festival of Mercè.

ONA

TANTO MONT

Fco PEDRO NAVIA

Decisive Dates

EARLY HISTORY: C.700 BC–AD 476

c. 700 BC The Iberians settled in the fertile area between the Riu Llobregat in the south and the Riu Besòs in the north.

c. 600 BC The sails of Greek ships appear off the Catalan coast. Among the Greek settlements is Empòrion on the Costa Brava.

c 300 BC The Carthaginians penetrate as far as Catalonia. According to legend, Hamilcar Barca, father of Hannibal, occupied the city and called it Barcino.

264 BC After the First Punic War between the Romans

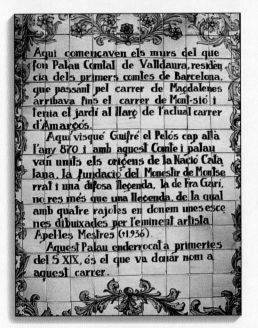

and Carthaginians, there are far-reaching changes in the Iberian peninsula. Hannibal crosses the Ebro in 217BC, and Romans troops capture Barcelona. In the peace treaty of 197BC the Carthaginians have to relinquish their Spanish conquests.

200 BC to AD 300 Barcelona flourishes, and a magnificent city centre develops around the forum (today Plaça Sant Jaume) on the small hill called Mont Táber. Around the time of Christ's birth, under the rule of Emperor Augustus, Barcino is renamed Julia Augusta Favencia Paterna Barcino.

AD 476 The Visigoths enter eastern Spain. They call the territory extending south of the Pyrenees Gotalonia. They capture Barcelona and make it their Iberian capital.

MOORISH RULE TO THIRTY YEARS' WAR: 700–1659

c. 700 The Moors from North Africa invade Spain, and capture Barcelona in 713, but are forced out by the Franks in 801. Arabic influence on culture and architecture in the city is considerably less marked than in other parts of Spain.

8th–9th century The Franks found the Marca Hispanica (Spanish Marches). Wilfred the Hairy (Guifré el Pelós) unifies the areas south of the Pyrenees. He establishes the House of Barcelona, a dynasty that continues in an unbroken line for 500 years.

985 Almansur, Grand Vizier of the Caliph Hisham II, reaches Barcelona and destroys large parts of it. Help comes from the Franks who free the city again.

988 The county of Barcelona declared autonomous. The foundation is laid for the development of an independent Catalonia. This year is celebrated as the birth of the state.

1137 Berenguer IV, Count of Barcelona, marries Petronilla, heiress to the throne of Aragón. Barcelona becomes capital of the kingdom of Aragón and enjoys a period of great success.

1284–95 The Catalan–Aragón confederation extends its power over the whole Mediterranean area as far as Naples 1295. A number of splendid buildings are erected in Barcelona (the Barri Gòtic).

14th century Catalonia has become one of the Mediterranean's most formidable maritime nations; its rule book, the Consolat de Mar, governs sea trade.

1359 The Corts Catalanes, a representative body of nobility, citizens and priests which had met at irregular intervals since 1289, is officially appointed. A body later given the name Generalitat de Catalunya, is set up to regulate financial and political matters.

1395 Annual competitions for poets and troubadors, called the Jocs Florals, are initiated. They are based on a similar event in Toulouse.

1469 Ferdinand II of Aragón marries Queen Isabella I of Castile, uniting the two kingdoms.

1492 The unification leads to the fall of Granada, the last bastion of the Moors. Under the developing absolute monarchy of the Catholic Monarchs – a title bestowed on Isabella and Ferdinand by the Pope – Catalonia and Barcelona become less important. Trade with the new colonies in the Americas goes via the Atlantic ports. Madrid becomes the national centre, while Barcelona suffers economic decline.

1639 The Thirty Years' War with France: Catalans rise up against the centralist rule of Philip IV, and are supported by the French king Louis XIII. Spanish troops are unable to recapture Barcelona until 1651.

1659 In the Treaty of the Pyrenees, all Catalonia north of the Pyrenees is ceded to France.

AFTER NAPOLEON

1714 Barcelona sides with Habsburgs in the Spanish War of Succession. The Bourbon king Philip V takes the city on 11 September, destroys the whole of the Ribera area, abolishes the Corts Catalanes and has a citadel built. This date (La Diada) is the national day of celebration in Catalonia.

1808 The inhabitants of Barcelona rise up against the French. Napoleonic troops destroy large parts of the city.

1814 onwards The city experiences an economic boom under Ferdinand VII. The industrial revolution has a positive effect and Barcelona becomes Spain's leading centre for technical developments.

1833 The country's first steam-driven engine is working in the city

1848 The first rail connection between Barcelona and Mataró is built.

1854–56 The citadel and the old city walls are razed to the ground.

1860 The building of the new city (Eixample), designed by Ildefons Cerdà, begins.

1873 The first electricity plant is constructed.

1888 Barcelona hosts its first Universal Exposition on the site of the former citadel. Numerous *modernista* buildings are erected throughout the city.

1901–9 Anarchism in the workers' movement results in general strikes by workers in 1901 and 1902, and the Setmana Tràgica (Tragic Week) in 1909, when widespread rioting leads to the destruction of 70 religious institutions.

1914 The Mancomunitat, a Catalan provincial government, is set up and Barcelona recovers administrative power. Industry flourishes during World War I.

1923 The military dictatorship of Primo de Rivera (1923–30) suppresses Catalan freedoms.

1929 A second Universal Exposition is held on the grounds of Montjuïc. Numerous buildings, including the Poble Espanyol, are built.

1931 Under the Second Republic Catalonia is granted its first statute of independence. Francesc Macià becomes president of the Generalitat de Catalunya. The statute barely takes effect, however, as the Spanish Civil War breaks out in 1936.

1936–39 After bitter fighting and widespread destruction, Barcelona falls. Franco's troops enter the city and dreams of independence give way to a harsh reality. Franco forbids the Catalan language and expres-

---

PRECEDING PAGES: Christopher Columbus returns with riches from the New World.
LEFT: a plaque commemorates Wilfred the Hairy.
RIGHT: Pasqual Maragall, city mayor until 1997.

sion of its customs. The statute of autonomy is revoked and the president of the Generalitat, Lluís Companys, is executed in Montjuïc Castle. Immigrants from southern Spain flock to Barcelona in search of work. A resultant uncontrolled building boom creates huge barren dormitory towns with consequent social problems.

1975 After Franco's death a constitutional monarchy is set up by plebiscite. Juan Carlos is proclaimed king. Catalan is recognised as an official language.

1978 Catalan Statute of Autonomy.

1980 Jordi Pujol, leader of the conservative Convergència party, becomes president of Catalonia.

1986 Barcelona is chosen as host for the 1992

Olympic Games. A massive wave of building activity gets under way and continues throughout the 1990s, presided over by Pasqual Maragall, the popular socialist city mayor .

1992 In the year when the 500th anniversary of Columbus' discovery of America is being celebrated, the Olympic Games are held in Barcelona.

1994 The Gran Liceu opera theatre devastated by fire

1995 Port Vell development completed. The Contemporary Art Museum (MACBA) opens

1997 Pasqual Maragall resigns and is succeeded by his deputy, Joan Clos.

1999 The new National theatre is completed. Maragall challenges Pujol in the Generalitat elections but the status quo is retained. The Gran Liceu re-opens. ❑

ORIGINS

From modest beginnings as a small Roman enclave,
the city rose to power under Catalonia's medieval count-kings

Barcelona has all the amenities of a great metropolis and the self-consciousness of a capital city, but much of its dynamism has come from always having had something to prove, and its history is very largely one of achievements incubated in frustration.

Its citizen-historians have attributed to it a myth of ancient splendour not justified by the facts. In the Middle Ages it was the centre of the greatest Mediterranean empire since Roman times, but never became a sovereign city in its own right, like Venice or Genoa. Until 1716 it was the capital of the nominally sovereign Catalan state and twice fought bloody wars against the rest of Spain to defend that status; but it never became a seat of government in modern times and, with the absorption of Catalonia into the Spanish monarchy, came to be ruled by its upstart rival, Madrid.

In the 19th century, it remained the centre of an increasingly vibrant Catalan national culture, which led to further conflicts – some of them bloody – over its constitutional relationship to the rest of Spain.

Mythical beginnings

The Barcelonans have never reconciled themselves to living in a provincial Spanish city and have always given themselves rival identities, be they Catalan, European or Mediterranean. In the past hundred years or so, Barcelona has risen in economic stature to become the heart of the biggest conurbation of the Mediterranean coastline, and in recent decades has been acknowledged as one of the liveliest artistic centres in Europe.

But the rapidity and fragility of this rise, and its dependence on Barcelona's role as a Spanish city, supplying goods to a protected Spanish market, have been obscured by the myths of a long and glorious history of continuous greatness and of fidelity to Catalan tradition.

Although the Roman colony that preceded

the modern city fed well off its "sea of oysters" and had such civilised amenities as porticoed baths and a forum with seven statues, it was a small town covering only about 12 hectares (30 acres). The walls, some of which are still standing, are dwarfed by those at nearby Tarragona and Empùries.

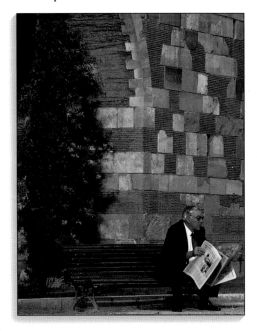

Catalan historians used to imagine antique greatness and "continuity" stretching back to the primeval forebears of modern Catalans. But, although the plain of Barcelona was well populated from neolithic times, and coins minted in the area prove the existence of a pre-Roman urban civilisation, no evidence of continuous settlement of the central site of historic Barcelona, on Mont Tàber, earlier than the 1st century AD has yet been found.

Pre-Roman Barkeno, a name found on early coins, may have been on the hill of Montjuïc: finds from here include an impressive Roman magistrate's seat, set ceremonially in the remains of some sort of stone enclosure.

LEFT: painting on a 16th-century altar urn.
RIGHT: parts of the Roman walls are still standing.

Quiet years

For half a millennium after the end of Roman rule, Barcelona's history remains sparsely documented. Of the occupiers of those years – the Visigoths, the Moors, the Franks – only the first seem to have esteemed the city highly. According to the earliest historian of the Goths, pity for the inhabitants of Hispania, smarting under the blows of less romanised barbarians, moved the Visigothic chief Athaulf to seize Barcelona "with his best men", leaving those "less adept in arms" to occupy the interior. This suggests that Barcelona was thought particularly desirable, or defensible, or both.

VISIGOTHIC POLITICS

Barcelona featured significantly in Visigothic history: Athaulf was assassinated and Amalaric murdered here, and, in 540, the city hosted a synod meeting.

Franks, seems to have been significant only as a frontier garrison or *ville-carrefour*. The city's potential for greatness only began to be realised when it was conquered, late in the 9th century, by the nascent Catalan state. This was a principality of regional importance, with its heartlands close by, its granary in the plain of Urgell and its defences in the mountains. Its warrior paladins adopted Barcelona as their favourite place of residence; they endowed it with religious foundations which stimulated urban growth; they

kept, and sometimes spent, their treasure there; and, as the state developed, they concentrated their court and counting-houses in Barcelona.

Its modest growth during the Visigothic period can be detected in the excavations under the Palau Reial. Evidence here suggests that between the 4th and 6th centuries the *intervallum* between the Roman building line and the ramparts was filled with new constructions. At the same time, streets were narrowed by building extensions. A building of noble dimensions appeared on the present palace site, which may have housed the royal assassination victims.

In this period Barcelona was still without long-distance commerce and, for the Moors and

Wilfred the Hairy

Of the man acclaimed as the "founder" of the House of the Counts of Barcelona, little trace survives in the modern city amid the attractive wine bars and galleries of the narrow Carrer d'Amargos, with its straggling balcony-plants and dangling laundry. You can still find a painted ceramic plaque proclaiming – almost certainly wrongly – that this was the limit of the palace of Count Wilfred the Hairy (who died in 898). The count, in a series of campaigns in the late 870s, united the hinterland of Barcelona with most of the other Frankish counties south of the Pyrenees.

By the early 10th century, Barcelona was already, in a sense, the "capital" of sovereign Catalonia. In about 911, Count Wilfred II chose a house of religion outside the walls for his mausoleum. His neglected grave, marked by an inscription discovered among rubble, deserved better treatment from the Barcelonans; for it was this sort of patronage, bestowing princely status on Barcelona, that began to turn the former hick-town into a medieval metropolis.

For the next 200 years, Barcelona's wealth continued to come mostly from war and the agricultural produce of the plain. Its courtly status was its main source of urban character.

The first known boom happened in the late 10th century. Most historians have assumed that this must have been the result of commercially generated wealth; but there is no evidence to support that conjecture and it is at least as likely that the simple presence of the knights, the court and the growing colony of clergy were the sources of stimulation.

Early expansion

The growth of the cathedral chapter is the first clue to the city's growth: there were six canonries in 974, 17 by 1005. The canons were growing in sophistication as well as in numbers: retiring to houses of their own; acquiring a reputation for erudition; building up libraries – since disappeared – worthy, in one instance, of attracting a reader as famous for his learning as the future pope, Gerbert of Aurillac. They were not the only people building in the city, and the first satellite villages began to grow up outside the walls.

In 989 Barcelona was a target of sufficient prestige to attract a raid by al-Mansur, the predatory vizir of Córdoba. The raid inspired traditional lamentations, with lists of buildings destroyed and martyrdoms incurred; but, except for Sant Pere de les Puelles, which was burned with all its inmates, real losses seem to have been slight and, by encouraging rebuilding, al-Mansur may actually have stimulated the boom. The Moorish threat did not long survive al-

Mansur's death in 1002. By 1010 a raid on Córdoba by an expedition of Catalans dramatically illustrated how the roles of victim and prey had been reversed. The empire of Córdoba was enfeebled by politics at the centre and eroded by usurpations at the edges. In the 1030s it dissolved into small, competing successor-states. Like much of the rest of Christian Spain, Barcelona began to enjoy a bonanza on the proceeds of booty, tribute, ransom, payola and the wages of mercenaries.

An detailed illumination in the *Liber Feudorum Maior* in the Arxiu de la Corona d'Aragó, (Almogàvers 77) shows Count Ramon

Berenguer I counting out coins from a lapful of gold into his hand, for the price of the counties of Carcassonne and Béziers, which he bought. The sort of expansion his forebears could contemplate only by conquest, he could undertake by purchase.

Golden age

By the 1070s, 95 percent of transactions in Barcelona were made in gold – a level never again attained in the city's history. Some of this money was invested in a maritime enterprise which for the next 500 years supplied the city's wealth and formed its character. In 1060, although Barcelona was already a "great town",

---

LEFT: Roman remains in the Plaça Vila de Madrid.
RIGHT: Wilfred the Hairy, who established the House of Barcelona in the 10th century.

according to the fastidious chronicler al-Bakri, the Barcelonans were still hiring their galleys from Moorish ports. By 1080 the counts possessed a fleet of their own, though it may not have been based in Barcelona.

Two charters of Ramon Berenguer III (who ruled 1082–1131) mention what sounds like substantial seaborne trade. In 1104 he granted a tenth of dues paid on "all goods that come in on any ship in all my honour"; in the following year four Jews were granted a monopoly of the shipping home of ransomed Moorish slaves. That some, at least, of this trade was going through Barcelona is suggested by the terms of

Architectural remains

Most of the buildings of this period were replaced in later eras of even greater prosperity: only Sant Pau del Camp, Santa Llucia and the Capella de Marcús remain. For a flavour of what Catalonia was like in the 11th and 12th centuries the visitor must go to the Museu Nacional d'Art de Catalunya (MNAC), on Montjuïc, where the collection of murals transferred from rural churches shows the high quality of work that Catalan money could buy.

In the streets, the explorer can match the map to documents that record the expansion of the 12th-century city. In 1160, Ramon Berenguer IV

privileges Ramon Berenguer granted to Genoa and Pisa in 1116, easing the tolls of goods beached in Barcelona.

Despite the deficiencies of its shoaly harbour, Barcelona was the point of departure for a fleet large enough to attempt the conquest of Mallorca – 500 vessels strong, according to the undoubtedly exaggerated report of the poet of the *Liber Maidiolichinus*, who accompanied the expedition and extolled its heroic failure in epic verse. International commerce continued to develop gradually and in 1160 Benjamin of Tudela reported the presence of vessels of "Pisa, Genoa, Sicily, Greece, Alexandria and Asia" off the beach of Barcelona.

gave permission for a new public bath outside the city wall, where today the Carrer dels Banys Nous (literally "street of the new baths") curves in the spectral shadow of lost ramparts: the profits of this enterprise were divided equally between the count and the Jewish investor.

Merits of conquest

The winds and currents of the western Mediterranean meant that Barcelona had to solve its problem of access to the Balearic Islands, to become a great centre of long-distance commerce, rivalling Genoa and Pisa. An illumination in Barcelona University library shows a leading merchant of the city entertaining the count-king "and the greater part of the nobles of Catalonia" in November or December 1228, and persuading them of the merits of conquering the islands.

In his extraordinary *Book of Deeds*, Jaume I (who reigned between 1213–76) identified his own motives for launching the conquest of the Balearics as essentially chivalric: there was more honour in conquering a single kingdom "in the midst of the sea, where God has been pleased to put it" than three on dry land. To chivalric and crusading satisfactions, the nobles who took part added substantial territorial rewards. The Barcelonans, however, and the other merchant-communities of the Catalan and Provençal worlds, needed little inducement. Their participation is explained by commercial motives: the anxiety to break the entrenched position of Moorish traders and their privileged partners from Genoa and Pisa.

Medieval building boom

Imperial exploits were matched by the city's desire to expand and embellish its territory at home. The new walls of the reign of Jaume I enclosed an area more than 10 times greater than those they replaced.

The cathedral is the dominant monument of the 13th century: the cloister portal, with its obscure carving of harpies and wild men dragging a half-naked, pudge-faced warrior, contrasts with the elegant High Gothic of the west front and the interior.

The early 14th century, when the profits of empire were perhaps at their height, was a time of frenzied building. The chapel of Santa Agata, in the count-kings' palace (the Palau Reial in the Plaça del Rei), was built by Jaume II (who died in 1327). The first stone of the church of El Pi was laid in 1322, that of Santa Maria del Mar, which still has its medieval glazing largely intact, in 1329.

Not even the Black Death – which killed half the city council and four of the five chief magistrates, could dent the city's confidence or interrupt the building boom. Never was the city so spectacularly embellished as in the reign of Pere III (1336–87); he built the vaulted halls – more reminiscent of Italy than Spain – of the

Saló de Cent (Plaça Sant Jaume) and the Saló del Tinell, with its martial wall-paintings, in the palace of the Plaça del Rei. Pere III also rebuilt the shipyards on a larger scale, where galleys for the Mediterranean war effort had been built since the reign of Pere II (1276–85): the eight great bays of the Drassanes at the foot of the Ramblas can still be visited, and now house the Maritime Museum.

Private builders were also active. An example of late medieval urbanisation, the Carrer de Montcada, was driven through the old town in a broad, straight line and promptly colonised by the aristocracy.

THE CITY'S RISE AND FALL

As with so many imperial adventures, Barcelona's acquisition of a Mediterranean empire, beginning in the Balearics and culminating in the conquest of Sardinia, marked the apogee of its achievement and sowed the seeds of its decline.

The marks of both are everywhere in the old city today; its rising success is evident in the great churches begun in the 13th and 14th centuries, and in vast ritual and even industrial spaces that survive from that time; its decline is marked by building works slowed or halted in the 15th century and in the decayed aristocratic streets of the late Middle Ages.

LEFT: Ramon Berenguer III, who presided over a period of prosperous seaborne trade.
RIGHT: a mural commissioned in the age of prosperity.

Price of conquest

The conquest by Barcelona's count-kings, or their subjects, of Mallorca (1229), Ibiza (1235), Sicily (1282), Menorca (1287) and Sardinia (1324), and the territorial extension by a series of treaties from 1271, gave the count-kings something like a protectorate over a number of Maghribi ports: these were the landmarks of an empire of grain and gold, of silver and salt.

As the empire grew, its costs came to exceed its benefits. Mallorca proved a thankless daughter, sustaining a turbulent political relationship with the count-kings and using Catalan knowledge to set up shipping, arms and textile indus-

count-kings' realms moved towards the city, the balance of population shifted. On the eve of the Black Death, Barcelona contained 20 percent of the population of Catalonia. The countryside could no longer keep the armies supplied with men or, perhaps, the city with food. In 1330 Barcelona experienced its first serious famine.

Never was a city more obviously the victim of its own success. Barcelona evinced the classic symptoms of the monster: corpulence induced by overfeeding, tentacles grown to uncontrollable lengths. Yet resolute civic spirit remains etched into the faces of the élite depicted, for

tries in competition with Barcelona's own. The ambition to control the western Mediterranean sea lanes caused wars with Genoa which were wasteful because Barcelona never had sufficient resources to exploit its victories. Above all, Sardinia was Barcelona's "Spanish ulcer"; the city seems largely to have borne the costs of conquest of the island by itself, with little support from the count-kings' other realms, while Sardinian resistance lasted, intermittently, for a hundred years, and exhausted the over-committed conquerors.

The empire which made a metropolis of Barcelona also sucked the rural life-blood out of Catalonia: as the centre of gravity of the

instance, in Lluís Dalmau's *La Verge dels Consellers*, painted in 1443 to project a magnificent image of the city magistracy in the intimate company of heavenly protectors. Today the painting can be seen in the Museu Nacional de l'Art de Catalunya (MNAC) in the Palau Nacional on Montjuïc.

The passing of glory

Like the similar problem of the "decline" of Spain in the 17th century, that of the decline of Catalonia in the 15th has to be treated cautiously. Though it appears with hindsight that by the end of the century the gravity of power in the Iberian peninsula had shifted forever towards the centre, the experience in Catalonia seems too mottled with short-term checks, leaps and lurches to justify the use of a sweeping term like "decline", except in a relative sense: especially in the late 15th century, the neighbouring kingdoms of France and Castile were developing the means to mobilise unprecedented strength. Barcelona's 15th century, however, was at best an "era of difficulties", redeemed only by the extraordinary mental resilience of an indomitable ruling class.

CIVIL WAR

The cataclysmic war of the 1460s had a devastating effect on the city's population; in 1500 there were only 5,765 households – the lowest since the Black Death.

the sympathy of the city governor for a movement to democratise the municipal institutions. The name of the incumbent party, the *Biga*, probably signifies a large beam used in the construction of a building; that of the challengers, the *Busca*, a piece of tinder or bunch of kindling. The names evoke the natures of the parties: the solidity of the establishment, the incendiary menace of its opponents. Their conflict in the 1450s did not in the long run unseat the traditional ruling élite, but left it enfeebled and embittered

In the century after 1360, not a decade went by without a recurrence of plague, sometimes accompanied by famine; from 1426, the yield of the customs and wool tax plummeted and did not recover until the next century. This protracted insecurity led to the first uncontrollable outburst – the pogrom of 1391, when the authorities were powerless to protect the Jews from massacre. In 1436 and 1437 popular agitations were suppressed, but by the mid-century the failures of the city's natural rulers had attracted

LEFT: a 15th-century painting depicts grain being shipped to Constantinople.
ABOVE: the tomb of the conqueror king, Jaume I.

against the count-king Joan II. His unpopularity had grown as he tried to exploit Catalonia in his attempts to meddle in Castile.

Failed pretenders

As a result, no part of the realm entered the rebellion of 1462 more wholeheartedly than Barcelona; none suffered so much from the results. The insurgents' cause became desperate as each of the pretenders they put up to challenge the king died or dropped out in turn.

The siege that ended resistance in 1473 left Barcelona devastated. "We see our city turning into something no bigger than a village on the road to Vic," the *consellers* wrote. ❑

AUTONOMY LOST, RICHES WON

After a series of unsuccessful rebellions, Barcelona entered a period
of industrialisation and steady economic growth

No visitor to Barcelona can fail to be struck by the relative dearth of great Renaissance and baroque buildings. There are examples of grandeur, but they are elusive: the Palau de la Generalitat hides its medieval core behind a Renaissance facade. Most of what survives in the city from the 16th and 17th centuries reflects private effort, rather than public wealth, and a history of slow recovery until 1640, before the terrible era of war, rebellion and the unrest that followed, which was to last until 1714.

Ports and palaces

In the 16th century, Barcelona kept closely enough in touch with fashion to earn praise from almost every visitor who left an account of the city. With the unremitting confidence that has characterised them in every age, the city fathers poured money into the creation of an artificial port in an attempt to recover lost trade: the task would remain incomplete for 300 years, but was never abandoned.

Private patrons like the Fivaller family could build splendid new palaces – theirs still stands in the Plaça de Sant Josep Oriol, where it now houses an Agricultural Association; and the Carrer Ample, which created a conspicuous straight gash across Anton van Wyngaerde's view of the town, was opened as a gesture to Renaissance town planning.

At the beginning of the century, Guicciardini commended the city for its great beauty while lamenting the decline of its commerce; by the end, a measure of recovery can be detected in the terms of Lope de Vega's praise: "Just as a splendid façade enhances the value of a building, so great Barcelona stands at the entrance to Spain, like a portico framing a famous threshold." This was despite the fact that the city was allowed no share of the rich booty plundered in Central and South America by Spain's

conquistadors. Joan II's son, Fernando II, had married Isabella of Castile in 1469, creating a powerful alliance rich enough to finance Columbus's first voyage in 1492. When Fernando succeeded to the Aragonese throne in 1479, Catalonia became increasingly regarded as merely an annexe of Castile.

Royal neglect

Barcelona's decline in the 16th century coincided with the progressive loss of the courtly status which, before the rise of the city's commercial importance, had been the foundation of its fortune. After the extinction of the ruling House of Barcelona in 1412, it had been governed by a series of kings whose main interests were in Castile or Naples and who spent ever less time in Barcelona.

For a while from Fernando II's succession in 1479 – and continuously from 1516 – her counts were also kings of Castile and, as such, were mainly concerned with the affairs of that larger and fiscally more productive country.

LEFT: a magnificent golden casket in Barcelona's Museu Nacional de l'Art de Catalunya.
RIGHT: the shield of a city-state.

Yet the patriciate never lost their sense of ruling the capital of a sovereign principality – or even a quasi-polis, a city with the potential, at least, to be a city-state like Genoa or Venice. From inside the Spanish monarchy, Barcelona affected the status of a foreign power and its representatives swaggered like the emissaries of foreign potentates.

When, for instance, a new viceroy of Catalonia was appointed in 1622, the congratulations of Barcelona were tendered by an ambassador, attended by 200 carriages, in what was rumoured to be the most magnificent procession ever seen in Madrid.

Twenty years earlier, the city's representative at court was honoured with so much pomp that "even the leading nobles of this court," he reported, "say that neither the nuncio of His Holiness himself, nor the envoy of the Emperor has ever been given such a reception… and the Castilians are all amazed that an ambassador who is a vassal of the king should be received with so much honour."

A similar war of protocol was carried on inside the city, where leading magistrates demanded the right to keep their hats on when in the king's presence and disputed seats of honour in church with the viceroy's wife. This was more than just play-acting. The privileges (*privilegis*) and liberties (*furs*) which meant so much to Barcelona were never systematically codified and are difficult to define.

Private laws

The Castilian models, and the different nuances of Castilian thinking, which could not be translated into Catalan, tended to mislead policy makers in Madrid into misunderstandings about the sort of traditions they had to deal with in relations with Barcelona. In Castile, civic liberties normally rested in a charter granted by the king: they were a negotiable commodity, revered but not written in stone.

Barcelona's identity, however, was bound up with the status in law of the principality of Catalonia as a distinct and equal partner in the Spanish monarchy. It had liberties not granted by the Prince as an act of grace, but governed by the *constitucions* – the statutes irrevocable except by the representative parliamentary assembly of Catalonia (the *corts*), which limited royal authority in the principality.

During the early years of the 17th century, when the Spanish monarchy was tottering under the inevitable effects of immoderate greatness, the growing need for money and manpower made the Catalans fearful for their immunities. At a time when to be a very good Catalan was to be "jealous of the country's privileges", the implicit constitutional conflict between the interests of Spain and those of Catalonia was bound to be noticed in Barcelona, where all the institutions of the statehood of Catalonia, inherited from the Middle Ages, were concentrated, and where a substantial body of professional lawyers more or less lived by watching the *constitucions*.

Catalan rebellion

The cost of the Thirty Years' War, and direct hostilities with France from 1635, brought the demands of the monarchy for money and men to a peak and the differences with the principality to a head. When Catalonia rose in revolt in 1640, and the rebels transferred their allegiance to Louis XIII of France, Barcelona was the head and heart of the rebellion.

Like the roughly contemporary rebellion in England, Catalonia's uprising was reluctantly supported elsewhere. An anonymous but representative diarist in Barcelona squarely blamed the king's bad counsel for what he saw as "the greatest sorrow this Principality of Catalonia has suffered" which was "to have been obliged to rely upon a foreign prince, moved by necessity, and to have had no other recourse... May God and most holy Mary be pleased to return us to the grace of our father and lord, Felipe."

However, as had happened in the English war, the Catalan juggernaut rolled out of control. The élite of Barcelona were forced to share power with popular elements, and 16 years of war devastated its land, depopulated its towns

A CATALAN REPUBLIC

In 1640, Barcelona spearheaded Catalonia's attempt to break from Castile and form an independent republic. This led to the disastrous War of the Reapers (1640–52).

In the second half of the 17th century, Barcelona had little respite. Civic-minded optimists like Feliu de la Penya had hardly begun to revive all things Catalan before the French wars of the 1680s and 1690s exposed her lands to yet more campaigns and the city to another crippling siege.

War of Succession

The War of the Spanish Succession was to plunge the entire monarchy into crisis. The Bourbon claimant, Felipe V, arrived in 1702, scattering rewards and promises with

and despoiled its wealth. The siege of Barcelona in 1652 was one of the most desperate episodes of the war and it ended only when the starving citizens were, literally, "reduced to eating grass".

However, the successful army commander, Don Juan José of Austria, was the architect of a remarkable restoration of the broken city and of Catalonia's national pride. Ironically, his very success was to raise the danger of another round of similar conflict.

a lavish hand; but he was suspected of an arbitrary disposition and absolutist plans – an impression finally confirmed in Catalan eyes by his failure to invite the chief magistrates to cover their heads in his presence. His insensitive viceroy, Francisco Fernández de Velasco, blundered into other infringements of the *constitucions*.

Despite the naturally peaceful inclinations of a mercantile élite, the majority of the leading members of Barcelonan society showed themselves to be willing to respond to Velasco's tactless rule with violence. Psychologically inclined to do battle, they were also ideologically equipped to do so.

LEFT: Felipe V, who refused to respect the Catalan statutes. **ABOVE:** the Battle of Lepanto against the Turks in 1571 gave Spain control of the Mediterranean.

Defeat

In Barcelona it seems, appetite for war *vient en mangeant* ("grew with eating"), and the Barcelonans, after their shy start, became the most committed opponents of the Bourbon claimant, Felipe V. They joined the allied cause in a calculating spirit but clung on when all the other allies had withdrawn. They dared beyond hope, endured beyond reason and reaped the usual reward of that sort of heroism: defeat.

The previous recovery of 1652 was fatally misleading: it encouraged the Barcelonans to believe that their liberties could be ventured again and that a hopeless resistance would save

them. The final siege lasted from August 1713 until 11 September 1714, when the city eventually capitulated (a date which is now celebrated by the Diada de Catalunya – Catalonia's national day).

The repression so hotly denounced by Catalan historians after Felipe's victory was actually rather mild: clerics and generals were its only individually targeted victims. But the *constitucions* were abolished; Barcelona was reduced to the rank of a provincial city and suffered the indignity of a permanent garrison – an occupying army was billeted in what is now the Ciutadella Park.

Drive to be rich

Defeat soon turned the energies of the citizens to a mood of *enrichissez-vous*. Although the city was prostrate and the revival slow, the 18th century as a whole was an era of forward-looking prosperity in which sustained economic growth began, thanks to new activities such as direct trade with the Americas, and the beginnings of industrialisation based on imports of American cotton.

Some of the palaces and villas of the Bourbon collaborators can still be seen: the finest of them, the Palau de Comillas, houses the Generalitat bookshop in the Ramblas; around the corner, the palace of the Comte de Fonallar enhances the commercial bustle of the popular shops in the Carrer de Portaferrissa.

The ensemble which probably had the most to say about Barcelona's 18th century was the Barceloneta district, the first industrial suburb, which was begun in 1753 to house a population then beginning to burst out of the dimin-

BARCELONA'S NATIONALIST INSTINCTS

Until 1714 and the final defeat of Barcelona by the forces of Felipe V, there was an almost unquestioned assumption among its people that Catalonia was a sovereign state with a right to secede from a monarchy with ambitions to control the whole country. Catalans' reading of their own history represented theirs as a contractual monarchy, in which the contract between people and prince, once broken, could be repudiated. By the end of the War of the Spanish Succession (1702–13), when Barcelona was under siege and left to fight alone, it was perhaps unsurprising that the city's inhabitants blamed the English for inveigling them into the fight with promises.

In fact, the trick relied almost equally on implicit threats: on 20 June 1705, the day Catalonia signed the treaty with England and Genoa in return for their support in Catalonia's fight for freedom, the guns of the British ships could be heard in local waters. Catalans came to see the episode as a typical instance of England's habit of acquiring by bribery or intimidation an ally she would later abandon. From their point of view, the sixth clause of the treaty was the most important, by which England guaranteed that "now and in the future the Principality of Catalonia shall keep all the graces, privileges, laws and customs which severally and in common her people have enjoyed and do enjoy".

ished city. The tight, neat grid of its streets, in contrast with the traditional cityscape of Barcelona, made it one of the earliest surviving examples of "enlightened" town planning in Europe. In recent years, however, Barceloneta has undergone massive changes.

In pre-industrial Barcelona manufacturing was a mainstay of the economy, but it was confined to the intimate society of the workshop and the master's home, and regulated by the powerful guilds. A visitor to the Museu de l'Història de la Ciutat in the Carrer del Veguer can see the images which dominated the mental world of the guilds: their art reflected pro-

Prestigious guilds

Everywhere the images of saints are reminders that the guilds doubled as devotional confraternities. Evidence of their prestige and wealth can be found around the city today: the shoemakers' palatial hall, for instance, in the Plaça de Sant Felip Neri, decorated with the lion of St Mark, who converted the first Christian shoemaker; the graves of the masters in the cathedral cloister, bearing the same emblem; the sumptuous premises of the silk weavers' guild in the Via Laietana.

The beginnings of the transformation of Barcelona's economy to an industrial basis can

fessional pride and devotion to their patron saints.

The book of privileges of the shoemakers is decorated with a huge but elegant gilt-bronze slipper with tapering toe; the silversmiths' pattern books record, in meticulous detail, the masters' copyright to thousands of intricate designs. The market-gardeners' book of privileges, begun in 1453, is flanked by busts of their otherwise obscure patrons, saints Abdó and Senen, and the gaudily painted coffer in which their relics were preserved.

LEFT: the Generalitat, seat of the Catalan government.
ABOVE: workers at a textile factory, a breeding ground of discontent.

be traced in the decline of the guilds. The 18th-century immigrants – most of them from communities in southern France, where languages similar to Catalan were spoken – "preferred factory life to subjection under the oligarchy of guild-masters".

The bridle-makers had 108 members in 1729, 47 in 1808 and 27 in 1814; the decline occurred during a period when the population of the city trebled and was at its most acute at a time of war and high demand for harnesses. In the textile industry, which was directly affected by reorganisation into factories, the decline was even more spectacular. By 1825, the cloth-dressers had only three members left, none of whom had either studios or workshops – indeed, all were too old to work.

In the last quarter of the 18th century a number of economic indicators accelerated. The rate of increase in wages between 1780 and 1797 was double that of Madrid. Manufacturers' profits, which had already doubled between 1720 and 1775, more than kept pace. When an English traveller visited in 1786, he was particularly impressed by the Bernis factory, which employed 350 operatives making woollen cloth for America; the following year, English economist and agrarian reformer, Arthur Young, could hear "the noise of business" everywhere.

The Peninsular War

After the defeat of the Spanish fleet at Trafalgar in 1805, and the abdication of King Charles IV of Spain, Napoleon put his brother Joseph on the Spanish throne. He attempted to win over the Catalans by offering them a separate government, with Catalan as its official language, but the Catalans were having none of it, and supported the Bourbon side throughout the war (1808–14). Napoleonic forces wreaked a great deal of destruction on the region, sacked the monastery at Montserrat, and destroyed a number of churches, before being forced back.

Inevitably, the war and its aftermath interrupted economic progress. Amid post-war unemployment, after a terrible yellow fever epidemic in 1821, the city council of Barcelona lost its habitual optimism and expressed public doubts that the city would ever recover. In fact, though recovery was socially painful, it was complete: in 1836, the first steamship rolled off the slipway of Barceloneta; and in 1848 Spain's first railway linked Barcelona to Mataró.

Social side effects

Working-class degradation and unrest accompanied economic change. The pattern of life in Barcelona in the mid-19th century was of fitful mass violence and intermittent plague. Ildefons Cerdà (the urban planner who was to create the Eixample and transform Barcelona) surveyed the working-class way of life in the 1850s and found that a diet of bread and potatoes, enhanced with the odd sardine, was all an average family could afford. Observers blamed the cholera epidemic of 1854, which claimed 6,000 lives, on overcrowding in insanitary conditions.

Disorder incubated with disease, and riots became a regular feature of the summer of 1854. Increasingly, they took on revolutionary proportions. The rioters' targets gradually changed: there had been various disturbances in the 18th century – in 1766, 1773 and 1789, when the targets had been grain speculators and the military service quotas. The insurgents of 1835 also attacked steam-powered factories, representatives of the government, and houses of religion; the disturbances of 1840–42 culminated in a political revolution by a coalition of the disaffected whose only rallying point was the call for protective tariffs: it was suppressed by force.

In 1854 a series of strikes and "Luddite" outrages began in defiance of the spectacularly fast automation of the textile industry. The riots were soon deflected into political channels by the fall of a "progressive" ministry in Madrid; respectable radicals joined the mob in resistance. The barricades of Barcelona were reconquered in the bloodiest scenes the city had witnessed since 1714. A conservative observer noted with satisfaction: "The rebels were massacred as they were captured… The spectacle was magnificent." ❏

LEFT: the rich paraded their wealth in La Rambla.
RIGHT: typical Catalan wall tiles showing the crafts and industries of the town and countryside.

THE MAKING OF MODERN BARCELONA

A strong Catalan identity has emerged from the repression of dictatorship and central government control. The result has been a new era of regeneration

By the middle of the 19th century, the resourceful Barcelonans had rallied and prospered once again. The new bourgeoisie, formed by old families of the urban mercantile aristocracy, cotton and iron industrialists, and makers of fortunes in the Americas, had now come into its own. At the same time, the bourgeoisie allowed the moderate government in Madrid to construct the Spanish state through the Constitution.

Barcelona expands

In this so-called "gold fever" period, trade and industry flourished with the spread of steam power and mechanisation. Gas light was introduced in 1842. Spain's first railway was built between Barcelona and Mataró, 30 km (19 miles) to the north, in 1848. Catalonia was now the fourth largest cotton textile producer after England, France and the United States.

Yet Barcelona was the most insanitary and congested city in Europe. It was still a strategic city, a walled stronghold watched over by two hated military enclaves, Montjuïc and the Ciutadella (the citadel built by Felipe V in 1714 after demolishing 1,262 dwellings for the express purpose). Strict military ordenances banned building outside the walls. Inside, every inch of space was occupied. Not even three major epidemics and violent outbursts of social unrest could stem the population explosion. Barcelona was bursting at the seams.

One obsession united all Barcelonans at this time, irrespective of ideology and social class: the need to demolish the walls and spread out on to the plain. But who was the legitimate owner of the plain outside the walls between the city and the burgeoning towns of Gràcia, Sarrià and Horta?

PRECEDING PAGES: clerics enjoying a game of football on a patch of waste ground. **LEFT:** Catalanism and autonomy became heated national issues.
RIGHT: workers on La Rambla discuss strike action.

Both Barcelona city council and the central government in Madrid felt they had jurisdiction over the building of the new city. In 1851 the council requested from the central government that Barcelona cease to be a stronghold.

Designing the new city

When progressive ideas triumphed in Madrid, the walls were demolished by Royal Order in 1854–56 and the central government then commissioned the idealistic civil engineer Ildefons Cerdà to draw up "Studies for the Extension and Reform of the City of Barcelona".

Not to be outdone, the city council held a competition for alternative projects to build the new city, which were exhibited to the public in October 1859. A project by Rovira i Trias won, whereupon in 1860 Madrid issued a Royal Order imposing Cerdà's plan. The Eixample was built by Cerdà but the council set about discrediting it and, ultimately, destroying it.

The Cerdà Plan extended to the limits of the hinterland towns with an extensive network of crisscrossing streets, parallel and perpendicular to the sea and broken only by two great diagonal avenues. Cerdà's egalitarian but, at the same time, grand layout was not inspired by any historical model; it was a utopian socialist dream, albeit with a scientific basis.

The forward-looking plan showed the corners sliced off from each block, which were designed for better visibility, for Cerdà foresaw the needs of fast steam engines. Only two sides of each block were to be built up, leaving ample space for parks and gardens. Entire groups of blocks were to be left free, too, for public amenities – schools, markets and churches. Passeig de Gràcia, the broad central avenue, was envisaged as a stylish residential street with small gardens.

Most of the criticisms of today's Eixample – that it lacks parks and gardens, for example – are the result of the progressive debasement of Cerdà's plan by the city council. Instead, the ravages of speculative greed held sway, allowing the blocks to be divided into smaller and smaller parcels and completely built up. The unfortunate result was a style and cityscape quite different from Cerdà's original design.

THE 1888 WORLD EXHIBITION

Barcelona's growing prosperity and the exuberance of the age were symbolised by the 1888 World Exhibition. The idea originated with a Galician entrepreneur who had seen the Vienna and Paris exhibitions, and it was taken up enthusiastically by Barcelona's Mayor Ruis i Taulet.

With less than a year to prepare for the exhibition, the city entered a period of frenzied building work. The head of the project, the architect Elies Rogent, incorporated what remained from the recently demolished citadel buildings with the newly constructed Arc de Triomf, celebrating the triumph of Catalan enterprise after so many years of defeat and humiliation.

As well as the buildings and cascade in the Parc de la Ciutadella, Sants and La Concepció markets, the Monument a Colom, the Palace of Justice and the Hospital Clinic were all built during this period. Activity was feverish, with electric light allowing building to go on all night. The Gran Hotel on the Passeig de Colom was built in 53 days, only to be knocked down again as soon as the Exhibition was over, to the astonishment of the young Josep Puig i Cadafalch. The hotel was his "first vision of that great Barcelona for which we are all working". The exhibition opened 10 days late but was a resounding success, drawing exhibitors from 20 countries and attracting well over 2 million visitors.

After the September Revolution of 1868, which swept the Bourbons from the Spanish throne, a period of relative social peace ensued. The movement for the recognition of Catalonia's distinctive institutions and the revival of its language and literature – later to become known as the *Renaixença* (Renaissance) – gained much ground, and Barcelona developed a café society with a flamboyant bourgeoisie. The fall of the monarchy also contributed to the shape of today's city, with the tearing down of the citadel.

GARRISON DESTROYED

In December 1869, the land on which the hated citadel had stood was handed over to the city for development into a public park – today's Parc de la Ciutadella.

The Eixample became the fashionable quarter of the city to which the new merchants and professional classes moved, abandoning the narrow streets of the Gothic quarter. An ambitious and complex policy of annexing the neighbouring municipalities was initiated. By 1897, when the city limits were redefined to incorporate the towns of the immediate hinterland, the official population figure was 383,908.

Antoni Gaudí (1852–1926, *see page 93*) graduated at a time when the city was hungry

A new era

Immigrants now began to pour into the city from the poorer and less industrialised parts of Spain. The establishment of democracy and the proclamation of the republic in 1873 gave an extraordinary impetus to the workers' movement. In the late 19th and early 20th century, the building of the Eixample – and the debasement of the Cerdà Plan – continued apace. Barcelona witnessed a display of capitalism at its most euphoric.

LEFT: Francesc Macià, Republican Generalitat leader.
ABOVE: President Lluís Companys,
RIGHT: an Italian bombing raid on Barcelona's port.

for architects with original ideas, as the new Eixample proprietors began to compete with each other for the most opulent and stylish buildings. The *modernista* style reflected an enthusiasm for new forms in art: the intricate, the elaborate and the capricious set against the coldness and rationality of the machine age.

To counteract the perceived monotony of Cerdà's Eixample, Gaudí, Puig i Cadafalch and others dreamed up breathtaking innovations for both facades and interiors. Domènech i Montaner refused to maintain the alignment within the Eixample grid pattern for his Hospital de la Santa Creu i Sant Pau, a stunning complex incorporating 26 buildings.

Revolution and anarchy

But by now, two separate forces operated in the city of Barcelona, one representing the new Catalan bourgeoisie, who sought modernisation and economic and political autonomy, the other the new class of factory and immigrant workers and artisans, who sought, ultimately, revolution.

Unrest grew with the loss of Spain's colonies and, therefore, the American markets in 1898. Anarchism took hold in the workers' movement. There were general strikes in 1901 and 1902, and in 1909 the city would suffer the Setmana Tràgica, a week of rioting and destruc-

tion, when 70 religious buildings were systematically burned by the anarchists.

Some of these tensions were reflected in the work of the *modernista* artists, the most representative being Ramón Casas (1866–1932), whose oeuvre includes a number of remarkable political paintings (many of which can be seen in the Museu d'Art Modern). His most famous work, *Garrote Vil* of 1893, records the public execution of a 19-year-old petty thief who had cut the throat of his victim. It caused a sensation when it was first exhibited in Barcelona.

For the Catalan painters and sculptors who gathered at the Quatre Gats café (today expen-

BARCELONA AND THE CIVIL WAR

The Spanish Civil War began on 17 July 1936. Barcelona rapidly became a Republican stronghold and it was not until January 1939, after a sustained bombing campaign, that Franco's Nationalist forces captured the city.

Early in the war, anarchists and communist militiamen effectively controlled the city – although the Catalan Nationalist leader Lluís Companys was nominal president of the Generalitat. Companys succeeded in disarming both communists and anarchists in May 1937 when, with the help of police loyal to the Republic, he laid siege to the anarchist-held telephone exchange in Plaça de Catalunya and negotiated a ceasefire between the warring factions.

There was much bloodshed in the city during this time; including the executions of more than 1,200 members of the Catholic clergy. Many churches, too, were desecrated, ransacked or destroyed.

After the 1938 Battle of the Ebro in southern Catalonia, the Republicans were unable to defend the city. Many of those who had been loyal to the Republic fled across the border to France, fearing for their lives as the Nationalist forces drew closer. Savage reprisals followed – around 35,000 people were executed for their part in the conflict, including Companys who was captured in France, returned to Barcelona and shot on Montjuïc hill.

sively restored in the Carrer Montsió), Paris was the capital. As well as a style of painting which emphasised light and mood, Casas and Santiago Rusiñol (1861–1931) brought from there a sense of the cosmopolitan world beyond the Pyrenees. This was the context in which the young Picasso was able to flourish, a context not available anywhere else in Spain.

Repression of Catalonia

In 1914 the Mancomunitat of Catalonia was formed as a confederation of the four Catalan provinces, whereby Barcelona recovered its administrative powers. With World War I the

with increasing repression, and the banning of the Catalan flag and public use of the language.

Meanwhile, work for a second International Exhibition in Barcelona – postponed several times – began, with Montjuïc the main setting for the new buildings. The event also had a decisive influence on immigration: from 1924 to 1930 Barcelona received around 200,000 immigrants, tipping the city's population over the million mark, with an enormous 37 percent born outside Catalonia.

When the left-wing coalition won Spain's 1931 general election, Alphonso XIII went into exile, and the Second Republic heralded a

city saw new opulence generated by supplying the warring countries. But after the war the market shrank, sparking an economic crisis. Barcelona became increasingly chaotic as the social conflict worsened.

Repression by the authorities triggered a period of terrorism practised by both workers and employers, and Barcelona came to be known as the city of bombs. The Catalan bourgeoisie supported the dictatorship of Primo de Rivera, initiated in 1923, only to be rewarded

LEFT: demanding Catalan independence in 1936.
ABOVE: victorious Nationalists in the Plaça de Catalunya at the end of the Civil War in 1939.

major step forward for Catalan aspirations. The socialist leader Francesc Macià returned from exile to become the president of the Generalitat of Catalonia, which won control over the police and the civil service, culture and local government, health and education. What Pau Casals would call "a veritable cultural renaissance" began. The years between 1931 and the Civil War were seen by Catalans as another golden age.

But Macià's ambitious plans for the city were cut short by the military insurrection of 1936. The Spanish Civil War ushered in one of Spain's darkest periods, and under Franco's iron hand the Catalan national identity was subjected to brutal repression.

Local government was in the hands of the collaborationist bourgeoisie, and Catalan culture was once again driven underground. Symbolically, Josep Viladomat's monumental sculptured allegory, *La República*, was consigned to a municipal storehouse.

Legacy of dictatorship

During the dictatorship, the middle classes worked hard, looking after their businesses and making money, firmly establishing Barcelona as the economic capital of the Spanish peninsula. Ironically, it was economic growth that posed the main threat to Barcelona's identity.

city and old neighbourhoods decayed. Access to the city was poor and the deficiency of public transport led to a steep rise in car use (the number of cars owned increased by a factor of 5 in 10 years). With 1,100 km (680 miles) of streets and an estimated 750,000 vehicles crammed within the natural boundaries formed by Montjuïc, the Collserola range and the Mediterranean, Barcelona was choking to death.

The only major force that had worked against Franco in the last two decades of the dictatorship were the communists, who had taken the lead in organising a clandestine union movement which, by the 1970s, was strong

Madrid, which held Spain's purse-strings, had neglected and underfunded "Spain's factory", allowing it to degenerate and lose its identity as vast waves of immigrants, mostly from impoverished Andalucía and Murcia poured in during the 1950s and 1960s, looking for work. The population more than tripled (to 1.8 million), and cheap and nasty housing was thrown up for the newcomers without a thought to infrastructure, amenities or social consequences. The uncontrolled building boom resulted in a ring of densely populated and poorly serviced outlying neighbourhoods, creating tremendous social problems. Shanty towns grew up on the outskirts, while the inner

enough to attempt political strikes. But, as it grew in numbers, the communist movement became ideologically diluted. The union elections of 1975 put apolitical leaders in control of most branches, and "responsible" unionism has been dominant ever since. With the onset of an economic crisis and rising unemployment, for the first time in years, Barcelona experienced emigration.

Autonomy for Catalunya

In the first democratic general elections of 1977, the Socialists and Jordi Pujol's Nationalist Conservative party emerged as the two main forces in Catalonia. The pressure for autonomy continued and in October of that year the president-in-exile of the Generalitat, Josep Taradellas, returned to a euphoric Barcelona after negotiating terms in Madrid.

With the new Spanish Constitution and Statute of Autonomy unveiled in 1978, Catalonia regained a measure of self-government. In the general elections of 1979, the communists won every working-class suburb of Barcelona, and the socialists took control of the city council; in 1980 the nationalist Convergència party was elected to the

A HEAD COUNT

The population of Greater Barcelona has fallen since its peak in the 1960s, and now stands at 4.2 million, with around 1.6 million in the city itself.

were offered for cleaning up facades, green spaces were to be restored, and public amenities built. The differences between the centre and the outskirts would be eliminated and the neighbourhoods preserved as cultural, economic and social units of the city. "Areas of New Centrality" would be created and the outskirts "monumentalised". The Horta Velodrome, Plaça Soller, Parc Joan Miró, Plaça dels Paisos Catalans and Parc d'Espanya Industrial are notable early examples of this policy.

Generalitat – a voting pattern that has continued ever since. The socialist-led council immediately set about tackling the legacy of dictatorship, and came up with radical solutions to the problems left behind, implementing a new, forward-looking urban policy

A policy for regeneration

Under the first democratically elected council, people and their quality of life rather than profit were to be the priorities. Grants and subsidies

LEFT: one of the many people who came to Barcelona seeking work and a better life. **ABOVE:** new homes had to be built to accommodate new citizens.

In 1986 the council made an agreement with the Generalitat for the renovation of significant spaces and buildings. The Caixa de Catalunya savings bank bought Gaudí's Casa Milà (better known as La Pedrera) and set about restoring it to its breathtaking pristine state.

Another key element in Barcelona's regeneration was the hosting of the Olympic Games in 1992. Barcelona's tradition is one of looking forward, so there was nothing new about using a big international event as a catalyst for development, modernisation and beautification of the city. The Universal Exhibitions in 1888 and 1929 had both helped to shape Barcelona. So in the late 20th century, what could beat hosting the Olympic Games and putting the city – and Catalonia – back on the international map where it belonged?

Post-Olympic city

After the euphoria of the Games, the anticlimax and the economic crisis bit hard. It is a measure of the popularity of the charismatic mayor, Pasqual Maragall, that he retained public loyalty even when the crisis necessitated large tax increases. Building work continued, subsumed under neat headings that took the word "*més*" – more – as a guiding thread. Barcelona was to have better communications; it was to be greener, more sporting, more cultured, cleaner, bluer (more open to the sea). In a word, said the Council, "*teva*" – yours.

And it has succeeded. As well as the high-profile undertakings – for example, the restoration of the Parc Güell and the rebuilding of the Liceu (badly damaged in a fire in 1994) – improvements are legion. Between 1992 and 1999, 19 new parks were opened. Between 1991 and 1998 the number of trees in the city rose by 26,680 (with schoolchildren taking part in some of the planting).

The metro network has been extended; a vast plan of action implemented in the Old Town,

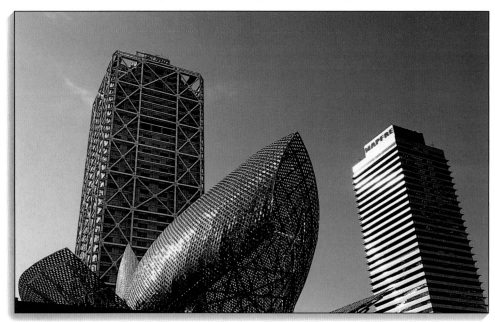

HOW THE 1992 OLYMPICS CHANGED BARCELONA

The city as a whole was viewed as the setting for the Olympics, not just the dedicated Olympic sites, so renovation and development took place throughout Barcelona.

The waterfront, the jewel in the Olympic crown, was at last reclaimed. The desperately needed ring road was built, linking up the four Olympic nerve-centres – Montjuïc, Pedralbes-Diagonal, Vall d'Hebron and the Olympic Village – as well as other points in the city, which eased chronic congestion and gave vastly improved access to the airport, motorways and towns of Greater Barcelona. The radical new road system also included the Túnels de Vallvidrera, a fast route to the towns and cities on the other side of Tibidabo.

Barcelona més que mai – Barcelona more than ever – was the rallying cry. The model for the new millennium was, above all, a city for people, and its citizens were regularly invited on tours to see the day-to-day transformation.

Through years of demolition and detours, dust and din, the city council insisted that it was the Barcelona of the future that was being built. What was involved was far more than a facelift. As Pasqual Maragall (the then mayor) put it: "Changing the outside of the city means changing the city inside. We don't want a city dressed up in clothes it cannot enjoy. Barcelona has to be more alive, more communicative, more accessible and more caring."

with the opening of the stunning Museu d'Art Contemporani de Barcelona (Contemporary Art Museum) in El Raval, and other cultural centres; Port Vell (the old port) has been redeveloped, with the Imax cinema, the Maremàgnum commercial complex, the Aquarium (not only a source of entertainment but a major research centre), and the Museu d'Història de Catalunya; fountains and squares have been created, monuments and facades cleaned and innumerable buildings restored throughout the city; bicycle lanes have been provided on major thoroughfares. The list of improvements goes on.

To the dismay of many, Maragall resigned as

Covering the waterfront

The most obvious and most stunning new development is the waterfront. The Olympic Village has become a smart residential district, the Olympic port a favourite haunt for eating and partying and enjoying the night. Within 10 years the number of visitors to the beaches nearly tripled. With its return to the sea, Barcelona seems to have distilled the essence of the Mediterranean city.

Late in 1998 a local street party was held to celebrate the completion of Carrer Marina, one of the principal arteries of the new Barcelona which finally links the Eixample directly with

mayor in 1997, and his position was taken by his deputy, Joan Clos, who was more of an unknown quantity, but policies have remained largely unchanged. In October 1999 Maragall challenged the conservative Jordi Pujol in the Generalitat elections. But despite Maragall's personal popularity he was narrowly defeated, and the status quo was retained. The election race will be run again in 2003 between Maragall and Pujol's "delfin" Artur Mas.

LEFT: ultra-modern towers and Frank Gehry's copper fish dominate the post-Olympic waterfront.
ABOVE: the Rambla de Mar in the redeveloped Port Vell.

the sea. The new Marina has been transformed into a citizen-friendly boulevard with wider pavements, a bicycle lane, new trees, new traffic lights, new urban furniture. Even the sewer system has been renovated.

Past the Sagrada Família and then the Monumental Bull Ring, Marina takes you through the "Area of New Centrality" around Plaça de les Glòries, the Eixample's main (and nightmarish) road nexus where Diagonal, Gran Vía and the Meridiana all cross.

In inimitable Barcelona style, only a stone's throw from the traditional Els Encants flea market is the gleaming new Glòries shopping centre, the neoclassical Teatre Nacional de

Catalunya and the Auditori de Barcelona – sleek, white, and yet somehow in no way out of place. Marina sweeps over what used to be the railway line: a few blocks along is the old Estació del Nord railway station, now a bus station, sports complex and park. By the bridge is a small football ground, home to many local football teams from the under-provided neighbourhoods. On Saturday morning, tiny tots play five-a-side football right under the bridge, and locals join supporters on the sunny tiers to watch "little league" matches.

From here you get an intimate view of Barcelona's inner life – the washing-festooned

backs of the apartment blocks, complete with pyjama-clad residents watching from their balconies. On the corner of Marina and Meridiana is the new Archive of the Crown of Aragon. The Parc de la Ciutadella is only a short walk away. Continuing down Marina, the brightness of the sky ahead grows, the old buildings give way to the green of the gardens of the Olympic Village to the left and Parc Carlos I to the right. The twin towers stand guard over the Olympic Port and Olympic Village, a gateway to the sea.

There are kilometres of promenades and beaches: to your left, the coastline stretches as far as the eye can see; to your right is the backdrop of Montjuïc.

The future

As you walk north towards the purification plant and Sant Andreu del Besòs with its unmistakeable trio of factory chimneys, you come upon a vast building site. *Veure per creure* proclaim the hoardings on the perimeter fence: seeing is believing. "Diagonal Mar. Barcelona's new neighbourhood. Live here and enjoy views of sea, park and city."

Once again, the city has a target: the Universal Forum of Cultures, otherwise known as Barcelona 2004. Organised by a Consortium formed by representatives of the Generalitat, the council and central government, and sponsored by UNESCO, the forum will have three main themes: multi-culturalism, building a culture of peace, and sustainable urban development. An International Arts Festival will also be staged, the main venue for which will be built at the mouth of the river Besòs.

The river itself will be cleaned and parks created on its banks. Energy and waste treatment infrastructures will be made eco-friendly. The Diagonal Mar development, with new commercial, residential and leisure areas, will be suitably environmentally aware: the whole project is to serve as a model for sustainable urban development.

A new gateway for Europe

All these outward changes and improvements, as well as being vitally important in themselves, are a reflection of the confident, self-assured spirit which guides the city – something that even a casual visitor is likely to pick up on.

Barcelona is not only the capital of Catalonia, but the centre of a much larger Mediterranean region with nearly 15 million inhabitants, from Marseille to Alicante. As such, its future must lie in the entire metropolitan area from the Besòs to the Llobregat. Here, the Delta Plan is providing the impetus for yet more redevelopment – major infrastructure work such as the enlargement of the port and airport and canalisation of the Llobregat river.

The future for Barcelona, says its council, is as the Southern Gateway of Europe, and its vocation is to be the model for all that a European city should be. ❏

LEFT: Joan Clos (right) became mayor in 1997.
RIGHT: keeping up with what's happening in the news: Barcelonans are keen newspaper readers.

PEOPLE

Life in Barcelona is characterised by dynamic commercial activity and a vibrant social scene – tempered, of course, by a dash of Catalan coolness

Catalans in general, and Barcelonans in particular, are famed for their business acumen, their passion for work, and their economic ability. In southern Spain they are seen as cold, tight-fisted and work-obsessed. The laid-back, *mañana* attitude of the popular Spanish stereotype scarcely exists in Barcelona. But then, as the Catalans will never tire of telling you, and as the history of their nation clearly shows, Catalonia and its capital city are definitely *not* Spain.

In Barcelona, 10 o'clock means 10 o'clock, not half past 11, which is bliss if you want to do some serious business. *"Anem per feina"* is a common expression, once pressed into service as a Catalan nationalist election slogan: "Let's get down to work."

Shop till you drop

Like the British, Catalonia has been dubbed a nation of shopkeepers and, indeed, Barcelona has a staggering number of shops. This is not so surprising when you consider that its background is purely mercantile, right back to the Phoenicians and Romans. This bourgeois city was built up through family enterprise and is now being promoted as one of *the* places to shop. The slogan that once graced the carrier bags of the famous Vinçon design store puts it in a nutshell: "I shop, therefore I am."

Barcelona exudes an air of prosperity and elegance and is no longer a particularly cheap city. The standard of living is high, but it has to be paid for, and the work ethic is especially noticeable if you come to Barcelona from elsewhere in Spain. You can see it in the comparatively early closing of bars and restaurants (early to bed) and the very long opening hours of shops. Efficiency, punctuality and deeply serious reliability are of the essence. Barcelona works *very* hard. It visibly bustles with immac-

ulately dressed and groomed urban professionals striding in and out of shops, offices and banks with document cases, folders and parcels, all with mobile phones clamped to their ears – this is life on the fast track.

In Andalusia they have a saying: "The Andalusian works to live, the Catalan lives to

work." But it is not so straightforward as this. For how do we square this view of Catalonians with the wild celebrations of the *Mercè*, for example, the week of festivities around 24 September, the day of Barcelona's patron saint, when giants and fantastical creatures parade around the city on stilts, the night sky blazes with fireworks, thousands dance to rock bands in (usually) rather sedate historic squares, and fire-breathing dragons chase reckless citizens through the streets?

On the other hand, in the cool light of day, Barcelonans actually tend to make self-regulating queues in shops, which comes as something of a surprise in Spain.

PRECEDING PAGES: a Catalan couple celebrate Sant Jordi (23 April); children at Carnival time.
LEFT: a new generation of shopkeepers in El Raval.
RIGHT: entertaining the tourists in La Rambla.

Prudence versus impulse

The Catalans call these apparently contradictory facets of their character *el seny* and *la rauxa*. The former is a combination of prudence, profound common sense and sensible judgement; the latter a fit, impulse or emotional outburst: a kind of attack of wildness.

You can see both sides of the Catalan character in the way they drive, for example. In contrast with other flamboyant cities, Barcelona traffic is, in fact, extremely disciplined and orderly. They keep

> ### AT WORK AND PLAY
>
> Barcelonans party until the early hours in designer bars but still get to the office at 8am to put in a good day's work. They do everything with energy, flair and passion.

of 1992 set out to show the world, Mediterranean high spirits and street life do not have to be synonymous with sloth and inefficiency, and Barcelonans are capable of first-class technology and efficiency without relinquishing any of their vibrancy and zest.

The key to this unique exuberance is that "passionate energy" noted by George Orwell in 1937 as he watched Barcelonan men, women and children build barricades in the civil war-torn city. Whatever they do, they give it everything they've got.

in lane and are very good at indicating. They stop on red, and go on green – fast. But if you hesitate for just a split second, or worse still, stall, you'll be deafened by furiously honking horns. When the traffic gets really snarled up, as it often can, the *rauxa* takes over. Patience is no longer high on the virtue stakes: you have to get going, be on the mark, have your wits about you. *Anem per feina.*

Passionate energy

Barcelonans may work till they're blue in the face, but they're still a Mediterranean people: wild, creative, fun-loving, noisy and gregarious. As Barcelona's celebrated Olympic Games

A clash of cultures

Barcelonans work hard all week, then sit in traffic jams every Friday afternoon so that they can enjoy weekends by the sea or in the mountains. They have little time for the wishy-washy: theirs are the strong, bright primary colours of Miró. They are efficient, enthusiastic, and resourceful. They are adventurous travellers, visiting the most remote corners of the world. They value and cultivate initiative and pioneering enterprise. Barcelona is intensely involved internationally in science, education, ecology and many other fields.

But they certainly come over as reserved and serious, even uptight, beside the large number of citizens originally from southern Spain, those immigrants who flooded in in the 1950s and 1960s in search of work, mostly from Andalusia. Co-existence has often been less than easy, with ethnic, class and cultural differences coming into play: the Catalan middle classes tend to take a dim view of the ebullient non-Catalan working class, and vice versa.

Known by the derogatory nickname of *xarnegos* (the original meaning of the word is a child of a Catalan and a non-Catalan), these "other Barcelonans" form a distinctive group, living in the outlying neighbourhoods of the city, with their own extrovert, boisterous

Barça fans

Barcelona Football Club is more than the city's football team, it is one of Catalonia's flagship institutions: during the repressive Franco years the dice were always very carefully loaded in favour of Real Madrid, and so Barça – "the army of Catalonia" – was the only possible outlet for the collective expression of Catalan national identity – rage, resistance and pride.

Now, Barcelonans and Catalans of all ages, classes, genders, shapes, sizes and persuasions happily unite to dance in the streets in wild celebration when Barça beats Madrid or wins some kind of cup or league. The red and gold of

lifestyle. Barcelona's *Feria de Abril* (April Fair), held near the city, is no longer a pale, homesick imitation of the Andalusian original but a big event in its own right that in recent years has attracted nearly a million visitors.

Moreover, it is largely thanks to the socialist voting habits of this huge community that Barcelona got its municipal act together under the socialist-led city council. And, of course, the second and third generations of these so-called *xarnegos* are Barcelona born and bred.

LEFT: solidarity for the cause of Catalan autonomy is widely felt.
ABOVE: a hotel doorman has to keep up appearances.

the Catalan colours combine with Barça's blue and maroon ("*blau grana*") in a swirling mass down La Rambla. Corks pop and champagne sprays while fireworks fizz and bang far into the night.

Taking to the streets

Like all good Mediterraneans, the Barcelonans are a street people. All it takes is a few tables and chairs squeezed on to a postage stamp of pavement, and there they'll sit for hours over their drinks and *tapas*, apparently oblivious to the fumes, traffic noise and even the dust and din of building works. When it rains, the milling throngs leap into cars and taxis, causing the traffic to "collapse", as they put it, in a cacophony of honking horns. Fortunately, it doesn't rain too often.

Dynamism rules

Barcelonans love dashing around, being busy and generally having lots of irons in the fire. It's their life blood. Ask them how they are and they'll say, breathless with pride: "*Vaig de bòlit!*" – literally, "I'm going like a bullet". One of the highest accolades a Barcelonan can receive is that he or she is *espavilat* or *espavilada*, which may be translated as a dynamic, bright, assertive person who goes out and gets

things done. This proactive zooming around encompasses not only work, of course, but a host of other activities – from culture, shopping and social life to voluntary work, chauffering children, sports... you name it, Barcelonans do it with gusto.

Tradition with a difference

The Barcelonans adhere fiercely to tradition and convention, as anyone witnessing them dancing the *sardana*, Catalonia's intricate national dance, outside the cathedral on a Saturday evening or Sunday morning will confirm. Yet, at the same time, they are refreshingly

DANCING THE SARDANA

The *sardana* is Catalonia's national dance, one which unites old and young, rich and poor, and which, in its present form, grew out of the 19th-century *Renaixença* when Catalans were rediscovering their cultural identity. No festival is complete without it, and every Sunday in every town and village, you will see it performed. In Barcelona the *sardana* is danced in the cathedral square each Sunday at noon and Saturday at 6.30pm, and in Plaça Sant Jaume on Sunday evening. First the band, the *cobla*, starts up: the leader plays a *flabiol*, a three-holed pipe, and has a *tabal*, a small drum strapped to his elbow. The woodwind players are seated, the brass players stand behind them; each tune

lasts about 10 minutes, and, just as you might think it is dying away, it starts up anew.

As the music gets going, a few people in the growing crowd will start to dance, sometimes just a group of four, forming a small circle, in the centre of which will be placed a bag of some kind. Soon others join in, making their own circles or joining existing ones, until the whole square is filled with dancers, linked hands raised high, solemnly counting the short sedate steps, which suddenly change to longer, bouncy ones. Real *aficionados* wear espadrilles with coloured ribbons, but most people dance in their ordinary shoes, be they Sunday best or the ubiquitous trainers.

open to innovation and creativity. These perceived contradictions are only skin deep.

Barcelona has always though of itself as a thoroughly cosmopolitan capital city, which is hardly surprising since, for most of its history, it *was* a capital city. Its traditions are inextricably bound up with Catalonia's defence of its identity as an independent nation – an advanced, cultured and tolerant nation which is always open to new ideas and influences, and constantly looking forward to new horizons.

LIVE AND LET LIVE

Locals refrained from making a particular fuss of the *infanta* Cristina, right up until her marriage (in Barcelona), out of respect for her wish to live an ordinary life.

This translates into a great respect for individual privacy. The *infanta* Cristina of Spain has lived in the Sarrià neighbourhood of Barcelona for years, living, working and having babies in the same way as anyone else, with no intrusive interest from the media or the proud but protective Sarrià locals.

Open-minded outlook

Barcelona is one of the most tolerant places in Spain. Gay and feminist movements were largely pioneered here, and alternative medi-

Catalan independence

This tradition places a high value on independence, both collective and personal. The mild climate allows Barcelonans to live life outside. They are masters of sociablity when out in the streets and squares, bars and restaurants; and they engage fully in the community life of offices and shops, parks and sports fields. However, they are fiercely protective of the privacy that they enjoy in their homes, which they view as a safe haven where they can finally collapse in exhaustion.

LEFT: local artists display their work in the Plaça Sant Josep Oriol. **ABOVE:** a walk in the park.

cine, self-help and New Age culture thrive. There is very little obsession with petty titles and nobility: Barcelona is more of a meritocracy than anything else. And look at Gaudí: far from being the archetypal misunderstood artist, he was positively sought out and encouraged in his fabulous creative flights.

Above all, good humour rules. Take a walk through any of Barcelona's markets. The stall holders have been up since dawn, buying goods at Mercabarna, loading and unloading their provisions, as well as cooking lentils, chick peas and the like. Yet they're filled with vitality and good cheer, cracking jokes and gossiping, their talk peppered with endearments like *rei, reina, maco, maca...* They may be Barcelona shop-keepers to the core, but you get the impression that they really are enjoying themselves.

Putting on a show

This good humour and flair for combining work, fun and creative imagination is the essence of life in Barcelona. On (pre-Lent) carnival Thursday, for example, it's business as usual at the big market on La Rambla – but in fancy dress. A cardinal in full regalia blesses the shoppers trundling their carts in and out. Ballet dancers, black chest hair bristling from their pink tutus, cart crates of potatoes around.

Plumed cavaliers slice ham and chorizo, while Roman emperors weigh out oranges and Moorish princesses gut fish.

But this is nothing. In the old districts of Gràcia and Sants the locals work hard all year round on the elaborate preparations for their *festa major* (annual fête) in mid-August. This time entire streets are turned into theme parks, with prizes for the best. Each street or square organises its own non-stop progamme of events. Old men drag tables and chairs out for chess and dominoes tournaments; the kids get puppet shows and hot chocolate parties; live *salsa* and rock bands play through the night. But during the day it's still business as usual:

except you'll go shopping in Jurassic Park, a space station, a medieval village, or something out of the Arabian Nights.

But the crowning achievement, the very epitome of the Barcelonan's personality, is surely exemplified by the Sant Jordi's day celebrations. Sant Jordi (St George) is the patron saint of Catalonia, and his day, 23 April, which is also the anniversary of both Shakespeare's and Cervantes' death, is celebrated by giving gifts of books and roses. What makes Sant Jordi such an inspired blend of culture, money-making and fun is that it's not actually a public holiday, so everyone is sucked into the festivities as they go about their usual business.

A day of roses and dragons

All the bookshops set up stalls in the streets and squares and give a 10 percent discount. It's a field day, too, for journalists and chat-show hosts, with round-the-clock live TV coverage from La Rambla, including celebrity signings and interviews. Massive public collections of books for hospitals are organised. The city's hawkers and panhandlers make a killing, too, selling roses in the metro stations and at traffic lights instead of cleaning windscreens or peddling strings of garlic. Kids in national dress, miniature hairnets, red caps and espadrilles, greet their caregivers at the school gates with paper roses and paintings of expiring dragons.

In the evening, Barcelona men of all shapes and sizes hurry home from work. Whether dressed in suits and carrying briefcases, plugged into mobile phones or Walkmans, in tracksuits or jeans and T-shirts, each bears a single red rose beautifully wrapped in cellophane and tied with red and yellow ribbon. At night there are discos and shows, parties and dances. And not to let the partying get in the way of business, record sales figures appear on the late-night news, of course.

Peaceful co-existence, solidarity, integration, caring, citizen participation, a plural society – these are just a few of the buzzwords bandied about by Barcelona's planners, policy makers and copywriters these days. Even Barcelona's animals and trees, they tell us, are citizens. And you can't get more integrated, plural and caring than that. ❑

LEFT: stallholders in La Boqueria market dress up at Carnival time.

A Cosmopolitan City

It's the after-lunch chat show on TV3. Over a dozen men and women from the five continents – Indians and Cubans, Africans and Scandinavians, Brazilians and Japanese – and the popular presenter listen intently to a young Chinese talking in Catalan about his experience of life in his adopted country. "My culture is very repressive about boys crying," he says. "I used to have everything bottled up inside. But after living in Barcelona for a year or so, I was finally able to cry. I feel so much better."

Barcelona has always worked magic on foreigners. Having been a busy port since its origins and close to the Crusade routes from western Europe, it has always been something of a melting pot. Most tellingly, Barcelona Football Club was founded on the initiative of the Swiss Hans Gamper and several other foreigners, in 1899. In his memoir, *Homage to Catalonia*, George Orwell chronicled the ideologically boiling Barcelona of 1936, filled with young foreigners from all over the world who had come to defend democracy. In the 1960s, as the Spanish-language publishing capital, the city was home to writers and intellectuals such as Gabriel García Márquez and Mario Vargas Llosa. The 1970s saw a huge influx of South Americans fleeing the vicious dictatorships in Argentina and Chile.

Since Spain's return to democracy, and especially since the break-up of the former eastern bloc and the formation of the EU, the foreign community has continued to grow. Irish pubs, Greek restaurants and Pakistani grocers and mosques abound. And Barcelona's popularity as a venue for trade fairs and international meetings of all kinds make for an exciting cosmopolitan buzz. Barcelona TV gives news broadcasts in Tagalog for the burgeoning Philippine community, while on the Catalan channels a flick of your remote pad will switch you from Catalan dubbing to the original soundtrack of *Dragon Ball*, *Neighbours* and foreign-language films.

Germans, French, British, Italians and Americans have always had a strong presence here. Barcelona's Lycée Français has long been one of the city's top schools. The German School has flourished for decades, as have Swiss, Italian, and several British and American schools. Many other nationalities are represented, too. The Japanese community, in particular, has grown rapidly and also has its own school. The inevitable ranks of teachers, writers, translators and tourist guides are now swollen by painters, actors and singers, as well as acupuncturists, hairdressers, psychiatrists...

As modern technology and telecommunications make physical location increasingly irrelevant, more foreigners are choosing Barcelona for their *pied à terre*, attracted by its mild climate and laid-back but vibrant lifestyle. The city's increasing importance as an international business centre has also translated into an influx of foreigners. To immigrants from the impoverished nations of northern Africa, Barcelona holds the hope of a better future.

Although the latest ranking of immigrants shows the Russian community to be the fastest growing. Population figures are notoriously hard to come by. The last official census (1996) gave 58,385 foreigners in the 10 city districts (not Greater Barcelona) but this only includes holders of residence permits. The real figure may be three times as high. The British Consulate – where registration is not obligatory – reports 15,000 British registered in Catalonia and Andorra, of whom roughly 4,000 are in Barcelona. Figures for other nationalities are similarly imprecise. But, as usual, Barcelona never fails to come up with surprises, such as the Jewish-Argentinian yoga guru, or the Catholic nuns who teach Zen meditation. ❑

RIGHT: new arrivals in the city find many different ways to earn a living.

LANGUAGE AND LITERATURE

*With a long and chequered history, the Catalan language
has a literary tradition dating back to the 12th century*

Despite several attempts to run it underground or wipe it out completely, the Catalan language finally came to the ears of the world during Barcelona's celebrated Olympic Games in 1992.

While spoken Catalan has a sharp, staccato quality that makes it sound very different from the more familiar Spanish, the good news for the visitor concerned with street signs, restaurant menus and so on is that on paper it looks no more incomprehensible than Spanish, French or Italian and a lot less so than German, Dutch and Swedish.

Catalan is a Romance language, derived from the Latin spoken in the Iberian peninsula in Roman times, and is therefore a sister language to Castilian (Spanish), French, Italian, Portuguese, Provençal and Romanian. Words such as *entrada* (entrance), *sortida* (exit), *urgències* (emergencies or casualties), *àrea de servei* (service area), *museu* (museum), *ciutat* (city), *església* (church), *pa* (bread), *carn* (meat), *aigua* (water), are some common examples of words that are easily recognisable.

Golden age

Today Catalan is spoken by at least 6 million people in Catalonia, the community of Valencia, the Balearic Islands, some border areas of Aragón and Murcia, the Roussillon region of France, Andorra (where it is the only official language), and in the city of Alghero in Sardinia. This last fact is not so surprising if we remember that Catalonia was a major commercial and naval power in the eastern Mediterranean in the 13th and 14th centuries: then Catalan enjoyed its greatest political and geographical expansion in the Iberian peninsula, when the Moorish kingdoms of Valencia and Murcia were conquered by Catalonia and Aragón. Mallorca, Sicily, Sardinia, Naples and Athens were also ruled by Catalan dynasties.

LEFT: the Catalan language has long been a hotly debated political issue. **RIGHT:** stacks of independence stickers – in Catalan, of course.

Catalan literature had its own Golden Age – the 15th century, when the language was honed into a splendid tool in both prose and poetry. Most people have heard of *Don Quixote*. But before Cervantes' masterpiece came *Tirant lo Blanc*, a novel of chivalry written in Valencia by Joanot Martorell in the second half of the

15th century. Highly praised by Cervantes and regarded by some critics as the best European novel of the 15th century, *Tirant* has been translated into many languages.

After the War of Succession (1705–15), Catalonia was punished by Felipe V for defending the Archduke Charles: all its government institutions were abolished and Castilian laws imposed. Castilian was now the official language and Catalan was relegated to religious and popular use. But with the industrial revolution and the emergence of a dynamic middle class in the 19th century, a national economic and cultural revival known as the *Renaixença* (Renaissance) took place. The Catalan language was recovered as a vehicle of culture thanks to major figures such as Jacint Verdaguer, Narcís Oller and Angel Guimerà. In 1907 the Institut d'Estudis Catalans was formed for "the re-establishment and organisation of all things relating to Catalan culture". This body drew up standard grammatical and spelling rules for the written language and in 1932 published a dictionary that was not to be updated until the 1990s.

The first third of the 20th century was an exciting, effervescent period, with *Modernisme*

LANGUAGE OF CURRENCY

Catalan is mistakenly thought by many to be merely a dialect of Spanish. In fact, it is a language in its own right – and gave the word *peseta* to Spain and the world.

(those who had escaped a massive purge) in a language that to many was "foreign" and imperfectly known. In some schools, children were even encouraged to report classmates caught speaking Catalan. The result was a generation of Catalan speakers unable to read or write their mother tongue.

A devastating "brain drain" took place, too, as artists, intellectuals and scholars flocked into exile. The Institut d'Estudis Catalans went underground, its remaining members meeting in private homes.

and the more conservative *Noucentisme* producing eminent artists and writers. With the establishment of the Generalitat (Home Government) in 1931, Catalan once again enjoyed the status of official language.

Catalan goes underground

But Franco's victory in the Spanish Civil War (1936–39) put a tragic end to all that. Catalan was banned entirely from public use and took refuge in the domestic sphere. Books, newspapers and films were subjected to draconian censorship. The enforced implementation of an all-Castilian education system meant that Catalan children were taught by Catalan teachers

Censorship eased somewhat in the latter years of the Franco dictatorship. To this period belong the works of Mercè Rodoreda, who lived in exile for many years. Her excellent 1962 novel, *La Plaça del Diamant*, set in the Gràcia neighbourhood of Barcelona, has been translated into more languages than any other Catalan work: its title in English is *The Time of the Doves*.

With the recovery of democracy, Catalan was established alongside Castilian as the official language of Catalonia, the Balearic Islands and the Community of Valencia by the Spanish Constitution of 1978 and the Statutes of Autonomy of those regions. The Catalan government set about implementing a policy of "linguistic normalisation" whereby Catalan was reinstated in all aspects of public life, government, education and the media. In 1990 the European Parliament passed a resolution recognising Catalan and its use in the European Union.

A modern-day language

Now, once again, Catalan thrives in the arts and sciences, the media and advertising. It is used by rock bands and on the Internet, in schools and universities, on TV and radio. Barcelona is a bilingual city, although different degrees of proficiency in different languages are evident.

The rationale behind the Generalitat's controversial linguistic policy is that if Catalan is not actively defended it will decay into a mere local patois. Its detractors allege narrow-minded nationalism verging on the totalitarian. There is some alleged discrimination against non-Catalan speakers in the job market but, in practice, for the most part the two languages happily co-exist, with most Barcelonans (including many foreign residents) slipping instinctively from one to the other, depending on who they are talking to. Courtesy and consideration rule, and very few Barcelonans will refuse to speak Castilian to non-Catalan speakers. ❏

Some older people educated before the Civil War may have an imperfect knowledge of Castilian, speaking a somewhat "catalanised" version of it. While Catalan is almost universally understood, older immigrants from elsewhere in Spain may not speak it. Many middle-aged people educated during the Franco years have difficulty reading and writing Catalan. Those schooled during the past two decades, including second and third generation immigrants, are generally proficient in both languages.

LEFT: book stalls and book shops do a thriving trade in Barcelona.

ABOVE: Jesus Ferrero, one of Catalonia's new writers.

A HAPPY CO-EXISTENCE

The Castilian and Catalan languages seem to thrive side by side in Barcelona. The weird Castilian coinages of teenage slang are happily and effortlessly Catalanised in classrooms, discotheques and Internet chats. Many writers and journalists, as well as actors, singers and TV presenters, work in both languages.

Barcelona's daily newspaper, *La Vanguardia*, is written in Castilian. The Spanish daily, *El País,* produces a Barcelona edition with several weekly supplements in Catalan. And now, thanks to advances in computer translation, the daily *El Periódico* publishes two separate editions, one in each language.

FESTIVALS ARE A TIME FOR SERIOUS FUN

The Catalans' reputation as sober workaholics is seriously undermined when one of the many annual festivals brings the streets to life

Hardly a month passes in Barcelona without at least one excuse to party, or a *festa major* (celebration of local patron saint), which calls for a public holiday, enormous family meals, flowing *cava* and noisy antics in the streets.

Depending on the *festa*'s status it will probably entail dancing *gegants* (giants), *dracs* (dragons), *dimonis* (devils) and legendary beasts, plus processions of dignitaries and mounted guards (*guardia urbana*), *castells* (human towers), as well as *sardanes* (the traditional Catalan dance) in public squares which are taken over by rock or jazz bands at night. Nearly always there is an air-raid of fireworks.

GOING TO EXTREMES

There are also more demure festivals, such as the Fira de Sant Ponç (11 May), when medicinal herbs, honey and crystallised fruits are sold. At the other extreme are the wild festivals like La Mercè, the *festa major* in September, which consists of a whole week of uproarious fun culminating in the *correfoc*, a pyromaniac's dream.

Such manifestations of Catalan culture were repressed under Franco, so since his death a lot of energy and public investment has been put into the reclamation of old customs and traditions. *Festas* are generally well organised, with children's activities and many side events, but the spontaneity remains and the atmosphere in the streets is quite intoxicating.

◁ **CHRISTMAS CHEER**
Children chant to this wooden Christmas *tió* and beat him until he produces presents.

△ **MARKET CARNIVAL**
Carnaval is an excuse to dress up and party before bidding farewell to indulgence during Lent.

△ KINGS OF THE ORIENT
The kings arrive by boat on the eve of Epiphany and parade through the streets tossing sweets to the delighted crowds.

▽ LITTLE DEVIL
Most Catalans grow up loving the noise of firecrackers, fire-spitting dragons and dazzling firework displays.

A DAY OF BOOKS AND ROSES

Sant Jordi, the patron saint of Catalonia, is celebrated on 23 April, a key date in the festive calendar. The long-term President Pujol is Jordi, most families have a Jordi, and on many a street corner or public building are statues of this revered saint.

Children draw pictures of the legend at school: the blood of the slain dragon transmutes into a rose, creating a basis for one of the most commercial yet poetic festivals. Men and women exchange gifts of books and roses in a ritual connected to this also being the anniversary of Cervantes' death. Streets are filled with bookstalls, huge vats of red roses and crowds of people, and the date has now been declared World Book Day.

The elegant Gothic courtyards of the Palau de la Generalitat (home of the Catalan govern-ment) in Plaça Sant Jaume are rose-filled and along with its 15th-century Sant Jordi chapel open to the public on this festive day.

MEDIEVAL GIANTS
During La Mercè, the *egants* from each district parade through the city streets (on stout young shoulders) and meet up in Plaça Sant Jaume.

◁ L'OU COM BALLA
A recently revived tradition at Corpus Christi: an egg dancing in beautifully decorated fountains in the patios of several Gothic buildings, like this one in the Palau de la Generalitat.

▷ HEADY HEIGHTS
The five-year-old *anxeneta* crowning a nine-storey *castell* is the most breathtaking and unmissable moment of a fiesta.

ART AND INSPIRATION

*With a ground-breaking artistic legacy and lively
contemporary aesthetic, art has never been more alive in the city*

To visit Barcelona is to breathe in a complex and exciting visual art history. The streets map the impressions that have inspired three of Spain's prime movers in the story of modern art: Pablo Picasso, Joan Miró and Antoni Tàpies. Ironically, Picasso only spent a few years here before moving on to Paris; Miró also came and went. Only the still-living Tàpies made his permanent base here, but the legacy left by these three great artists is clearly appreciable through the work of young contemporary Catalan artists.

Pablo Picasso

Pablo Ruiz Picasso (1881–1973) was born in Málaga, Andalusia, in southern Spain. His family soon moved on to La Coruña in Galicia before arriving in Barcelona in 1895, where Don José Ruiz took up the post of Painting Professor at the city's La Llotja School of Art.

One department of this school can still be found in Carrer Avinyó, and the story goes that a brothel located in this street inspired the title (and content) of Picasso's landmark painting *Les Demoiselles D'Avignon* (1906–7). Curiously, Picasso and Miró had several teachers in common, most prominently Modest Urgell, a master of light and landscape whose work can still be enjoyed at the Museu d'Art Modern in Ciutadella Park.

Picasso's precocious genius is legendary: at the age of 14 he entered his father's school, completing the month-long entrance exams in a single day. He was to repeat this feat two years later at the Royal Academy in Madrid before abandoning his studies and setting out as a painter in Paris. Meanwhile, he was to encounter and devour Barcelona's artistic circle that met at the now famous Els Quatre Gats (The Four Cats) café. It was here, on 1 February 1900, that Picasso exhibited for the first time.

The 150 drawings of friends included portraits of Jaume Sabartés, Picasso's life-long friend and secretary. The Museu Picasso in Barcelona was initially founded largely thanks to Sabartés donating his personal collection of the artist's work. Picasso also designed the menu cover for Els Quatre Gats, which was

stylistically influenced by Henri de Toulouse-Lautrec (1864–1901). This influence was just one stage of many during Picasso's phenomenal development. Picasso entered his melancholy Blue Period (1901–4) after the death of his Catalan friend, Casagemas, before emerging into the warmth of the Rose Period (1904–6).

Then came the pioneering breakthrough into Cubism, which Picasso was to develop over the next 20 years. He returned to Catalonia on several occasions, to Horta de Sant Joan on the Delta de l'Ebre, and donated a considerable number of paintings (almost all the works from his youth and the *Las Meninas* series from the 1950s) to the Museu Picasso in Barcelona.

PRECEDING PAGES: no object is too humble for artistic embellishment: a bench in Parc Güell.
LEFT: an illustration from Picasso's *pointilliste* period.
RIGHT: the young Picasso, drawn by Ramon Casas.

The 15th-century palace which houses the Museu Picasso is one of several in the same street which serve as art venues, including the Galeria Maeght. The Maeght family opened the Barcelona branch of their empire in 1973. As well as an exhibition space, it includes a bookshop selling their output on such big names as Miró, Tàpies and Chillida. Opposite is the Sala Montcada, a contemporary art space funded by the prestigious La Caixa bank. This large cultural foundation is worth noting for its many and varied exhibitions, particularly in its new cultural centre, CaixaForum, in a magnificent modernista building on Montjuïc.

native" gallery spaces. Only a few remain, but the vast Metrònom space in Fussina still promotes experimental art and video.

Joan Miró

You only have to walk out of Barcelona airport to find one of Joan Miró's large ceramic murals, which was made in collaboration with his friend Llorens Artigas. Born and bred in Barcelona, Miró (1893–1983) was to return here throughout his life, during periods spent either in Paris or Mallorca, where he eventually moved permanently. While studying at La Llotja School in Barcelona he passed through

City of art

Barcelona is exceptional for the quantity and quality of exhibition venues in proportion to its size and is a sheer delight for any visitor interested in art. You will find well-produced catalogues, usually with texts in English, and shows on a par with those in most capital cities. Start at the Palau de la Virreina in La Rambla for information about current shows, or go to the Santa Mònica Centre at the end of La Rambla. Both these venues put on fascinating and sometimes controversial exhibitions, often promoting local national art trends.

At the end of Montcada is the Passeig del Born, an area which has been prolific in "alter-

the Cercle Artistic de Sant Lluc, which still exists today. Here he met Joan Prats, who was to become a friend for life and an art dealer.

Miró was already aware of Dada at this time, though Fauvism, Cubism and Paul Cézanne (1839–1906), in particular, were the major influences on his work. Catalan landscapes featured strongly. *The Farm* (bought by Ernest Hemingway and now in Washington), a major painting of his "detalliste" period, portrays the family farm of Mont-Roig near Tarragona. It features many of his subsequent motifs: stars, everyday objects, insects and animals, as well as showing a characteristic respect for manual labour. Gradually, realism gave way to suggestion and poetry, a progression aided by his contact with French Surrealism.

Like Picasso, Miró suffered greatly during the civil war, such that he produced (among other things) the "Aidez L'Espagne" poster to raise funds for the Republic. Picasso and Miró were friends in Paris, although Picasso at times viewed his friend's curious "constellations" of signs, symbols, women and birds, and deceptively simple palette with amusement. In fact, Miró's works, showing limited use of certain colours, were precisely composed. He also had wide ranging skills, turning his hand to theatre design, printmaking, tapestry, ceramics and

la Santa Creu is worth a visit: around the Romeo and Juliet courtyard is the exhibition hall where Miró celebrated his 75th birthday show; the present Massana School of Art occupies much of the hospital where Gaudí died, and La Llotja School of Art has its printmaking department here.

Showcase for art

The Fundació Miró building must surely be a candidate for any "Best Art Space" award and is testimony to the close understanding Miró had with his friend Josep Lluís Sert, who designed both this and Miró's studio in

bronze sculptures as well as painting and drawing. The magnificent permanent collection at the Fundació Miró on Montjuïc amply covers all of these areas.

You will find evidence of him all over the city, whether walking over his ceramic pavement in La Rambla, admiring the monumental *Woman and Bird* sculpture in the Parc de Joan Miró, or simply noticing the La Caixa bank logo he designed. If you happen upon Carrer Hospital, just off La Rambla, the Hospital de

LEFT: a Picasso design on the exterior of Collegi d'Arquitectes. **ABOVE:** Miró's *Dona i Ocell* (*Woman and Bird*). **RIGHT:** on display at the Fundació Miró.

MIRÓ AND THE SURREALISTS

An apocryphal story about Miró tells of how, in his desperation to be considered a member of the Surrealist group, he went about trying to get himself arrested – the surest way to attain credibility among his peers. Although he was a pacifist by nature, Miró summoned up the courage to walk around the streets of Paris shouting: "Down with the Mediterranean".

Miró was using the Mediterranean as a symbol for the "cradle of Western civilisation", but his choice of words was ironic given the importance of Mediterranean light and colour in much of his work. Of course, no one arrested him and the rest of the group scorned his efforts.

Mallorca. It is a powerful celebration of Miró's work, and showcases a varied programme of temporary exhibitions as well as important works such as Alexander Calder's *Mercury Fountain*, the Joan Prats room and the Homage to Miró section.

Antoni Tàpies

Antoni Tàpies (born 1923) is probably Spain's best-known living artist. His work forms an artistic link between Miró's generation and the new work being produced by the Catalan art world. Tàpies knew Miró and revered his work; the latter's influence is clearly seen in Tàpies'

early work, on view at the city's Fundació Tàpies. The museum, which carefully re-deploys an important Domènech i Montaner building, has a permanent collection of work by Tàpies as well as high quality contemporary exhibitions.

Tàpies is "deeply committed to pluralism and diversity" in art, a fact which is reflected by the excellent exhibitions and the library – accessible to scholars by appointment only. The first thing to strike you when you arrive at the building is the mass of metal wires perched on the roof. This represents a "Cloud and Chair" and is Tàpies' emblem for the building.

THE PHENOMENON OF STREET ART

Street art is prevalent in all areas of the city, thanks to a recent initiative to create new parks and urban spaces. Chillida's newly restored heavyweight sculpture, *Elogi de l'Aigua,* in the Parc Creueta Coll is a fine example. Artist-poet Joan Brossa is ever-present in the city: his giant-sized letters are scattered about the Passeig Vall d' Hebron, and his bronze tribute to "Barcino" (the Roman name for Barcelona) is set in front of the cathedral.

In the Passeig Picasso, Tàpies pays homage to his idol with a large glass cube containing planks, a piano and painted blankets. The cube itself was designed by the great-grandson of Lluís Domènech i Montaner.

On the beach at Barceloneta is Rebecca Horn's reminder of the original beach huts and restaurants which were torn down to make way for the new waterfront development. Models of the huts, cast in bronze and lit like beacons from within, lie piled one on top of the other.

Also down by the port is Lichtenstein's *Head*, just in front of the main post office. This massive piece uses Gaudí's technique of setting broken pieces of ceramic into cement to impressive effect but was originally intended to be placed in the Parc de Collserola so that it could be viewed from a distance. In its present location it rather towers above onlookers on the street below.

A dirty aesthetic

During the repression under Franco, when all Catalan culture was effectively illegal, methods of expression were forced to become highly creative. In 1948 the Dau al Set (Dice on Seven) group was set up, with members Tàpies, Tharrats, Cuixart, Ponç, Puig and Brossa. The "visual poems" of Joan Brossa, a long neglected, now deceased Catalan artist-poet, have been at the forefront of recent Catalan art – in his seventies Brossa represented Spain at the Venice

ART AUTRE

Paintings that rejected figurative or geometric forms in favour of more spontaneous techniques were first dubbed "Informal Art" in 1952 by French critic Michel Tapié.

Povera and Art Autre, or Informal Art, Catalan Informalism combines existentialist ideas with simple materials to result in what is termed a "dirty aesthetic".

This aesthetic still reigns in Barcelona, and materials such as wax, marble dust and varnish are prevalent. If you visit the Joan Prats Gallery in Rambla de Catalunya you will find representative work from contemporary and older generation artists. Or try the commercial gallery street, Consell de Cent, around the corner from the Fundació Tàpies.

Biennale (with Valencian Carmen Calvo). Fascinated by magic, alchemy, the writings of medieval Catalan mystic Ramon Llull and Surrealism, it made sense, given the political climate, for these artists to resort to codes to veil their messages.

Catalan artists also employed street graffiti to voice dissent. The use of signs and symbols, already seen to different effect in Miró's painting, emerged in the work of Tàpies. In keeping with the international movements of Arte

FAR LEFT: Double Face (1956), Palau de la Virreina.
LEFT: Núvol i Cadira (Cloud and Chair) by Tàpies.
ABOVE: Miguel Barceló, an artist with vision.

The art scene today

The Informalist legacy is tempered by Catalan Conceptualism nowadays, as represented in the Museu d'Art Contemporani's (MACBA) permanent collection. There is also work from the Dau al Set group, and the bed-piece hanging at the entrance is, of course, by Tàpies.

There have been changes in the directorship of the museum since its opening in 1995 – the collection was deemed to be outdated and the shows too esoteric, although there have been some huge successes, such as Miguel Barceló's retrospective.

This youngish Mallorcan painter now carries the torch for art in Barcelona. His stays in Mali,

West Africa, have produced some epic "relief" paintings. If you visit the theatre at the Mercat de les Flors and look up at the ceiling you will be able to get some idea of Barceló's vision.

Pere Jaume's panoramic exposition brought in the crowds, as well. His work is great fun, neatly fusing questions of representational art and how to frame it. This theme is on permanent display at the Gran Teatre del Liceu, newly rebuilt and reopened in October 1999, after a fire five years earlier, where Jaume designed the ceiling.

> **URBAN REGENERATION**
>
> In response to the presence of new museums – like MACBA and CCCB – in El Raval, small galleries have sprung up in the gentrified streets of this once run-down quarter.

Susana Solano, another internationally known Catalan artist, finally gained an ample retrospective of her sublime and enigmatic metal constructions here in the late 1990s. Other artists representative of established trends include the painters Xavier Grau, Ràfols-Casamada, Hernàndez-Pijuan and Grau Garriga – the latter combines textiles with painting, in keeping with Catalonia's textile industry and Miró's heritage. Artists who are producing work in multi-disciplinary techniques include Carlos Pazos, José Manuel Broto, José María Sevilla and Sergi Aguilar.

The Museu d'Art Contemporani is right next door to the Centre de Cultura Contemporània de Barcelona (CCCB). This labyrinthine and wonderfully restored building was set up as a force for social, urban and cultural development, promoting shows on themes as diverse as the World of Television, Pessoa's Lisbon, Kafka's Prague, and the Cosmos.

Preserving the past

On Montjuïc hill, not far from the Miró Foundation, the Museu Nacional d'Art de Catalunya (MNAC) is unmissable. The recently restored building offers a fabulous opportunity to marvel at Catalonia's wealth of Gothic and Romanesque painting and sculpture. Many of these items, which include sections of medieval wall paintings and carved beams, were removed from the region's churches and monasteries amid much protest and cries of desecration, but, had they been left *in situ*, they may have crumbled away completely.

Another delight undoubtedly worth including in a visit to Barcelona is the Thyssen-Bornemisza collection. The majority of this collection, first loaned to the Spanish state and then permanently acquired in 1993, is housed in Madrid, but a substantial part of it is exhibited in the Monestir de Pedralbes, a work of art in itself (*see page 223*).

It contains some wonderful pieces of medieval sculpture, and numerous paintings by Florentine Renaissance artists, among which are the exquisite tempera panels of St Claire and St Catherine. The 16th century is best represented by the works of Titian and Tintoretto, and the northern Europeans by Lucas Cranach (1472–1553). Outstanding among the European baroque works in this collection is the enormous *Christ on the Cross*, by Spanish artist Francisco de Zurburán (1598–1664).

"The act of creation in itself transcends the individual to become a vehicle of universal communication, and this is why I believe that...works of art should be accessible to everyone," said the originator of this collection, Baron Hans Heinrich Thyssen-Bornemisza – an attitude which seems to be widely shared in this city. ❏

LEFT: ancient horrors in the Museu Nacional d'Art de Catalunya. **RIGHT:** Barcelona produces 80 per cent of Spain's comic strips.

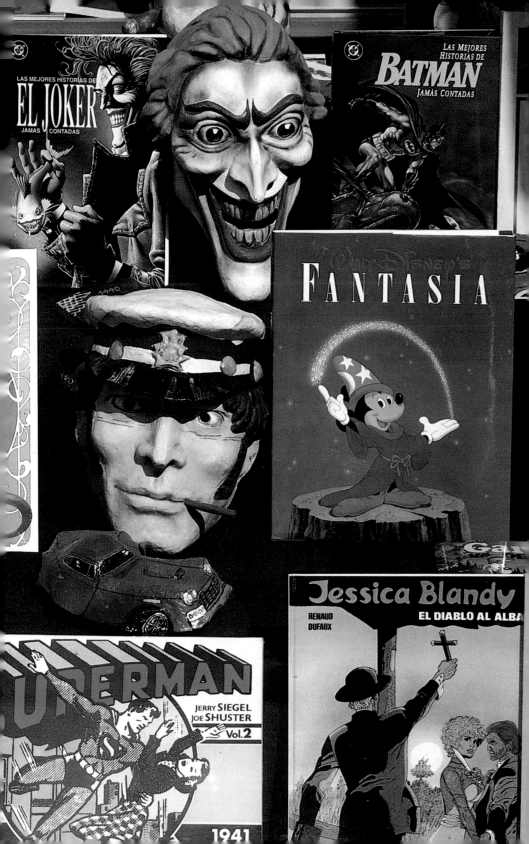

ARCHITECTURE AND DESIGN

A spate of exciting new buildings and urban design projects
has helped to rejuvenate the city's image

In 1999, the Royal Institute of British Architects awarded their annual gold medal – widely perceived to be the most prestigious award for architecture in the world – not to an individual but, for the first time, to a city: Barcelona. The award stated that: "Inspired city leadership, pursuing an ambitious yet pragmatic urban strategy and the highest design standards, has transformed the city's public realm, immensely expanded its amenities and regenerated its economy, providing pride in its inhabitants and delight in its visitors."

Since the early 1980s Barcelona has attracted the attention of architects from all over the world for its commitment to building an astonishing number of fine pieces of contemporary architecture and urban design, and implementing a vast and effective programme of renewal. The effect has been to catapult the city from a dusty European backwater to a shining example of how cities should be managed.

Architecture has always been on any visitor's agenda due to the works of Antoni Gaudí. However, his work, extraordinary though it is, comprises only a small part of the rich architectural heritage of present-day Barcelona. Catalans have long considered architecture as the most durable way of representing their culture. They use it to express their independence of thought and liberalism compared to the rest of Spain, as well as to create a strong connection with the rest of Europe.

Understanding the city

Situated between the sea and the Collserola mountains, and contained by Montjuïc to the south and the River Besòs to the north, Barcelona is the most densely populated urban area in Europe. At its heart lies the *Casc Antic*, the old medieval area which, up until the middle of the 19th century, contained the entire city within its walls – the oldest of which date back

to the Romans. For complicated political reasons the city was not permitted to expand until 1850, by which time the density of population was comparable to 10 times that of contemporary London. In the narrow streets of this area are found most of Barcelona's pre-19th-century buildings.

Catalan Gothic has a distinctive character: dignified but somewhat dour. The interiors of the buildings are often strikingly large. Some are very fine, embodying the secular and religious splendour of the time. Not to be missed are the Saló del Tinell with its enormous arches, in the Palau Reial Major, the Museu Marítim/Drassanes, where the galleons of the Armada were made and, of course, the Església de Santa María del Mar for its elegance and serenity.

The area's dwellings are incredibly mixed; dingy flats opening on to interior lightwells rub shoulders with splendid merchants' palaces in Montcada, which now houses the Museu Picasso and other notable institutions.

LEFT: Ricado Bofill, Barcelona's best-known modern architect. **RIGHT:** the Palau Reial Major exemplifies the Catalan Gothic style.

Inventive restoration

Restoration of such palaces has been carried out as part of the city's regeneration programme. Contemporary insertions and details now sit proudly and comfortably beside medieval structures in a style that does not seek to create exact replicas. The purpose has been to complement the existing buildings rather than trying to imitate past architectural styles.

This attitude is prevalent in all restoration work done in the city. A notable example is the Casa de la Caritat, in El Raval, the restoration of which was carried out by architects Vilaplana and Piñon.

made their fortunes building speculative housing. The quality of housing was graded depending on location; the fashionable streets became the sites for some extremely grand *modernista* blocks, with glazed balconies and tiled and carved facades. In the more obscure locations are poorer imitations – badly built narrow, dark flats, usually with similar but smaller layouts and sometimes with a touch of *modernista* detailing on the ground floor entrance and facade. All sides of the blocks were developed, and the internal spaces, originally intended as communal parks, became factories, workshops and, later on, car parks.

A radical solution

In the 1850s, with the liberation of the city from Madrid's control, it was necessary to build an expansion, or "Eixample", to relieve overcrowding. Engineer Ildefons Cerdà proposed the laying out of an enormous grid that would spread out over the surrounding plain, intersected by avenues lined with trees. The project was radical at the time, proposing a vision of the city that would be full of sunlight, air and open spaces, well ordered and with integrated public facilities and transport networks.

The existing Eixample, however, is very different. Almost as soon as the grid was laid out, plots of land were bought up and families

The Eixample development has been a continuous process from the early *modernista* housing, through 1960s architecture, to contemporary blocks of flats. The height restrictions and building lines of the strict grid layout have generally been maintained, resulting in a lively but homogeneous urban design.

The population of the Eixample is great enough to sustain the small shops and bars that give the place its pulse, and the area has adapted well to changes in transport and lifestyle. Recent measures to reduce the traffic have improved conditions, and industry has been discouraged, allowing new parks and open spaces to be reclaimed.

Village life

The city has a number of outlying "villages", such as Gràcia, Sants and Sarrià. Although enveloped by the Eixample, these areas still manage to keep a strong and vibrant identity, with their own local history, fiestas and culture. The buildings are generally smaller in scale, with narrower streets, small squares and parks, four-to five-storey blocks of flats and even a small amount of single occupancy housing. The whole city is ringed by blocks of flats built in

was already receiving international attention for its architecture and urban design programme. Design was clearly the highest consideration, with dramatic architectural solutions retaining existing positive elements in the city. Barcelona has changed, but not beyond all recognition.

Each of the city areas was subject to a plan based on a detailed study of all aspects of the urban fabric, from provision of schools and parks to traffic organisation and major infrastructure projects. The plans proposed a number

the 1960s to house the thousands of immigrant workers from the rest of Spain. These are variable in quality and some estates have severe social problems.

Architectural regeneration

After the stagnation of Franco's rule (ending with his death in 1975), the new Ajuntament (City Council) of Barcelona was quick to implement plans for the city's regeneration. By the time the Olympic bid was won in 1986, the city

THE MIES VAN DER ROHE PAVILION

Built by Ludwig Mies van der Rohe (1886–1969) for the 1929 International Exhibition on Montjuïc, this pavilion challenged contemporary notions of space. It had no windows, doors or walls in the conventional sense; steel columns supported the roof, and the space flowed seamlessly from interior to exterior rooms. Frameless glass blurred the concept of thresholds, with panels and screens used to create particular spatial effects.

Probably one of the most influential buildings of the 20th century, it still appears very modern. Controversially, a replica of the original was built in 1986 to mark the centenary of the architect's birth.

LEFT: glossy tiles were an integral part of *modernista* architecture: these are on Gaudí's Casa Batlló.
ABOVE: the Mies van der Rohe Pavilion.

of ways in which each area could be improved, from the the creation of parks and squares to the building of a motorway interchange at Plaça de les Glòries. The improvements were carried out either within the public works department or as commissions by local architects.

International profile

For the very high-profile public buildings, and to lend international status to the programme, "star" architects were invited to contribute: Japanese architect Arata Isozaki

THE NEW WATERFRONT

The city's coastline has been transformed. Promenades and reclaimed beaches now lead to the Vila Olímpica, which has been integrated with Cerdà's original grid.

built the Palau Sant Jordi, a huge steel and glass indoor arena with a levitating roof, on Montjuïc hill; English architect Norman Foster built the Torre de Collserola, now an icon of the Barcelona skyline, and sometimes known as the Torre Foster; US architect Frank Gehry constructed the huge copper fish glittering on the sea front, while another American, Richard Meier, designed and built the city's new contemporary art museum (MACBA). Unlike Meier's previous buildings, which are on open sites, MACBA is

ARCHITECTURE OF THE VALL D'HEBRON

The Vall d'Hebron Olympic site, located at the end of Metro Line 3 at Montbau, is home to some of the most interesting, if lesser known, Olympic buildings.

The most impressive is the Velodrome, built by Esteve Bonnell. It is a beautifully simple, modern interpretation of an ancient, essentially Mediterranean, building type, set in a landscape surrounded by cypress trees. It was built in 1984, at a time when post-modernism was prevalent, incorporating a characteristically classical pastiche and superficial decoration, using high quality materials such as stone, marble, steel and glass. The site also contains the now-dilapidated archery range by Enric Miralles and

Carme Piñon, and a replica of the 1937 Pavilion to the Spanish Republic, designed by Josep Lluís Sert for the Paris Exhibition, and used to exhibit Picasso's *Guernica*. Sert established modern architecture in Barcelona in the 1920s and 1930s, after coming into contact with other European modernist architects, most notably Le Corbusier, but was later exiled to the United States.

The pavilion was rebuilt using the original cheap materials of thin steel sections and asbestos panels, but is nevertheless very sophisticated. It creates a sense of enclosure while capturing the flavour of a traditional Spanish courtyard house.

very much an urban building, forming the side of a square and cleverly framing vistas from the surrounding streets with the sculptural elements on its facade.

Home-grown talent

Also extraordinary is the confidence and sophistication of the work undertaken by many virtually unknown Catalan architects, who often had little or no previous experience of building. It seems that the trust invested in them by the planning authorities and the support of the city's inhabitants, as well as a close appreciation of their cultural and architectural heritage,

City of interiors

Barcelona is also full of beautiful, architect-designed interiors from all periods; throughout the city you will encounter bars, cafés, restaurants, shops and galleries, all with careful attention paid to their design. Due to a fairly static population and the culture of small businesses, many original designs have been retained and are still in use today.

Catalan architects have always designed more than just buildings. The structure of the profession, with technical architects dealing with the more day-to-day constructional aspects of building, allows more time to to be spent on

have enabled them to flourish creatively as the rest of the world looks on in admiration.

At the Olympic sites on Montjuïc and the lesser known Vall d'Hebron are located many new buildings constructed for the 1992 games. Most notable among these is the Institut Nacional d'Educació Fisica de Catalunya (INEFC), a kind of sports university designed by Catalonia's most renowned contemporary architect, Ricardo Bofill (who also designed the Teatre Nacional).

LEFT: the steel and glass structure of the Palau Sant Jordi on Montjuïc. ABOVE: the so-called Walden 7 development by Ricardo Bofill.

design and innovation. Street furniture, kiosks, paving slabs, tree grills, shop fronts, and even men's ties are architect-designed, often to be reused in other projects just as Gaudí and others before him did. Architects' work still tends to be craft based, and the existence of small metalworking shops, marble masons and stained-glass artists, combined with a lack of prefabricated building products, allows buildings to be more creatively detailed.

Recent projects

Although in the post-Olympic period there has been a slowing down of building work, the regeneration programme still continues. Newer projects are now coming to fruition. One such is the area around Plaça de les Glories, now the site of the Auditori de Barcelona by Rafael Moneo, and Ricardo Bofill's Teatre Nacional, built like a neo-classical temple.

The port area of Barcelona has also been opened up as a major shopping and leisure area, along with the construction of the World Trade centre at the end of La Rambla. Several large new shopping centres have been built, such as L'Illa, also by Moneo, and the latest in Diagonal-Mar,

> ### ARCHITECTURAL GUIDES
>
> Recommended guidebooks to the city's architecture include *Guide to Architecture in Barcelona* and *Barcelona Design Guide*, both published by Editorial Gustavo Gili.

Scottish Parliament, Bernadetta Tagliabue is completing his avant-garde projects like the Santa Caterina market after his premature death.

There is an extensive "*Posat Guapa*" ("Make it Beautiful") campaign in the *Casc Antic*, with an emphasis on restoring facades and houses. EU grants have been obtained for the purpose. Parks are still being constructed in peripheral areas, the Sagrena area is being regenerated to accommodate the high speed rail link to France and a spate of new hotels are on the drawing board.

the new seaside neighbourhood. These projects have nearly all been commercially led and, although still design conscious, tend to lack the energy and freshness of earlier work carried out in the city.

Current projects

Barcelona's city council, however, is still building. There has been renovation of the city's food markets, remarkable when the rest of Europe is becoming more and more oriented towards a supermarket culture. The flea market at Plaça de les Glòries is being relocated inside the motorway interchange, while the widow of Enric Miralles, architect of the new

City of light

Barcelona has an ideal climate for fine architecture, the strong light allowing sculptural forms to be read more clearly. The lack of weathering also makes flat facades and the use of rendering and tiling appropriate.

The population of Barcelona has a high degree of design consciousness, linked to their desire to be regarded as progressive and modern. The factors that made Barcelona the City of Architecture and Design in 1999 are complex, but even if nothing else were built for many years the last two decades of the 20th century have left an impressive architectural legacy. The city has always nurtured her architects, indulged their idiosyncrasies and encouraged them to be forward thinking and individualistic in their approach. Catalan architects understand the history of their capital city's architecture, they love Gaudí, Domenèch i Montaner and the Saló del Tinell, but they are not intimidated by them, building alongside and within this legacy in a confident and contemporary style. Their achievements are as good or better than their predecessors', and have their roots in the same traditions of attention to detail and local craftsmanship, so that surfaces and materials always have an impeccable finish.

The best way to see the city's architecture is simply to walk around its streets. To help you on your way there are some very good architectural guidebooks, obtainable from the basement shop in the Col.legi d'Arquitectes opposite the cathedral in Plaça Nova, many of which have now been translated into English. ❏

LEFT: reflective glass plays a major role in the design of Maremàgnum on the waterfront.

Urban Spaces in Barcelona

In 1981, architect Oriol Bohigas was asked to establish a new department of urban design for Barcelona city council. Previously, he had been the head of the city's School of Architecture so took with him his most able students, who become known as the Golden Pencils.

Each architect was allocated an area of Barcelona and asked to develop a plan for its regeneration. Throughout the city there was a desperate shortage of public space and, since buildings were expensive, parks and squares became the focus of the regeneration. The proposals ranged from small areas of paving to large parks on derelict land, and from the opening up of the Eixample blocks to the renovation of traffic interchanges. Bohigas' young architects and others commissioned by the council were allowed to keep authorship of the projects, the design and originality of which were regarded as crucial in order to achieve high quality results.

When walking around the city, you will come across many of the completed projects; some are now in need of repair, while others look fantastic as their planting has matured. Almost without exception, they are well used and have become a positive focus for their area.

Plaça Fossar de les Moreres (Grave of the Mulberry Trees) by Carme Fiol, was created next to the Gothic Església de Santa María del Mar, and commemorates the Catalan Martyrs of 1714. The paving design reflects the existing geometry of the site and surrounding streets, while the red granite wall is reminiscent of a gravestone and has a commemorative inscription.

The Parc Creueta del Coll by Martorell Bohigas Mackay is in the site of an old quarry in an outlying area of the city (at Vallcarca, Metro L3). Its somewhat rugged quality is in marked contrast with its urban context, but good use is made of the site. An enormous sculpture suspended above a pool by Eduardo Chillida has been reinstalled after its controversial collapse.

Now fully mature, the Parc de l'Escorxador on the site of the old abattoir near Plaça d'Espanya covers the area of a Eixample block. What was once a rather dry and dusty space has been trans-

RIGHT: Oriol Bohigas, who established a new department of urban design.

formed into a series of rectilinear terraces and walkways, highlighted by an enormous Miró sculpture. The park is difficult to categorise, but has been described as falling somewhere between a formal garden and a wild Mediterranean landscape.

In Gràcia, architects Bach and Mora have redesigned each of the eight existing but neglected squares. As a result, Plaça del Sol now has lampshades that look like the setting sun, while the design of Plaça del Diamante contains references to the famous book of the same name, including a rather nondescript figure of the book's heroine.

A more recent work is the Plaça Islàndia by architects Arriola and Fiol, built in the not-so-glamorous

Sant Andreu district just steps away from the main arterial route into Barcelona. It is set along Carrer Bofarull which, although almost obliterated by the superimposed Cerdà grid, was the original route of the aqueduct from the river Besòs into the *Casc Antic* in Roman times.

The aim of the redesign was to acknowledge the older historical context within the more recent Cartesian grid. Water was introduced as a symbolic element, while trees, paving and furniture designed by the architects were laid out so as to reflect the Roman waterway. The name derives from the fact that the central pool contains an artificial geyser which was sponsored by the Icelandic government and opened by its president. ❏

GAUDÍ AND MODERNISME

The modernist style has become synonymous with Barcelona,

and Gaudí is the movement's most celebrated exponent

Modernisme is *the* architectural style of Barcelona, and modernist buildings are one of the city's main tourist attractions. Yet the concept of *modernisme*, although widely discussed, is notoriously difficult to define. As an artistic and architectural style, it bears some similarities with parallel artistic currents which were developing elsewhere in Europe at the end of the 19th century, such as the English Arts and Crafts movement, French Art Nouveau, and German and Austrian *Jugendstil*.

All these movements shared a common preoccupation with sinuous line, organic form and ornament. But *modernisme* was more than just a Catalan version of these European-wide trends. Its distinctive quirkiness, rooted in local tradition, set it apart from developments north of the Pyrenees.

A modern movement

Modernisme may be a convenient label, but it does not denote a homogeneous style so much as a shared desire to develop something completely new or modern. The modernist movement spanned the work of three generations of architects who were helping to shape the new face of Barcelona from the 1880s to the second decade of the 20th century.

The three big names of Catalan *modernisme*, Lluís Domènech i Montaner, Josep Puig i Cadafalch and Antoni Gaudí, were extremely diverse in their interpretations of what this "new" style might be, and they held radically different ideologies. Domènech i Montaner, for example, wished to emphasise Catalonia's place within a modern and expanding Europe created by capitalism, and he was happy to design optimistic, technologically experimental buildings for the city's new wealthy industrialist élite.

PRECEDING PAGES: intricate decoration was a typical component of *modernista* architecture.
LEFT: the sumptuous Palau de la Música Catalana.
RIGHT: shops also received the *modernista* touch.

On the other hand, Gaudí tended towards more visionary, utopian solutions, which he saw as a cure for the problems of urban life rather than a celebration of it. Whatever their personal philosophy, Barcelona's modernist architects were presented with plenty of occasions to exercise their craft.

From the second half of the 19th century, the city swelled to accommodate a population that was growing rapidly as a result of industrialisation. There was an explosion of building in new areas such as the Eixample, which created a plethora of opportunities for architects to experiment with new materials and forms.

Cultural and political nationalism had also begun to develop within Catalonia. Wealthy flag-waving patrons such as Eusebi Güell wanted to show their commitment to Catalan power and ingenuity, and they invested huge sums to patronise previously unknown architects who promised to create a new order of originality – a second Catalan "Golden Age".

Architectural influences

Modernist architects drew upon various elements in the Catalan tradition, including the Gothic style, which harked back to the Catalan golden age at the end of the Middle Ages. There are, not surprisingly, excellent examples of Gothic architecture in Barcelona's Barri Gòtic. Reusing or "quoting" elements of this style was a reminder to the architects and their public that their predecessors had been among the most daring in Europe.

Another local building style to which modernists turned for inspiration was Islamic or *mudéjar* architecture, developed by the

For the designers and architects themselves, the most minute decorative details became an obsession, and the complexity of detail in their buildings is quite stunning. The Palau de la Música Catalana (*see page 155*), by Lluís Domènech i Montaner, considered one of the most remarkable examples of modernist architecture, is a particularly fine example.

Most visitors who see this extraordinary building only from the outside (guided tours of the interior are, in fact, available) are unaware that the ornamental theme is continued inside. Gigantic winged Pegasuses fly from the columns of the upper balcony; the ornate

medieval Moorish craftsmen whose people occupied Spain for several centuries. This style proved particularly important for its use of tiles and ceramics. Gaudí's Casa Vicens is a fine example of a neo-*mudéjar* decorative trend. Just as William Morris in England actively promoted the work of craftsmen, so Barcelona's modernist architects took pride in local workmanship; the use of crafts in their buildings even led to a revival in decorative ceramics, ironwork and stained glass.

"When one contemplates a building, a sculpture, or a painting, that which is most noticeable is its decorative content," wrote A. Cirici Pellicer, one of the first modernist academics.

stained-glass ceiling is a masterpiece; and a long roll-call of sculptures and ceramics is dedicated to musical muses.

Domènech i Montaner

The oldest of the three chief modernist architects, Domènech i Montaner, became director of the Escola Superior d'Arquitectura de la Llotja. He often worked with teams, installing a group of architects, ceramicists, sculptors, and glass- and iron-makers in a community workshop. Beginning with the site of the Museu Zoològic, a castle-shaped building in the Parc de la Ciutadella, his personal catalogue includes not only the Palau de la Música Catalana, but also Casa Fustes, Hotel Espanya, La Rotonda and the monumental Hospital de la Santa Creu i de Sant Pau, not far from the Sagrada Família. Domènech i Montaner's influence extended to his pupil, Josep Puig i Cadafalch whose highly eclectic works show the influence of the domestic architecture of Charles Rennie Mackintosh and the Viennese Secessionists combined with reminiscences of Catalan and Central European medieval and baroque architecture. His creations include the Casa Terrades (or Casa de

SERPENTINE BENCH

Ironically, one of the best-loved features of the Parc Güell, the bench that snakes its way round the central square, was executed by Gaudí's assistant, Josep Jujol.

Gothic and Moorish architecture, but he went on to develop a highly personal language which transcended historical reference.

His buildings have an organic quality, probably because the fluid forms appear to follow the flowing lines found in nature. A playful feeling animates his most fantastic and bizarre creations, which are often encrusted with mosaics of tiles, scales or broken bottles.

Gaudí was born in Reus, near Tarragona, but spent most of his career in Barcelona. Shortly

les Punxes), Casa Macaya, and an industrial building, Casaramona, now CaixaForum, the new culture centre of the La Caixa Foundation.

Antoni Gaudí

However, it is the highly personal style of Antoni Gaudí (1852–1926) that has become the hallmark of Barcelona's *modernisme*, even though Gaudí would certainly not have called himself a modernist. Gaudí's earliest works, such as the Casa Vicens, were inspired by

LEFT: Antoni Gaudí's Casa Milà (La Pedrera).
ABOVE: Casa Viçens, Gaudí's first work.
RIGHT: the dining room in Casa Lleó Morera.

after his graduation he met the wealthy industrialist Eusebi Güell, who gave him a major commission to create the Parc Güell, a development which was intended to emulate an English garden suburb.

The park was to have 60 houses, but only two were actually completed, one of which Gaudí took for his family home. Now the Casa-Museu Gaudí, it is an excellent place to see Gaudí's furniture *in situ*. The municipal park, with its fanciful tilework and richly coloured pavilions, has become one of Barcelona's main *modernista* attractions.

Eusebi Güell also commissioned Gaudí to design the Palau Güell – a most extraordinary building with clearly visible iron supports, and wonderfully glazed and decorated chimneys.

Gaudí's other residential projects include the ceramic-covered Casa Batlló, which was commissioned by a textile manufacturer, and an apartment block designed for Batlló's partner, Milà. The Casa Milà's nickname La Pedrera, (the quarry), was inspired by the almost sculptural quality of the undulating facade which resembles a cliff face eroded by waves. The Espai Gaudí, in its roof vaults, has a permanent display on Gaudí's

NO HEAD FOR HEIGHTS?

Gaudí's patron, Eusebi Güell, could not have properly appreciated the artistry on the rooftop of his own palace, for it is said that he never ventured up there.

life and work. The vaults lead to the roof with its bizarre chimneys and ventilation stacks.

Antoni Gaudí's religious fanaticism found an outlet in the overwhelmingly ambitious project of his later years – El Temple Expiatori de la Sagrada Família (*see opposite*). Gaudí devoted himself exclusively to the Sagrada Família after 1914, giving up all other commissions. He spent his last years living unwashed and unkempt in a shack on the site until he was run down by a trolley bus in the Gran Vía in 1926. Taken to a nearby hospital, he was initially mistaken for a tramp. The large-scale celebrations of 2002 International Gaudí Year, featured exhibitions and previously unseen works.

The block of discord

The best place to appreciate the diversity and decorative richness of modernist architecture is the so-called Mansana de la Discòrdia (there is a pun here, as *mansana* means both "apple" and "block", and this is the Block of Discord) on the Passeig de Gràcia between Aragó and Consell de Cent, where visitors can see the best works of the three leading modernist architects standing almost side by side.

On the southern corner is Domènech i Montaner's Casa Lleó Morera, a profusely ornamented residential building. Two entrances further north is the Casa Amatller by Puig i Cadafalch. Next door to that is one of Gaudí's best-known buildings, Casa Batlló, the most original of the three. Gaudí's work is unique in being completely free from previous and contemporary influences, and marked by his distinctive sinuous expressionist shapes and judicious use of ceramics. It is obvious from the shape, both inside and out, that Gaudí never had to think of mundane details such as where a desk might fit. This lack of attention to practicalities explains why modernist buildings can be difficult to rent.

Next door is the colourful, geometric facade designed by Puig i Cadafalch. First planned when the architect was only 21, Casa Amatller was completed 10 years later, in 1900. Both the facade and the interior demonstrate Puig i Cadafalch's ability to combine neo-Gothic and modernist influences. The majestic entranceway is heavily Gothic, while passageways within are neo-*mudéjar*. The first-floor library is impressive for its stained glass and the enormous fireplace covered with mythical figures.

Both the facade and interior of Domènech i Montaner's 1905 Casa Lleó Morera have definite similarities to the Palau de la Música in their attention to detail and use of stained glass, mosaics and tiling. Unfortunately, at street level the building is rather disfigured by a shop.

In the years immediately following its heyday, *modernisme* was considered to be the epitome of bad taste, but today the pendulum has swung back again, and modernist buildings have become symbols of a vibrant city. ❑

LEFT: chimney detail on Gaudí's Casa Batlló.

The Sagrada Família

The Sagrada Família, Gaudí's most famous work, was actually begun in 1882 as a neo-Gothic structure under the direction of the architect Francesc P. Villar. Gaudí took over the project a year later, using Villar's plans as a starting point, but greatly expanding their scale and originality to include a central tower some 180 metres (590 ft) high, massive transept facades, a nave 95 metres (310 ft) long, and a decorative scheme of bizarre intricacy.

The enormously ambitious undertaking became Gaudí's main project for the rest of his life. He realised long before he died (as a virtual recluse) that he would not live to see its completion, admitting: "It is not possible for one generation to erect the entire temple; let us then leave such a forceful example of our passing that the coming generations will feel the urge to do as much or more." At the time of his death in 1926, only the crypt, apse and part of the Nacimiento facade and one tower had been completed. As a mark of respect, Gaudí's body is entombed in the crypt.

Many people believe the temple should be left as an unfinished monument to its famous creator. Why, they ask, is the work of one of the greatest 20th-century architects being finished in a style which often has little to do with his life, his time and his ideas? Yet such is Barcelona's commitment to the temple – which has acquired an almost iconic status – that work, under the auspices of members of Gaudí's original team, has continued on its construction for more than 70 years after his death, apart from a break during the Civil War years. Gaudí made it clear that his disciples should have complete liberty to carry on in whatever manner they deemed suitable for their time.

Today the work progresses under the control of Jordi Bonet Armengol, the son of one of the maestro's long-standing aides. Because of the complexity of Gaudí's work, and the absence of detailed plans indicating precisely what he intended, every stage of construction is preceded by involved conceptual and engineering investigation by the team of architects.

Once each step has been approved, draughtsmen draw up plans using models designed and built by Gaudí. Their work has been seriously ham-pered as many of the models were smashed during the Civil War and have had to be pieced together from mountains of fragments. Up to 15 percent of the work has been designed from scratch.

The Sagrada Família has three facades: the Pasión (Passion) on Carrer de Sardenya, the Nacimiento (Nativity) on Carrer de Marina and the Gloria (Glory) on Carrer de Mallorca. The first two, with their soaring mosaic-topped towers, are closest to completion. The restoration and continuation of the sculptures on the Nacimiento facade is being undertaken by a Japanese sculptor, Etsuro Sotoo, in a spirit which is remarkably faithful to Gaudí's original work.

Those on the Pasión facade, however, designed by local artist Josep M. Subirachs after 1952, have aroused less enthusiasm. The Gloria facade, which was originally planned as the principal entranceway and is orientated towards the midday sun, is slowly beginning to take form.

Also being considered is the construction of the central tower, which is planned to soar way above the existing ones. Early experimentation has indicated that this massive project would require 50 workmen to pour up to 1,000 tonnes of cement a day into subfloor pylons, which would need to weigh at least 8,000 tonnes each to sustain the tower during an earthquake or in gale force winds of 160 kph (100 mph). ❑

RIGHT: modern sculptures on the Sagrada Família are faithful to the spirit of Gaudí's work.

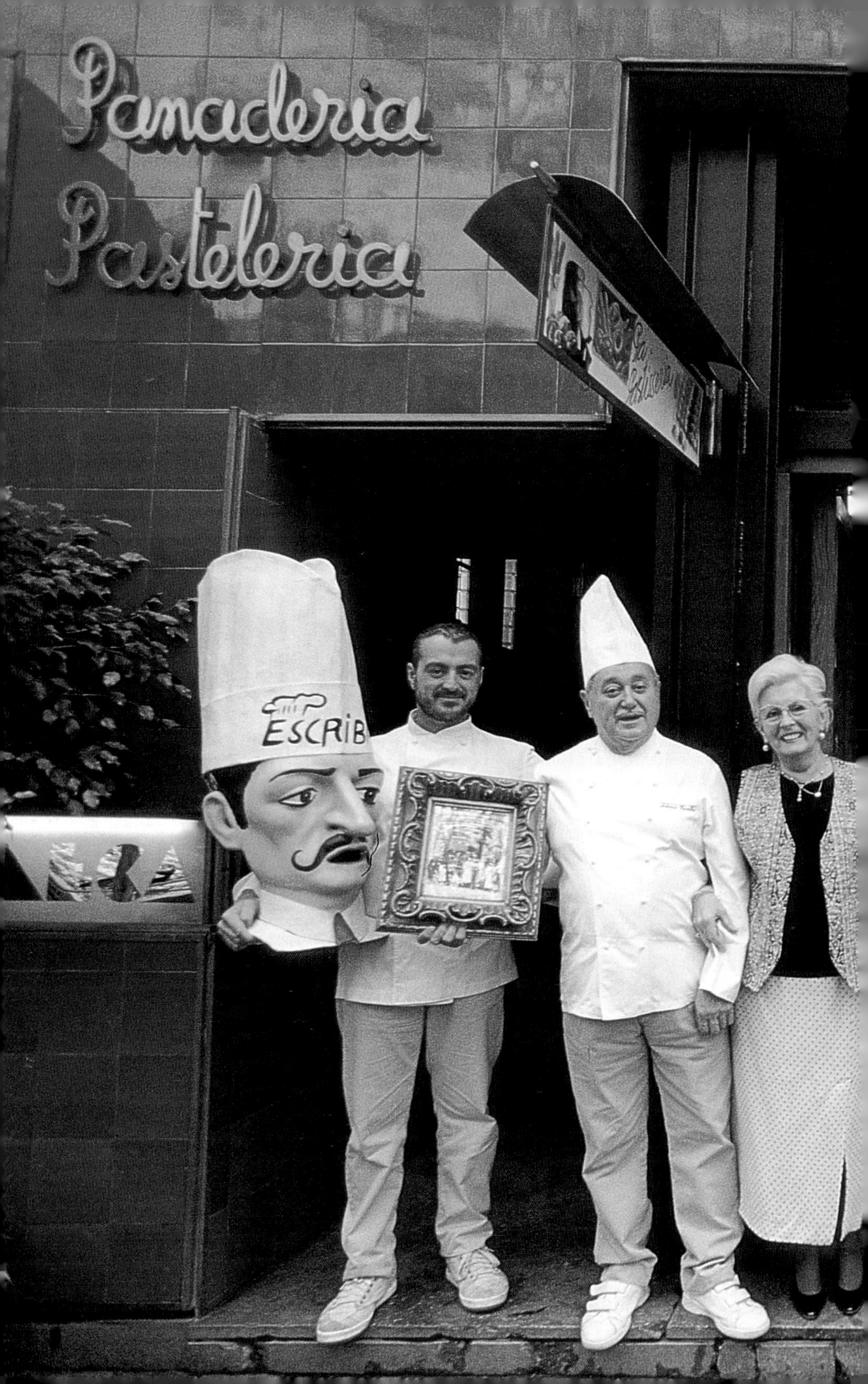
Panaderia
Pasteleria
ESCRIB

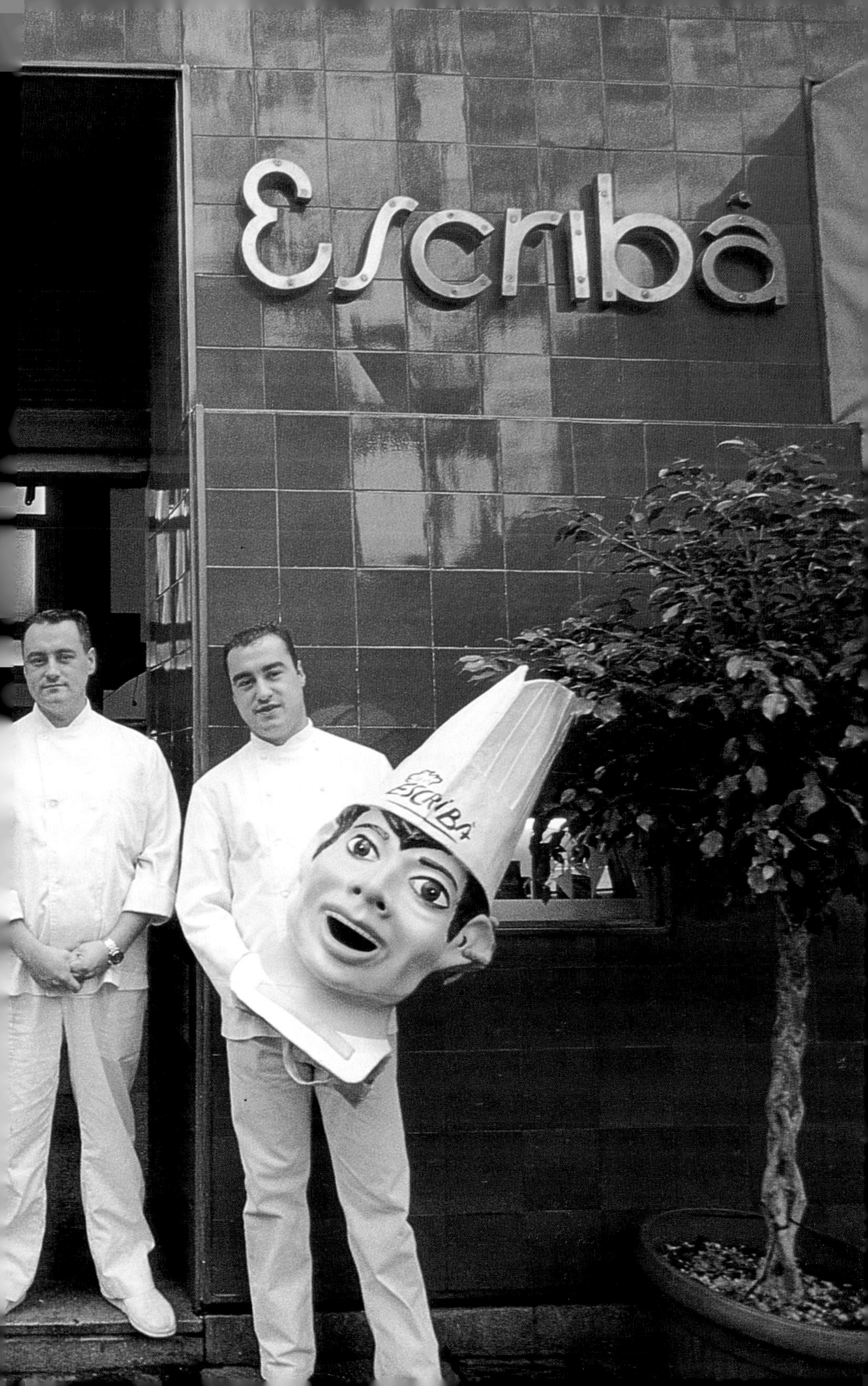
Escribà
ESCRIBÀ

FOOD

From hearty traditional fare to elegant nouveau dishes, food is a matter of great importance to the people of Barcelona

No one should visit Barcelona without making some attempt to get to know Catalan food. The experience would be incomplete, and any assessment of its people merely superficial. Eating is an important part of Catalan culture, something to be valued, taken seriously and enjoyed to the full, in true Catalan style.

The acerbic political commentator, eminent writer and novelist Manuel Vázquez Montalbán is passionate about food; he bestows a certain grace on any restaurant at which he chooses to eat. In his opinion "Catalan cooking is one of the most distinguishing signs of the national identity". It is also a composite of the nation's past, embodying the many influences of the different peoples and cultures that have swept through, settled in or bordered with Catalonia, to say nothing of lands dominated by Catalonia over its millennial history. The original fusion food, perhaps.

Nature's bounty

Catalan cooking is also a reflection of the geographical and physical characteristics of the country. Many dishes have their basis in the nuts, garlic, olive oil, tomatoes, herbs and dried fruits indigenous to these lands. Catalans are justifiably proud that their country can offer miles of rugged coastline and sheltered beaches, as well as awesome mountain ranges and rich valleys, and all within easy reach of each other.

Similarly the cooking combines the natural products of the sea, the fertile plains and the mountains in a style known as *mar i muntanya* (sea and mountains). It makes for strange sounding, though delicious tasting, marriages on the menu, such as *mandonguilles amb sèpia* (meat balls with cuttlefish), or *gambes amb pollastre* (prawns with chicken).

The Mediterranean diet is almost a cliché these days, and a selling point in many an advertising campaign, but here it still exists in its pure unadulterated form. One of the most famous Catalan dishes is perhaps the most simple, yet one of the best: the ubiquitous *pa amb tomàquet* (fresh peasant bread rubbed with

tomato, a trickle of virgin olive oil and a pinch of salt) is the Mediterranean answer to Northern Europe's thinly-sliced bread and butter, and not surprisingly provokes a certain amount of Southern pride. It is a delicious accompaniment to meals, or eaten as a snack, served with anchovies, cured meats or cheese.

Getting to know Catalan food is hardly a chore. Along with Basque cooking its reputation ranks highest in Spain. And with nearly 3,000 restaurants in Barcelona, choice is not a problem. Sightseeing and museum visiting both can and should be interrupted to recharge the batteries, and experience the culinary offerings of the city.

PRECEDING PAGES: the famous Escriba chocolate family outside their shop in the Gran Via.
LEFT: airy interior of the Senyor Parellada restaurant.
RIGHT: *bacallà*, salt cod, tastes better than it looks.

Do as the locals do

Try and adapt to local timing to get the best results: have breakfast when Barcelonans do, lunch with them, even have "tea" with the old ladies and children and then you will easily be able to wait until after 9pm for dinner.

Breakfast veers wildly from being a dull, cursory affair of milky coffee and biscuits, to a full-blooded *esmorzar de forquilla* (fork breakfast), which is a mid-morning meal of hearty dishes, like pigs' trotters and bean stews. More of a rural market-town tradition, not meant for an efficient morning in the office. It is common, though, to have a large ham sandwich or

The advantages of conforming and having a lunch (*dinar*) are manifold: the food has just arrived from the market and is at its best; it can be slept or walked off; the whole city is tuned into lunch – a sacred quiet descends, especially on Sunday; and most offices, shops and museums are closed until 4 or 5 pm. So there is no danger of missing anything.

Peak lunchtime is 2pm lingering on to 4pm or even later at weekends – although after 3.30pm there is a danger of not being served. Lunch is also the most economical meal, when nearly every restaurant has a *menú del dia* (set menu). Even the most basic of these offers a

wedge of *truita* (the traditional Spanish omelette) with a glass of wine around 10am, and the morning coffee is chased by a *conyac*. For the faint-hearted, bars and cafés serve good *cafè amb llet* (large coffee with milk), *tallat* (a shorter version) or *cafè sol* (small and intense) with a range of pastries or croissants.

Visitors can indulge in what is more of a weekend treat for residents: an aperitif around 1pm. This consists of a drink such as red vermouth, often with soda, served with olives and other *tapes* (snacks) like *boquerones* (pickled anchovies) or tinned *berberechos* (cockles). The temptation to turn this into a light lunch is where visitors often lose the local rhythm.

PASTRY HEAVEN

In Barcelona the number of pastry shops per square metre must rank among the world's highest. For each feast day and festival there is a corresponding traditional sweetmeat: *bunyols* (a small doughnut) during Lent, *la mona* (a sort of brioche, often with fancy decorations) for Easter, *panellets* (little marzipan cakes decorated with pine nuts) for All Saints and for *castanyades* (autumnal parties centred around roasting chestnuts). Throughout the long summer months the different neighbourhood and village feast days are celebrated with an abundance of fireworks, *cava* and *cocas* (pastries covered in sugar, crystallised fruits and pine nuts).

choice of starters (soup, salad, or vegetables), a main course of meat or fish, a dessert and wine, beer or a soft drink. Obviously the standard and the price vary according to the establishment, but it is invariably good value. For around €6 or 7 (£4–£5 or US$6–7.50) you can have an excellent, balanced meal.

Sauces may be rich but can be outweighed by crisp fresh salad, and fruit to follow. The option of simple grilled fish or meat, garnished with a *picada* of garlic and parsley is hard to equal, especially when accompanied by *allioli* (a strong, garlic mayonnaise which is also served with rice dishes).

broad beans stewed with herbs and pork and sausage meats (best in spring); *canalons*, a Catalan tradition brought from Italy, always eaten on 26 December; *fideuà*, an excellent and lesser known variation on paella, noodles cooked in a fish stock; and a strictly winter dish *escudella*, the most traditional Catalan soup, usually followed by *carn d'olla*, that is, the meat and vegetables which have been cooked to make the soup. Now a traditional Christmas dish, it used to be part of the staple diet of every Catalan household.

Among the main courses, be sure to try the very Catalan *botifarra amb mongetes*, a tasty

Local specialities

Look out for *menús* that include any of the following: as starters, *arros negre* (black rice, a more interesting version of *paella* made with squid and its ink); *escalivada*, grilled peppers and aubergines dressed with oil; *esqueixada*, salad of raw salt cod, onions and peppers; *Xató*, a salad from Sitges of *frisée* lettuce with tuna, salt cod, anchovies and a *romesco* sauce; *espinacs a la Catalana*, spinach sautéed with raisins and pine nuts; *faves a la Catalana*, small

sausage served with haricot beans; *fricandó*, braised veal with *moixernons*, a small, delicate wild mushroom; *bacallà*, salt cod served in many ways like *a la llauna* (garlic, parsley and tomato) or *amb xamfaina* (tomato, pepper and aubergine sauce, also served with meat); *suquet*, a seafood stew; *calamars farcits*, stuffed squid; *oca amb naps*, goose with turnip; *conill*, rabbit, either grilled and served with *allioli*, or stewed; *xai*, lamb – the cutlets (*costelletes*) are especially good.

Fish (*peix*) and shellfish (*marisc*) should not be missed in Barcelona: the simplest and perhaps the best way is grilled (a mixed grill, *graellada*, is a good option for two) or done in

LEFT: a Pepe Carvalho meal at the Casa Leopoldo.
ABOVE: the elegant lines of one of Barcelona's more up-market *tapes* bars.

the oven, *al forn*. It is worth going to a good restaurant for a *paella*; cheap imitations are usually disappointing.

If you have any room for dessert, don't miss the famous *crema catalana,* a cinnamon flavoured custard with a burnt caramel top. Other traditional *postres* include *mel i mató,* a curd cheese with honey; *postre de música*, roast nuts and dried fruits usually served with a glass of *moscatel*; and *macedonia* (fruit salad).

The advantage of the light lunch option is being able to face a *berenar* (afternoon snack). From around 5 to 7.30pm *granjes* (milk bars) overflow as people manage to drink extremely

sive than at midday. If you've had a good lunch, this is the ideal time to "do *tapes*" – visit several bars for a glass of wine and a snack in each.

The *tapes* tradition

Although it's not originally a Catalan tradition, there are nevertheless many bars offering *tapes*, including a new wave of Basque bars and some Catalan ones which specialise in *torrades* (large slices of toast), with which you can make your own *pa amb tomàquet* and request different toppings. Choose with care, especially with mayonnaise-based dishes in the summer. A delicious safe bet is *pernil salada* or *jamon*

thick chocolate (the authentic one is made with water and needs to be "drunk" with a spoon) and very creamy cakes. For a classic *berenar* try the cafés around the Plaça del Pi, especially in Petritxol, or sit at a marble table in the Granja M.Viader in Xuclà, the oldest *granja* in Barcelona, where *cacaolat* (a children's favourite) was invented.

Shops and offices are open till 8 or 9pm, so family dinner is around 10pm, and is usually quite light: soup and an omelette, for example. Restaurants serving dinner before 9pm are probably oriented towards tourists and best avoided. Restaurants do not usually have a set menu at night, so eating out can be more expen-

serrano (cured ham cut from the bone – *Jabugo* is the best), *llonganissa, fuet* (spicy sausages) or cheese (try *manchego seco* for a strong flavour, *cabrales*, a potent blue cheese from Asturias wrapped in vine leaves, or *cabra*, goat cheese).

Other favourites are *tortillas,* Spanish style omelettes, which may be *española* (potatoes and onions); *espinacas* (spinach); *payés* (mixed vegetables); *ajos tiernos* (young tender garlic). *Francesa* is the classic French omelette without a filling. Also *patatas bravas*, fried potatoes with a hot spicy sauce, or garlic mayonnaise; *ensaladilla*, Russian salad, with potatoes, vegetables and mayonnaise; *pescaditos*, small fried fish; *pulpo*, octopus, a speciality from Galicia.

International influences

Apart from these traditional dishes, the creative spectrum is broadening into many variations on the basic Catalan theme, in *tapes* and main dishes. There is a new generation of chefs, seemingly inspired by internationally renowned Ferran Adrià of *El Bullí* restaurant on the Costa Brava. Their rebellious spirit combined with the essential Catalan love of food, and passion for the Mediterranean is a formula that makes for exciting results. Chef Felip Planas would look more at home at a heavy metal concert than in a kitchen, yet he waxes lyrical about cooking. He experiments with whatever is

are restaurants from other regions of Spain, particularly Galicia, from top-notch, top-price *Botafumeiro* with fine oysters and fish, to the average corner bar. And then there are French, Italian, Greek, Lebanese, Mexican, South American, Indian, Pakistani, Chinese and Japanese, and a growing number of improved vegetarian restaurants. There really is no excuse to resort to one of the fast-food outlets, insidiously taking root in some of the most historic streets and squares of the city - the latest sign of cultural colonisation. So get out and immerse yourself in local culture in one of the most enjoyable ways possible. ❏

available in the market, introducing ingredients from other countries into Catalan dishes, and adding a strong dash of *"amor y arte"*. His artichoke soup with lime and black pepper ice-cream and Palamos prawns won a prize among young chefs in Spain. Defying convention, in his restaurant *Ot*, in Gràcia, customers are given no choice, yet they flock to its doors.

As an increasingly cosmopolitan capital, the broad range of restaurants in Barcelona reflects the tastes and demands of its inhabitants. There

LEFT: Miguel has been serving at the famous L'Egipte Rambla for many years. **ABOVE:** tempting window displays make pastries hard to resist.

OCTOBER HARVEST

October is a great time to be in Barcelona, because it's mushroom season, when fans of wild fungi will be in their element. The market stalls are rich in autumnal colours and the smell of damp woods is intoxicating. The generic name for the various wild mushrooms is *bolets*. *Rovelló* is one of the best, especially just grilled with garlic and parsley, but also delicious in stewed meat dishes at this time of the year. For the best range of fresh, dried (or if need be frozen) mushrooms, and unusual fresh herbs, go to Petras, Fruits del Bosc, at the very back of La Boqueria market. Ignore the arrogant service and enjoy the superior products.

WINE

Spanish wine is no longer a poor relation of the French, and Catalan producers are among the industry's new leaders

There was a time when Spanish wine meant plonk, *sangria* was associated with packaged holidays on the Costas, and the only Spanish vintage to have any international acclaim was Rioja. Today, these misconceptions are well buried in the past, and anyone who believes in the importance of accompany-

ing good food with a decent glass of wine will be aware that Spain has many different wine-growing regions, producing a range of interesting and increasingly high-quality wines.

One of these is Catalonia, which itself has nine wine regions officially classified as D.O. (*Denominació de Origen,* similar to the French *appelation contrôlée*): **Empordà-Costa Brava,** near the French border; **Alella,** almost on the outskirts of Barcelona in the Maresme, a tiny area known for its white wines; the well-known **Penedès,** to the south-west of Barcelona; the most recent **Pla de Bages,** near Manresa; **Conca de Barberà,** with its *modernista* wine cellars, in the province of Tarragona; **Costers**

del Segre, home of Raimat wines, to the west in Lleida; and **Tarragona, Terra Alta** and the **Priorat** with its terraced vineyards on steep hillsides in the south.

A flourishing industry

With over 68,000 hectares (178,000 acres) of vineyards the Catalan wine industry is one of the most important in Spain, yielding twice as much wine annually (350 million litres) as La Rioja. In a bid for stronger identity in the international market a recent controversial move by the large companies backed by the Generalitat (Catalan autonomous government), to introduce a denomination for the region as a whole, *D.O.Catalunya,* has been approved. As with Bordeaux wines, the smaller denominations will continue to exist within it.

The Catalan region with the highest profile abroad is the Penedès, mostly due to the giant Torres, a family firm in Vilafranca del Penedès, that exports wine to more than 90 countries, has vineyards in Chile and California and is held in high esteem in the wine world. With the sixth generation of the family now in the business they continue to produce award-winning wines, like Gran Coronas Black Label, Fransola, Gran Viña Sol and Viña Esmeralda.

The Penedès is also the largest region (26,400 hectares/65,990 acres) where about 100

THE CORDONIU EMPIRE

Ninety-five per cent of Spain's *cava* production is from Catalonia and the greater part from the Penedès, where it was first created by Josep Raventós in 1872. From that celebrated first bottle grew the Codorniu empire, which, shares with Freixenet the title of undisputed leaders of the *cava* industry. This sparkling wine made by the *méthode champenoise*, is obligatory at fiestas and almost essential for Sunday lunch, usually accompanying the dessert. Regarded as one of the world's great sparkling wines, *cava* is warmer, earthier and less acid than Champagne. (See the trip to Sant Sadurní d'Anoia on *page 237*.)

companies produce 65 million litres of still wine annually. And that's not including the *cava* (*see below left*).

In the last few years there has been a lot of activity in previously lesser-known regions and among the smaller *bodegas* across Catalonia with experimentation, new techniques, introduction of different grape varieties and maximising the indigenous grapes like *xarel.lo* and *macabeo* (white), and *carinyena*, *garnatxa* and *monastrell* for red wines. It is reflected in improved quality and some notable wines are emerging.

VILAVINITECA

This small shop, bursting with over 3,000 brands of wine and spirits, is in Agullers 7, near Santa Maria del Mar, and well worth visiting.

A visit to Barcelona is the perfect opportunity to taste some lesser-known wines from different regions, which are probably not available in the large supermarkets back home, but which are increasingly gaining prestige and respect amongst oenologists. In a restaurant the house wine (*vi de la casa*) may be good. It is often a young wine, or in rural areas a strong, dark red country wine; locals tend to drink it with *gasosa*, a light fizzy lemonade. If you find it rough there will be no objection to changing it for something different. Be guided by the staff.

Up-and-coming labels

One of the most fascinating areas is the Priorat, which after years of neglect, is now experiencing a boom. Traditionally it was known for the cheapest, strongest wines bought from barrels in the dark bodegas of Barcelona. Now Priorat wines are demanding the highest prices. Large companies from La Rioja and the Penedès have started working there and some highly-prized wines are emerging from its low-yield, high-alcohol content grapes. International wine buffs are paying attention and the locals are blinking with amazement at the influx of visitors to the small, neglected villages, whose street names remain in Castilian from the dark ages of Franco as if the Generalitat language policies have not yet reached this "remote" part. In fact it is only a couple of hours from Barcelona and makes a wonderful weekend excursion.

Along with Priorat wines, some recent labels from Conca de Barberà, are now found in the highest price range too. **La Ermita** from Riojan

winemaker Alvaro Palacios who started working in the Priorat in the early 1990s, retails at a mere £100 (US$160). Other wines to look out for, though not necessarily so highly-priced, are **Cervoles**, a red from Costers del Segre, **Can Rafols dels Caus**, **Can Feixes** and the ecological wines **Albet i Noia** from the Penedès, and from another up-and-coming area, the Empordà, where outsiders are developing new wines. Watch out for **Oliver Conti**.

Catalans are proud of their wine but not over-serious about it. They do like to accompany a

well-cooked meal with a wine that does it justice, yet it could easily be a simple, home-grown country wine. At an important family gathering you may still see the *porró* in use (a shapely glass bottle with a spout, used for communal drinking).

Don't be surprised in summer if the red wine is served chilled: according to Quim Vila who runs VilaViniteca (*see above*) "wine is not a consommé…chilling a young, fruity red wine becomes it". Whatever your view on this, there is no doubt that the recent burgeoning of the industry in Catalonia is driven by an increasingly discerning home market as well as by international market demands. ❑

LEFT: roll out the barrel: the Catalan wine industry is very productive. **RIGHT:** take your choice of local wines.

MORE THAN JUST A GAME

Barça, the Barcelona Football Club, has long been a focus of Catalan nationalism as well as the home of world-class football

Barcelona Football Club, known throughout the sporting world as Barça, was founded in 1899 by Hans Gamper, a Swiss living in Barcelona. It is one of the oldest clubs in Europe, and during its long and chequered history it has played a surprising political role, championing Catalan nationalism and liberty; it is the city's army, opera and ballet all in one and all Barcelona celebrates with its victories and weeps with its defeats.

The team lost no time in becoming well established. By 1922 it already had its own stadium, recognised at the time as one of the best in Europe, and it signed up two of the most sought-after players of the time: forward Samitier and goal-keeper Zamora.

Even at this stage matches between Barça and rival teams, such as the club Español (founded in 1900, also in Barcelona), and the Madrid team, were studded with incidents. At times the rivalry was so heated that the public was not permitted to attend.

Suppression

In 1925 a band from a British warship played the Royal march *Himno de la España Monàrquica* just before the game. Even before the band had completed the opening bars the public started jeering and whistling – a spontaneous reaction against the Spanish monarchy that had accommodated the dictatorship of General Primo de Rivera. Rivera's policy had been to suppress not only personal freedom but cultural events and, more important still for the fans of Barça, the Catalan national spirit. After the incident the government ordered the Barcelona football ground to be closed.

Needless to say, popular dissatisfaction reached even higher levels during the long dictatorship of General Franco. The year 1939 saw a Franco loyalist nominated as the club's pres-

---

PRECEDING PAGES: a Barça match never fails to fill the stands.
LEFT: Barça celebrated its centenary in 1999.
RIGHT: Kubala, Barça's star player in the 1950s.

ident and up until the 1950s the board of directors was kept under control by the obligatory presence at meetings of a Falangist and a member of the armed forces. However, even though the vast majority of the club's presidents and governors were government vigilantes, they all became ardent followers of Barça's fortunes.

In 1941 a serious incident occurred during the cup match between Barcelona and Madrid. It had been pre-ordained that Madrid should win. As a gesture of the absurdity of the fixture, Barcelona allowed them to win by 11 goals to one. The Barça goal-keeper was suspended for life for waving his cap on high each time he allowed the Madrid team to score.

Star sharing

Barça's fortunes really improved with the signing of the player Kubala in 1951. So powerful was the team becoming that the government ordered the removal of the equally skilful Di Stefano, also a new signing. The club's president Martí Carreto was threatened to such an extent that he eventually had to agree to share Di Stefano (known as the *Saeta Rubia* – the "blond arrow") with the Madrid team. The pact had the player alternating between the two teams – an absurd situation almost unparalleled in world football.

Martí Carreto came under intense pressure at the time. He was ordered to Madrid by the president of the Spanish Football Federation and told that the financial operation carried out to pay for Di Stefano's transfer was illegal. The Federation's president, with the National Sports Delegate General Moscardó, phoning every

Europe with a seating capacity of 98,260.

Barça has also been "more than just a club" (a slogan popular during the last years of the Franco regime) by playing a key role in Catalanising the enormous numbers of immigrants who have flooded into the city over the years. It is also, literally, more than just a football club, maintaining nine other sports sections, including basketball, hockey (on roller skates), handball teams and since signing a contract with the NFL (National Football League) even has an American football team, the FCB Dragons.

Barça has always extended its activities beyond sporting events. During the last years of

few minutes to increase the pressure, also threatened Carreto with reprisals against his textile industry. In the end the entire board of directors of Barça resigned in protest at the forcible removal of the great Di Stefano.

Cradle to grave

The unusually high number of Barça members – 105,000 – is proof enough of the club's popularity. It is the world's largest organisation where memberships pass from father to son and where new-born babies are made members only hours after birth. No fewer than 80,000 of the members have permanent seats in the impressive Camp Nou stadium, one of the largest in

POLITICAL FOOTBALL

The extent to which Barça became a focus of Catalan nationalism may seem strange, but, in fact, its political role demonstrates the importance of sports in general as a way of helping countries to make their mark at an international level.

Members of the Welsh rugby team regularly put their small country – and its fervent champions of nationalism – on the European map; the former East Germany overcame some of its political stigma by winning Olympic medals; and more than one country in the developing world has made its mark through the achievements and triumphs of its athletes.

the dictatorship the club came to symbolise freedom. For decades thousands of members and fans frantically waved the blue and garnet flag of Barça as a substitute for the forbidden Catalan flag. A victory over Real Madrid was equivalent to a victory over the oppressive central government.

In this spontaneous fashion Barça became the focal point for Catalan nationalism, and the nationalists were able to use the matches to maintain their fervour with much less risk than if they had organised a rally or demonstration. The re-establishment of democracy has done nothing to lessen the strength of support for

because of its roots and the social structure upon which it is firmly built, Barça has proved to be one of the most demanding clubs in the world. Great players have come and gone, although not all of them managed to withstand the pressures surrounding the club.

Maradona, Romario, Ronaldo, and more recently, Rivaldo are just some of the great names any football fan associates with the essence of the game. It is only fair to say, however, that they all played in extremely talented Barça sides, alongside players from all corners of the globe and the homegrown talent in which the Barcelona crowd take so much pride.

Barça. Indeed, the enormous social and financial back-up of Catalan society provides the basis for its power. The recent creation of a foundation enables Barcelona to remain a football club, whereas other Spanish clubs have inevitably begun the transformation into limited companies.

Superiority and strength

Recent history is also a true reflection of the club's insatiable appetite for victory at both national and international level. However,

LEFT: a floodlit match at the state-of-the-art Camp Nou. **ABOVE:** fans off to celebrate after another victory.

The club has a history of great managers, too, though Johann Cruyff was the last to truly make his mark. Now, armed with a team of exceptional quality, and having just celebrated its 100th anniversary, Barça is continually looking to prove why it is considered one of the greatest clubs in the world.

Football fans will inevitably, and understandably, be drawn to the Camp Nou, and the club's museum, the second most visited in the city (open Mon–Sat 10am-6.30pm, Sun 10am–2pm; entrance fee). Getting to see a game shouldn't be too difficult, though tickets for a fixture against arch rivals Real Madrid are virtually impossible to find. ❏

PLACES

*A detailed guide to the entire city, with principal sites
clearly cross-referenced by number to the maps*

Barcelona is everything you have ever heard about: Gaudí and the Sagrada Família, *modernisme* and contemporary design, Olympic achievements, nightlife, thrusting Catalans and Mediterranean quality of life. But it is a lot more besides. The Places section will guide you through itineraries that go beyond the main tourist attractions (though by no means overlooking them) to what goes on behind the scenes, in an attempt to get closer to real life on the streets of this dynamic city. When exploring the Gothic Quarter you'll be guided to the best cup of coffee, or taken past an interesting shop you might otherwise miss; visiting one of the latest, most dazzling museums, MACBA, we'll make sure you are aware of the network of streets behind it where people struggle for a living. You can follow a route all along the waterfront, see its past and future, yet be encouraged off the beaten track for one of the best snacks in town. Few venture "above the Diagonal" (or below it, depending on your viewpoint), but you can find out why, and why it's worth it.

The geography of Barcelona is easily fathomed. If you can get to one of its high points early in your visit – Montjuïc, Tibidabo, the Carretera de les Aigües, the Park Güell, or even Columbus' column – it will put the city into focus. It is not surprising that this is one of the world's densest cities (15,230 inhabitants per square kilometre): packed in between the Collserola range of hills and the Mediterranean, and bordered by Montjuïc and the River Besòs, all the available space has been consumed. Parks tend to be in rocky knolls where no building could have been erected, or created latterly in disused industrial spaces. Inevitably, the latest developments are centred on the sea, with planned extensions to the port and reclaiming land by the Diagonal Mar.

The map of the city tells the same story, and now shows how the ring road, split into Ronda de Dalt that goes round the top, and Ronda Litoral below, circumscribes the city almost like another symbol of its limits, even though it is a practical and much quicker way out.

Finding your way around

Whether Plaça Catalunya is the centre of this metropolitan mass or not, it is certainly a good place to get one's bearings and work out the next move. From this crossroads between the old town, the **Ciutat Vella** and the new town, the 19th-century **Eixample**, it is easy to get a sense of place and history. Below is the old town, within which is an even older Gothic Quarter, the **Barri Gòtic**, partly surrounded by Roman walls, a testimony to Barcelona's first civilisation.

PRECEDING PAGES: an historical view of the city; the Palau Nacional with its magical fountain; the Parc d'Espanya Industrial.
LEFT: old-fashioned transport will take you sightseeing.

The original city spread beyond the Roman walls, to a later medieval wall, but by the mid-19th century there was pressure to break out from these limits. The prosperous middle class, on the back of the industrial boom, wanted to build; the Cerdà plan to extend the city was approved and work began on the Eixample in 1859.

Based on a grid system, its geometric precision is evident on the map, extending over the area between the Old Town and former outlying districts like Gràcia and Sarrià. Standing in Plaça Catalunya, or looking at the map, the contrast is striking: the old streets meander down towards the sea, getting narrower, darker and denser, with a jumble of architectural styles. The "new" streets, leading up towards the Diagonal and the Collserola range glimpsed behind, have an immediate elegance and structure, albeit regimented and inflexible.

Most of the *modernista* gems are in this area and the streets rich with details, making it resemble an open-air museum, complemented by art galleries, elegant shops and fine restaurants. Yet it is also several *barris*, or neighbourhoods, with markets, grocery shops, community centres and schools, where normal life goes on. And that can be just as fascinating as "tourist sights".

The Old Town, containing most of the city's historical landmarks, is divided into the **Barri Gòtic**, **La Ribera** and **El Raval**. The Barri Gòtic (Gothic Quarter) is in the middle, bordered by **La Rambla** and **Via Laietana**; La Ribera is the district of medieval mansions on the other side of Via Laietana, and El Raval lies on the other side of La Rambla, where convents turned cultural centres rub shoulders with the notorious **Barri Xino**.

Plaça Catalunya, like an all-encompassing terminal, is also a good departure point for most excursions. Airport buses and trains arrive there, buses to most parts of town and beyond can be caught on one of its sides, two metro lines run through it and the FGC trains to take you up town or through the hill to the Parc de Collserola leave from it. Even trains to the coast and the mountains depart from beneath this central square.

Directions in this section are given as the Catalans would give them: streets are rarely called streets, *carrers*. Instead they are referred to just by their name, like **Bonsuccés** or **Hospital**. Someone living in the Eixample will describe the location in New York style, as **Girona**, between **Aragó** and **València**, or suggest meeting on the corner of **Balmes** with **Provença**. On the other hand, the words *Plaça*, *Passeig* or *Avinguda* are rarely left out.

The city is very manageable on foot, which is the best way to discover details and absorb the atmosphere. However walking can nearly always be backed up by the highly efficient and economical public transport system, of metro, bus and the FGC lines, to say nothing of funiculars and escalators to help up hills. Should you be stranded far from one of these options, rest assured that a black and yellow taxi will not be far away, and the rates are fairly moderate. ❑

RIGHT: a good overview of the city from Montjuïc's cable car.

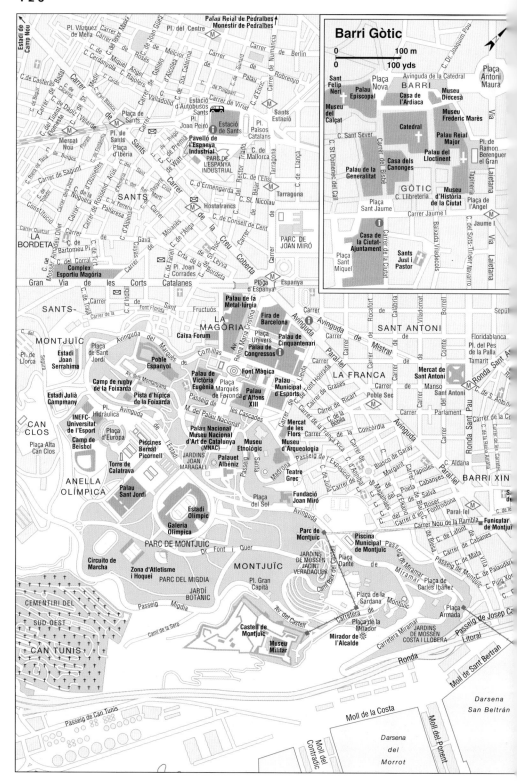

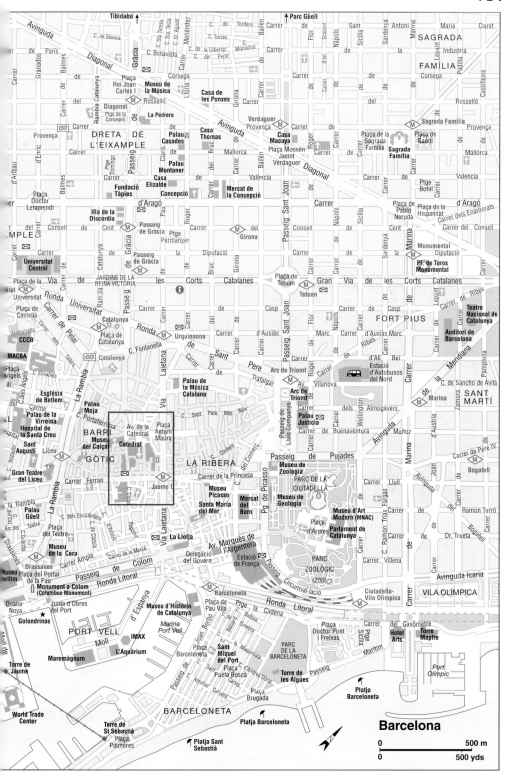

Barcelona

LA RAMBLA

*The life and pulse of the city are perfectly reflected
in the spectacle and colour of this celebrated promenade
leading down to the waterfront*

Map
on page
126

At the northern end of La Rambla lies the **Plaça de Catalunya ❶**. It is not the kind of picturesque square that you might make an effort to visit, but it *is* the kind of place you inevitably do visit on any trip to Barcelona. Whether arriving from the airport by bus or train, coming into the city from other parts of Catalonia, visiting the Old Town from up town or vice versa, Plaça de Catalunya is bound to be part of the trajectory. It is more of a pivotal *plaça* acting as a logistical centre for the city's transport.

From the top

Here you'll find the Metro underground train service; FGC trains (the Ferrocarrils de la Generalitat de Catalunya, which run to uptown areas and outside the city); RENFE trains; public and privately run buses like the Tombús; and tourist coaches and taxis. A world of underground corridors, confusing and exhausting to start with, leads to the trains, so allow time when travelling. The main Barcelona City tourist office is also here, marked by a tall "i" above ground. Run by the tourist board, it offers an efficient and helpful service, dishing out leaflets, maps and all kinds of information, as well as a hotel reservation service, money exchange and an Internet connection. For many, Plaça de Catalunya also marks the beginning of another inevitability in Barcelona: a walk down the famed avenue of **La Rambla**.

Before embarking on that flow of humanity down to the sea, pause a moment in the welcome shade of Plaça de Catalunya's trees, or in the bright winter sunshine that fills it with a light and warmth which barely reaches the narrowest of the Old Town streets. As well as being the hub of Barcelona in terms of transport and city communications, this *plaça* is the centre of the city in a wider sense: if you look in the middle of the square itself you'll find paving stones arranged into the shape of a star which, they say, marks the centre of the capital of Catalonia.

Pigeons flock here to be fed by children and old ladies. Tacky stalls sell plastic toys and caramelised nuts. Families wander around aimlessly, lovers meet beneath the gushing fountains and predatory youths lurk, with an eye on swinging handbags and cameras. On the newly paved and urbanised outer rim, men gather to play chess beneath the monument to a much-loved Catalan leader, Macià, designed by contemporary sculptor Subirachs, accompanied by electronic Andean pipes relentlessly churning out the "Sound of Silence", making you yearn for the real silence of the *altiplano* where the air is pure.

But the square is more of a created centre than one with a real Catalan heart. Consider its history. When the medieval wall of Barcelona was demolished in

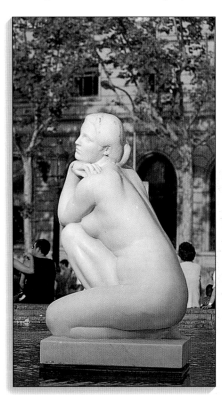

PRECEDING PAGES:
Plaça de Catalunya.
LEFT: chatting
with friends.
BELOW: the goddess
in the square.

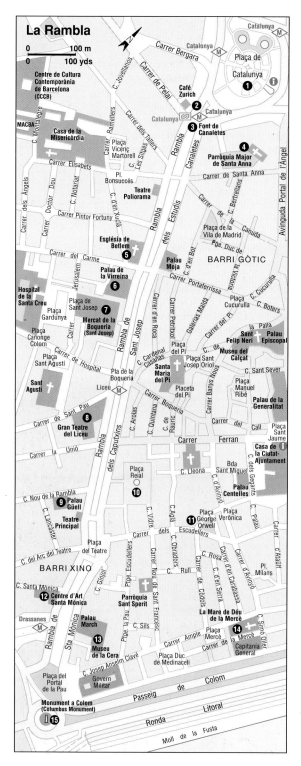

La Rambla

0   100 m
0   100 yds

Centre de Cultura
Contemporània
de Barcelona
(CCCB)

MACBA

Casa de la
Misericòrdia

Carrer Elisabets

Hospital
de la
Santa Creu

Sant
Agustí

Pl.
Bonsuccés

Teatre
Poliorama

Església de
Betlem ⑤

Palau de
la Virreina ⑥

Plaça de
Sant Josep ⑦

Mercat de la
Boqueria
(Sant Josep)

Plaça
Gardunya

Plaça
Canonge
Colom

Plaça
Sant Agustí

Liceu Ⓜ

Pla de la
Boqueria

⑧
Gran Teatre
del Liceu

Carrer la Unió

C. Nou de la Rambla

⑨ Palau
Güell

Teatre
Principal

Plaça
del Teatre

BARRI XINO

C. Santa Mònica

⑫ Centre d'Art
Santa Mònica

Palau
March

⑬
Museu
de la Cera

Drassanes Ⓜ

Plaça del
Portal
de la Pau

Monument a Colom
(Columbus Monument)
ⓘ ⑮

Catalunya Ⓜ

Carrer Bergara

Plaça de
Catalunya ① ⓘ

Café
Zurich ②

Catalunya Ⓜ ③ Font de
Canaletes

④
Parròquia Major
de Santa Anna

Carrer de Santa Anna

BARRI GÒTIC

Plaça de la
Vila de Madrid

Palau
Moja

Carrer Portaferrissa

Plaça
Cucurulla

Santa
Maria
del Pi

Placeta
del Pi

Sant
Felip Neri

Museu del
Calçat

Plaça Sant
Josep Oriol

la Palla

Palau
Episcopal

C. Sant Sever

Plaça
Manuel
Ribé

Palau de la
Generalitat

Carrer del Call

Plaça
Sant
Jaume

Casa de
la Ciutat-
Ajuntament

Palau
Centelles

Plaça
George
Orwell

Plaça
Verònica

La Mare de Déu
de la Mercè

Plaça
Mercè

⑭

Capitania
General

Pl.
Milans

Parròquia
Sant Sperit

Passeig   de   Colom

Ronda

Moll de la Fusta

Litoral

1859 and work on the **Eixample** began, the *plaça* was a large field outside the city, traversed by a mountain stream (the stream bed later formed the foundations of La Rambla) and connected to the inner city by means of an entrance called the Portal dels Orbs. The entrance was later renamed the **Portal de l'Angel** because, so the story goes, when Sant Ferrer crossed through this doorway with his followers, he was greeted by an angel. The 19th-century Plan Cerdà, a project for the redevelopment of Barcelona, called for the creation of a square a little further inland, at the junction of **Passeig de Gràcia** and the **Gran Via**.

Another rival project presented by Antoni Rovira i Trías proposed an enormous *plaça*, 800 by 400 metres (2,600 by 1,300 ft) to be called the "Forum Isabel II". Yet another plan for a *plaça* similar to that which we know today was designed in 1868 by Miquel Garriga.

While the authorities were endeavouring to reach an agreement, the owners of the corresponding plots of land got fed up with waiting and began to build. In 1902, Lord Mayor Ledesma ordered the demolition of all these buildings but it was another quarter of a century before the *plaça* took on its current appearance. Based on a design by Francesc Nebot, the square was officially opened by King Alfonso XII in 1927.

Ever since this uneasy birth, the winds of change have swept through the square, taking away any vestiges of nostalgia and tradition. Now it is bordered by banks and giant shopping institutions that seem to have been transplanted from Madrid and elsewhere like some kind of late 20th-century colonisation. On the corner now dominated by the Hard Rock Café and the latest branch of the El Corte Inglés empire stood the almost mythical Maison Dorée café. Such was the character of this establishment that, when it closed its doors in 1918, another café of the same name opened at No. 6. "It was never the same," wrote Lluís Permanyer, city historian, who relates that it was here that a tradition of "five o'clock tea" was introduced to Barcelona.

Another meeting point of intellectuals was the old Hotel Colón, which has since become the headquarters of the Banco Español de Crédito (Banesto). Older generations of Republicans remember when the facade of the hotel was covered in portraits during the Civil War. With giant posters of Marx, Lenin and Stalin, there was no mistaking that this was the headquarters of the Unified Socialist Party of Catalonia (PSUC), then the leading socialist group.

Map on page 126

Shopping emporia

It's difficult to miss the monumental department store **El Corte Inglés**, which has now taken over the whole of the northern side, and has a new branch in the former Marks & Spencer. The store is so named ("The English Cut") because its distant origins lie in a humble Madrid tailor's shop, a far cry from today's exhausting air-conditioned expanse of goods and madding crowds. On the opposite side, where a broad new pavement makes a tenuous link between La Rambla and **Rambla de Catalunya**, two other favourites, the Cine Vergara and the Café Zurich were subsumed into what is now **El Triangle**, a large commercial centre redeemed, perhaps, by the FNAC, several slick floors of books, music and technology and a *quiosc* on the ground floor with a vast range of magazines.

At the point of the "triangle" where **Pelai** meets the top of La Rambla is a newly built **Café Zurich ❷**, a complete replica of the original on the same spot. Thanks to its vantage point at a busy crossroads, and with the same old bad-tempered waiters, it may yet take on the persona of the former landmark.

Whether seated on the Café Zurich's terrace, or emerging blinking from the Metro exit at the top of La Rambla, contemplate the panorama ahead. This is La Rambla, one of the most famous boulevards in Europe, and for many one of the

El Corte Inglés department store has taken over the northern side of Plaça de Catalunya.

BELOW: the new Café Zurich.

TIP

Take a seat, if you can find one free, fixed at casual angles in the first stretch of La Rambla. It makes for an unbeatable floor show.

distinguishing features of Barcelona. This kaleidoscopic avenue throbs day and night, exerting an undeniable magnetism which attracts both visitors and locals, and which never fails to entertain.

The best advice is to plunge in, go with the flow and enjoy the constant weird and wonderful activity all around you. Let yourself be carried past lottery ticket booths, shoe shiners, cheap *pensions,* human statues, northerners in frocks in December, and locals in sharp suits. Let your senses be assailed by the squawking of caged birds, the perfumed air of the flower stalls, the chatter of the gossips and the shrieks of the lads delivering fruit to the market. Don't miss a thing, especially the ubiquitous pickpockets who inevitably prey on such a bountiful crowd. Being aware and strapping cameras and bags tightly to your body is usually enough to deter thieves.

River to road

Originally, La Rambla was the river bed (the Latin name *arenno* was replaced by the Arab word *ramla*) that marked the exterior limits of the city fortified by King Jaume I. But when the city expanded during the 15th century, La Rambla became part of the inner city.

In due course, a number of religious houses were built throughout the surrounding areas and the river bed came to be known as the "Convent Thoroughfare". It was not until the beginning of the 18th century that La Rambla was to become a more clearly defined street, after permission was granted to build on the ancient walls in the Boqueria area. In 1775 a section of the city walls was torn down and a central walkway built, lined with poplar trees and higher than the roadway that ran along either side.

BELOW: drinking at the Font de Canaletes.

LA RAMBLA BY NIGHT

As night falls La Rambla takes on a nocturnal persona, losing nothing of its daytime energy and pace: the flow of human traffic at 3am is much the same as at midday. After dark it becomes the main artery for anyone going *de juerga* (out for a wild time) in the Old Town. There are the young ones going out for a dose of *leche de pantera* (a dangerous mix of hard alcohol and milk), yuppies on their motos or mobiles off to the new nightlife of Maremàgnum, the cocktail set coming out of Boadas and off to dinner, immaculately coiffed middle-class ladies in fur coats on their way to the opera, and after 2am the dance crowd in search of techno. After important victories Canaletes roars with jubilant Barça fans, climbing lampposts and waving banners in front of TV3 cameras, who film it every time.

Witnessing the goings-on through impervious eyes are the newspaper kiosk attendants, who replace yesterday's papers with today's first editions in the small hours. And while the fun continues, out come the municipal cleaners in force, like some kind of eco-angels, sweeping, collecting rubbish and vigorously hosing down the gutters in preparation for a new day on La Rambla. Woe betide any *juergistas* who get in their way.

Within the small and densely populated area of the ancient fortified city, La Rambla was the only street of any significance, and it became the city's focal point. Renovations were constantly underway during the 19th century, and the street settled down to become more exclusive and aristocratic; this change of status was aided by the disappearance of some of the surrounding buildings and convents, creating space for new squares and mansions.

La Rambla assumed its present shape between 1849 and 1856 when all the remaining fortifications were torn down. The first plane trees, brought from Devesa in Girona, were planted in 1851 and the street became "the fashionable promenade route, where the cream of Barcelona parades on foot, by carriage or on horseback," according to the 19th-century journalist Gaziel. Today's promenaders are more mixed and much more cosmopolitan, though the "cream" can still be spotted wrapped in furs on their way to the opera at the Liceu. Since the prettification of the Old Town in the 1990s, more up-town residents are now venturing down to these "picturesque" parts.

Between the top of La Rambla and the Columbus monument where it ends there are five different parts to the promenade. The first, **Rambla de Canaletes**, is named after the **Font de Canaletes ❸**, one of the symbols of Barcelona. A small brass plaque at the foot of this 19th-century cast-iron fountain confirms the legend that all those who drink its waters will be enamoured of Barcelona and always return. It is a favourite meeting place, and posses of retired men regularly gather here for *tertúlies* (chatting in groups and putting the world to rights – often around a table after a large meal). The font is at its most jubilant when Barça football fans of all ages gather there to celebrate yet another victory by their heroic team.

Map on page 126

Bar Nuria is a long-established presence on La Rambla and a good spot for a late breakfast.

BELOW: putting the world to rights.

Tucked just inside Tallers, the first street on the right, is **Boadas**, the oldest cocktail bar in town and probably the most atmospheric, with its 1930s décor and walls lined with caricatures of the original owner. His daughter, Dolors Boadas, still mixes a mean *mojito,* a skill inherited from her father who learned his art in Cuba where, like so many Catalans in the 19th century, his parents had emigrated. At the next junction, with Bonsuccés, is the *modernista* pharmacy of Dr Masó, and across La Rambla are the diverging streets Santa Anna and Canuda, the former a good pedestrian shopping street.

Just down here, through a half-hidden doorway on the left, is the **Parròquia Major de Santa Anna ❹** (open Mon–Sat 9am–1pm, 6.30–8pm; avoid weekends, the time for weddings and masses), an oasis of peace amid the traffic. The Romanesque church and Gothic cloister are marvellous examples of the architecture of their time. Return to La Rambla via **Plaça de la Vila de Madrid**, reached from the narrow street Bertrellans almost opposite the church: it is an attractive newly landscaped square with some Roman ruins and a wonderful jacaranda tree. On the corner, at Canuda No. 6, is the **Ateneu Barcelonès**, a traditional cultural enclave with walk-in exhibitions in a building dating from 1796. Steal a glimpse of the hushed library and the romantic rear garden.

Rambla dels Estudis

Back on La Rambla, the crowd gets denser and the noise level rises as it passes through a corridor of caged birds, fish and small rodents, against a background of large hotels which were modernised for the 1992 Olympics. This is the Rambla dels Estudis, so-named because the 16th-century university was here. The Reial Acadèmia de Ciències i Arts on the right also houses the **Teatre**

BELOW: Dolors mixes a *mojito* in the Boadas bar.

Poliorama with regular performances and good shows for kids on Sunday mornings. On the exterior of the building, which was designed by Josep Domènech i Estapà, is the clock which has been the official timekeeper of the city since 1891. The decoration at the **Viena** next door is not genuine, but the coffee is. Of all the vast conglomeration of the former university, only the **Església de Betlem** ❺ (beyond the Filipino tobacco company) remains, a long and rather depressing bulk. The baroque facade on **Carme** was built in 1690 but the main structure was not completed until 1729.

Opposite is the **Palau Moja,** an important neoclassical, 18th-century building converted into offices of the Department of Culture of the Generalitat (the Catalan government). Under the arcades is the official Generalitat bookshop, with a few titles of general interest amid the weighty tomes of statistics on Catalonia. Next door is the semi-helpful Catalan cultural information centre.

At the corner, **Portaferrissa** leads into a world of commerce and numerous fashion shops, cafés selling hot chocolate and sticky confectionery, and the central part of the **Barri Gòtic.** To the right of La Rambla is Carme, an interesting street going into the heart of **El Raval**, worth a brief detour for **El Indio**, a textiles shop (at No. 24) founded in 1870 and little changed since. Inside there are long wooden counters for proper display of the cloth, and wooden chairs for stout ladies to rest their legs.

Back on the **Rambla de Sant Josep** (better known as the Rambla de les Flors), the air smells sweet. During the 19th century this was the only place where flowers were sold, and each vendor had his favourite clientele. The Catalan Impressionist artist Ramón Casas (1866–1932) picked out one of the flowersellers here to be his model, and later his wife.

TIP

The Teatre Poliorama has a good Sunday morning season for children, often with mime or music that dodges any language barriers.

LEFT: the best place for a stroll.
BELOW: human statues need patience.

The old music store next to the Palau de la Virreina is a little modernista *gem.*

BELOW:
a colourful fruit and vegetable stall in the Boqueria market.

On the right is the **Palau de la Virreina** ❻, a magnificent 18th-century rococo building set back from the road for greater effect. In 1771 Manuel Amat, Viceroy of Peru, sent a detailed plan from Lima for the construction of the house that he planned to build in La Rambla. The final building was not completed until 1778 and the Viceroy died only a few years after taking up residence. It was his young widow who was left to enjoy the palace, which became known as the palace of the "Virreina" or vicereine. Today it is an excellent exhibition venue, the official information centre for all cultural events in Barcelona, and a booking office. Wander into its handsome courtyard: around fiesta time there is usually some *gegant* (giant) or *drac* (dragon) lurking, before being brought out on parade. Designer souvenirs of Barcelona and good books are available in the shop. Next to it is a charming, ancient music store.

Get back on to La Rambla to fully appreciate, half a block further down, the entrance to the city's most popular and famous market, the **Mercat de la Boqueria** ❼, or Mercat de Sant Josep. The first stone was laid on 19 March 1840, Saint Joseph's day, to appease the saint whose convent in the same spot had been burned down in the 1835 riots. Again, take plenty of time to enjoy shopping there, or simply to observe. Discerning shoppers – restaurateurs early in the morning, housewives mid-morning and the men in charge of the Sunday *paella* on Saturdays – queue patiently for the best produce, bark their orders and refuse to be fobbed off with anything below par. The fishwives also shriek, trying to seduce passers-by into the day's best catch. It is a heady experience, and despite the frantic crowds, exceedingly heart-warming: there is something quintessentially Mediterranean about the noise, human warmth and the serious business of buying and eating wonderfully fresh produce.

On the opposite side of La Rambla is the **Palau Nou**. The total antithesis to La Boqueria, it is an ultra modern building that is supposedly completely automated, including "robot parking" on nine levels underground. It also provides a short cut through to the **Plaça del Pi**, and effectively frames the beautiful Gothic tower of the *plaça*'s church, Santa Maria del Pi.

Map on page 126

Executioner's spot

Continuing on down, La Rambla enters the **Pla de la Boqueria** (marked only by a widening of the Rambla, and a break in the shady avenue of trees). This was the site of executions in the 14th century, when it was paved with flagstones. The name dates from the previous century when tables selling fresh meat, *mesas de bocatería,* were erected here ("*boc*" was the Catalan for goat's meat). In the 15th century the tables of gamblers and cardsharps replaced the meat stalls.

Today the flagstones have been replaced by a Joan Miró (1893–1983) pavement created in the 1970s – look out for his signature. On the corner is the **Casa Bruno Quadras**, built by Josep Vilaseca in 1891. The colourful, extravagant decoration includes umbrellas, fans and a great Chinese dragon, demonstrating the Oriental influence felt by the modernists.

At this point the **Rambla dels Caputxins** begins, so-called because, until 1775, the left side was the site of the Capuchin Convent and its adjacent vegetable garden. The mood changes slightly now, as this stretch is dominated by the **Gran Teatre del Liceu ❽** (to book tel: 90 233 2211; for information tel: 93 485 9913), cathedral of the *bel canto* in Spain and launch-pad for names such as Carreras and Caballé. The original building, dating from 1861, was badly damaged by fire in 1994, but still peeks out of the enormous new edifice by

BELOW: the splendidly refurbished Gran Teatre del Liceu, reopened in 1999.

which it is now enclosed (*see page 139*). With its new technology and second stage, the opera house now takes over a whole block.

The **Café de l'Opera** opposite retains all the charms you would expect of one of the few remaining old-fashioned cafés in Barcelona. Opened in 1929, it is a good place to read the newspapers in the morning – subdued and peaceful – yet builds up to a giddy pitch late at night.

The Gran Teatre del Liceu ends opposite Ferràn, one of the most elegant streets in Barcelona in the first half of the 19th century. Remnants of this time can still be seen despite the invasion of fast food outlets and souvenir shops. Now pedestrianised, the street leads up to the Plaça Sant Jaume at the heart of the Barri Gòtic. The **Hotel Oriente**, a little further down La Rambla, preserves the structures of the Collegi de Sant Bonaventura, founded by Franciscan monks in 1652. The convent and cloister, built between 1652 and 1670, are there in their entirety. The cloister is now the hotel ballroom, surrounded by the monks' gallery. A wall plaque reminds readers that this was the first public place in Barcelona to use gas lighting.

In the first stretch of **Nou de la Rambla** is the **Palau Güell ❾** (guided tours only Mon–Sat 10am–5pm (winter); 10am–6.30pm (summer); entrance charge), built by Antoni Gaudí between 1885 and 1889 as the home of his patron, Count Güell. With this structure, the architect embarked on a period of fertile creativity. Here, Gothic inspiration alternates with elements of Arabic influence; the palace could be the set for a horror film. The building is structured around an enormous salon, from which a conical roof covered in pieces of tiling emerges to preside over an unusual landscape of capriciously placed battlements, balustrades and unusually shaped chimneys.

*One comfort of summer coming to an end is that mushrooms and sweet potatoes (*moniato*) arrive in the market, heralding autumnal days when braziers roasting chestnuts and sweet potatoes appear on strategic corners in La Rambla.*

BELOW: making a considered choice at the flower stall.

Map on page 126

Popular square

Back on the other side of La Rambla, an arcaded passageway leads to the infamous **Plaça Reial** , another Barcelona landmark and one of the most handsome yet decadent of its squares. Attempts to "clean it up" it have done little to change its character, so tourists on terrace bars still jostle with junkies, and backpackers share benches with tramps. Up-town yuppies, queuing for the stylish yet economic restaurant **Quinze Nits**, are typical of a new panorama in the Old Town. Restaurants and bars predominate, and the well-established **Jamboree** jazz club is here, along with its sister club **Tarantos** for flamenco, and other good places for dancing. The buzz never lets up, day or night.

On Sunday, stamp and coin collectors gather around the **Font de Les Tres Gràcies** and the two *fanals* (street lamps) designed by Antoni Gaudí. Inspired by the French urban designs of the Napoleonic period, this is the only one of the many squares planned in Barcelona during the 19th century that was built entirely according to its original plan. Its uniform, arcaded buildings were constructed by Francesc Daniel Molina on the plot where the Capuchin Convent once stood. Return to La Rambla through Passatge de Bacardí (the Cuban rum was created by a Catalan), noticing the **Herbolari Ferran** with its array of spices in small wooden drawers. On the corner with La Rambla is Arpi, a highly regarded photographic shop.

Tacky territory

The terraces that line La Rambla along this stretch are spurned by locals, but as long as you don't expect the ultimate culinary experience it is a temptation to sip a cool drink and watch the world go by. Where the promenade opens up

BELOW:
Plaça Reial, the hub of the Old Town.

TIP

If you want to avoid the queues at the best bars and restaurants, aim to eat at northern European times – which will be somewhat earlier than those of the local Barcelonans.

again into the **Plaça del Teatre**, or **Plaça de les Comèdies**, another notorious street leads off to the left, **Escudellers**. A kind of a cross between engrained seediness and 1990s trendiness, it is representative of many parts of Barcelona today. Walk along it to feel the pulse of the harsher elements of the city, and to observe its present evolution.

Escudellers opens up at the far end into a newly created square, **Plaça George Orwell ⓫**, the result of dense housing demolition, where several trendy bars and an excellent pizzeria have opened. The supposedly "surrealist" sculpture here is by Leandre Cristòfol.

Return back down Escudellers, passing Pakistani supermarkets, falafel bars, discos and dives. Narrow, fly-blown streets lead off to the right and left, most hiding extremely late-night bars and one, leading back to the Plaça Reial, an African restaurant. Particularly recommended are **Zoo**, which has a buzzy atmosphere and is good for light, alternative snacks; the more traditional restaurant **Los Caracoles** (with sizzling chickens on a blazing grill on the exterior wall); and newish **La Fonda**, which is related to Quinze Nits in the Plaça Reial and has the same effective formula – reasonably priced Catalan food, served in an attractive interior of palms and pale wood. The long queue at peak times is filled with the kind of locals you don't expect to see down this street.

Back on La Rambla you reach the spot where, in the 16th century, the city's first theatre was built. The present **Teatre Principal** replaced the old wooden theatre, which was for many years the only stage in Barcelona. A 2,000-seater, it was built on the site of the historical Corral de les Comèdies, a popular early theatre, although it never appealed to the bourgeoisie. Opposite is a monument to Frederic Soler "Pitarra", founder of the modern Catalan theatre.

BELOW: passing through, and passing time.

The few prostitutes remaining in this area choose the small square that surrounds the monument to offer their charms – almost as an epilogue to what used to be and a prologue to what still exists throughout the adjoining streets that make up the **Barri Xino** (Chinese Quarter, still better known as the Barrrio Chino). The area has been much cleaned up in recent years but some prostitutes remain, and the neon signs of sex establishments are still very much in evidence. The square marks the beginning of the **Rambla de Santa Mònica**, the last stretch of La Rambla before it reaches the harbour.

Map on page 126

To the waterfront

At this point the pace of the human river slows, as if reaching its delta, and the personality of La Rambla seems to fade. The Rambla Santa Mònica is lined with caricaturists and artists, portrait painters and artisans, and a craft market is held here at the weekend. Along these few metres the threads of past history and future events intertwine. This is where, in 1895, films were first shown publicly in Spain by the Lumière brothers. Some handsome buildings have been restored and new ones built, notably on the left for the university of Pompeu Fabra. On the right is the **Centre d'Art Santa Mònica** ⓬, a former convent redesigned as a Generalitat exhibition space by the highly regarded local architects Piñón and Viaplana, who have been instrumental in much of the new Barcelona. Opposite is the **Palau March** (1780), today the Generalitat's Department of Culture.

Just before the Santa Mònica art centre, a small street, Santa Mònica, heads off into Barri Xino to seedy old bars, newly fashionable old bars and even techno discos. Before going too far, however, pause for some French nostalgia in the timeless **Pastís** at No. 4. An evocative French atmosphere and suitably

BELOW: there's room to sit and enjoy the harbour in the refurbished Plaça Colom.

**Map
on page
126**

Gallic sounds are on offer here, except on Tuesday at 11.30pm when the ba
transforms itself into a corner of Buenos Aires by playing live tango music.

Towards the end of La Rambla, on the left, an old-fashioned ticket booth
loudly proclaims and sells tickets for the **Museu de la Cera** ⑬ (open daily
10am–10pm in summer; closed lunchtime in winter; entrance charge), in the
Passatge de la Banca. The roof of Barcelona's wax museum sports Superman
poised to leap from the top of the building, and the exhibits never fail to delight
children. Inside are more than 360 waxworks, giving an insight into some of
Catalonia's historic personalities. Youngsters love it, especially the spooky bits
but it is probably best to save it as a treat for a rainy day.

Around this part of La Rambla there is usually a horse and carriage waiting
patiently to whisk tourists off for a trot around town.

Our lady of mercy

A long street on the left, Ample, leads to the 18th-century church of **La Mare
de Déu de la Mercè** ⑭, usually known simply as **La Mercè** (like many Catalan women) and patron saint of Barcelona. A dramatic statue of the Virgin and
child stands on the top of the church, creating a distinctive element in the waterfront skyline. The square was one of the first urban spaces (1983) to appear as
a result of the socialist city council's long-term project of demolishing old buildings to open up dense areas.

It is at its most festive on 24 September, the day of La Mercè, when *gegants*
and *castellers* greet the dignitaries coming out of mass, before the real *festa
major* of Barcelona takes off. Every member of the Barça football team, whatever his creed, comes here to pay his respects to the Virgin after important victories, before going off to parade the trophy in front of
adoring fans in Plaça Sant Jaume.

The last building on the left side of La Rambla (now
occupied by the armed forces) has a curious history. In
1778 the foundry of the Royal Artillery, as well as its
workshop, were transferred to this building, popularly
known as El Refino. The foundry was one of the most
renowned cannon factories of its time. From 1844
until 1920 it was occupied by the offices of the Banco
de Barcelona (the first private Spanish bank) and,
since the Spanish Civil War (1936–39), it has been
converted into the offices of the military governor.

Making a challenging end to this long walk down
La Rambla is the steep climb to the top of the **Monument a Colom** ⑮ (open daily 9am–8.30pm in
summer, Mon–Fri 10am–1.30pm, 3.30–6.30pm,
Sat–Sun 10am–6.30pm in winter; entrance charge),
which stands at the centre of Plaça del Portal de la
Pau. Fortunately, it has an internal lift as well as a
great view of the city and port.

Cross the busy traffic here and you will reach the
relative peace of the waterfront, where an antique
market is held at weekends. From this point there is a
choice of diversions: the **Golondrinas** for trips around
the harbour or to the Olympic Port, or the **Rambla
de Mar**, a floating extension of La Rambla that con-
nects with the Moll d'Espanya and the Maremàgnum
leisure and commercial centre (*see page 183*). ❑

BELOW: the
Museu de la Cera is
a treat for children.

The Liceu

The origins of Barcelona's famous opera house, the Gran Teatre del Liceu, are curious. Philanthropist Manuel Gibert i Sans, a national militia commander, started the "Liceo Dramático de Aficionados" with the aim of organising soirées to raise funds for his battalion. The theatre company was housed for a while in the former convent of Montsió, where the first opera staged was Bellini's *Norma,* on 3 February 1838.

In 1842, looking for a bigger venue, they bought the land of the former convent of the Trinitarios on the Ramblas. Around this time the militia was dissolved and the company became a wholly artistic and social foundation. Gibert recruited the aristocrat Joaquim de Gispert i Anglí and the banker Manuel Girona i Agrafel, a principal representative of the new industrialist monied class, as backers for his project.

Construction began in 1844 of an enormous project second only to that of La Scala of Milan, with space for 4,000 spectators. The theatre boxes were sold for 15,000 pesetas each, in perpetuity, to the grand families who collaborated in the venture.

The Liceu was inaugurated in 1847, but a fire partially destroyed it and it was refitted in 1862. In the same year the Círculo del Liceu, a club that functioned as a meeting place for the city's power brokers, was started. It was described by the American social historian Gary Wray McDonogh in his book *The Good Families of Barcelona*: "The club was isolated [from the Liceu] as a prerogative of the upper class... The boxes, an extension of the family dwelling, were the dominion of the women where they held their meetings and socialising. El Círculo itself, on the other hand, was converted into an extension of the men's offices. Both were central parts of the Liceu as an institution."

Every type of performance, from musical galas, operas and ballets to rowdy carnival dances, were held in the theatre, attended by all classes of society, carefully segregated in their respective areas.

Some of the world's greatest musicians and artists have performed in the Gran Teatre del Liceu, including Igor Stravinsky, Manuel de Falla, Enrico Caruso, Maria Callas, Alfredo Kraus, Placido Domingo, Luciano Pavarotti and Catalonia's own Pablo Casals, Montserrat Caballé, and Josep Carreras, who made his debut here.

On 31 January 1994 a season of *Turandot* was interrupted by a dramatic fire which gutted the interior. After the initial shock, emotional reactions and not too much questioning about the fire's origins, the city authorities announced that the opera house would be rebuilt. Funded by a financial consortium, plus donations from individuals who felt very strongly about the future of their theatre, the renovation went ahead.

Architect Ignasi de Solà Morales modernised the acoustics, lighting and stage, and doubled the theatre's overall size to 350,000 sq. ft (32,000 sq. metres), while keeping to the original style. Appropriately, the theatre reopened with a performance of *Turandot* in October 1999, to much public acclaim. ❑

RIGHT: Montserrat Caballé, who is delighted that the Gran Teatre del Liceu has reopened.

BARRI GÒTIC

*There's no finer introduction to Barcelona's Golden Age
than a stroll around the warren of narrow streets
that constitutes the oldest part of the city*

Map
on page
144

The jewel of the Old Town, the Gothic Quarter or Barri Gòtic, is a dense nucleus of historic buildings that has formed the central part of the old city since Roman times. Today it represents the centre of municipal administration and is home to the Catalan autonomous government. The oldest part of the city, it is built around **Mont Tàber**, Taber Hill, a misnomer for what is little more than a mound in an otherwise flat city. This section of the Old Town is surrounded by the remains of Roman walls, within which very little has changed for centuries. Layer upon layer of different architectural styles illustrate the different periods of Barcelona's history, from remnants of the Roman city to contemporary architectural solutions seen in renovation work and extensions to old buildings. The Gothic period predominates, reflecting the glorious medieval period when Catalonia was at its height.

This route is designed to take in the key sites, and constitutes an enjoyable walk through the present day Gothic quarter – its residents, musicians and artists, its cafés and commerce. Alternatively, you can simply absorb its atmosphere by wandering aimlessly around its narrow streets, feeling the sense of history and observing the day-to-day comings and goings of the local people.

Approach from Plaça de Catalunya down **Portal de l'Angel**, a wide paved street full of shoe shops, fashion shops and the hi-tech branch of El Corte Inglés, which specialises in music, books, sport and computers, and is housed in a grandiose building reminiscent of long ago department stores. The wide space lends itself to street performances, bound to waylay you. Bear left at the fork at the bottom, past the *modernista* gas board offices, an Aladdin's cave of a toyshop, and the **Col.legi d'Arquitectes,** the architects' association, a 1960s building with friezes designed by Picasso, although they were executed by Norwegian Carl Nesjar.

Plaça Nova

The street leads out into **Plaça Nova ❶** and there, in front, is one of the main Roman gates to the old city, the **Portal del Bisbe**, or Bishop's Gate. The towers date from the 1st century BC but the name came later, from the nearby 18th-century bishop's palace. The sculpted letters by Catalan artist Joan Brossa spell out "Barcino", the Roman name for the city, like a caption for this historic image.

Here Plaça Nova merges with **Avinguda de la Catedral**, newly paved and streamlined into a wide open space spreading out at the foot of the Cathedral steps. The paving hides an underground car park and successfully highlights the drama of the ancient facades, which rise theatrically above the Roman walls. Sit on one of the polished stone benches or the

PRECEDING PAGES:
an ornate courtyard
in the Barri Gòtic.
LEFT: a shady Old
City street.
BELOW: tending the
window boxes.

A quiet corner of the Romanesque courtyard of the Palau Episcopal.

terrace of the **Hotel Colón** and take it all in: the constant movement of children footballs, bicycles, the clicking and whirring of cameras, the balloon vendor and beggars. An antiques market takes place here on Thursdays, and at the weekend the gatherings of Sardana dancers form large, impenetrable bouncing circles (6.30pm on Saturday, midday on Sunday). All this is played out against the surprisingly neo-Gothic front of the Cathedral, which was tacked on to its 13th-century origins in the 19th century.

Into the Barri Gòtic

Enter the Gothic quarter through the Roman gate in Plaça Nova, up the slope into **Bisbe**. On the right is the **Palau Episcopal,** built in 1769 around a 12th-century courtyard, which is the only remaining evidence of the original palace after centuries of modifications. The frescoes on the facade (facing the Carrer Montjuïc del Bisbe) date from the 18th century, while the triple recess windows and large *flamígero* window in the courtyard are from the 14th century.

Opposite the palace entrance a short street, **Santa Llúcia**, leads towards the cathedral. On the corner is a chapel dedicated to Santa Llúcia, patron saint of the blind and, curiously, of seamstresses. Built in 1268, it is one of the oldest parts of the Cathedral and a fine example of Romanesque architecture, with images of the Annunciation and the Visitation decorating the facade capitals. The holy water font inside the chapel is from the 14th century. A rear doorway leads into the cathedral cloister. The **Fira de Santa Llúcia**, a Christmas arts and crafts fair, takes over the narrow streets from early December, and the Cathedral square is filled with Christmas trees of all shapes and sizes, plus everything you could possibly need to make your own nativity scene.

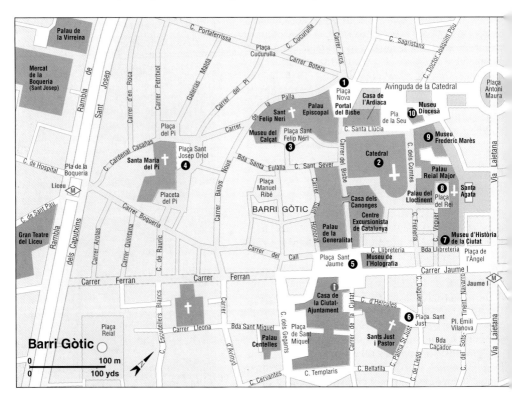

The Cathedral precincts

Map on page 144

Opposite the Capella de Santa Llúcia, on the other corner, is the **Casa de l'Ardiaca** (Archdeacon's residence), built in the 15th century on Roman ruins. It has one of the most evocative patios in the city. A tall, elegant palm tree rises high above a fountain, which is decorated with flowers at Corpus Christi and the setting for a curious tradition, *l'ou com balla*, in which a fragile egg "dances" on the spouting water. The building contains the **Municipal History Archives,** a valuable collection of historical chronicles and documents. Recent extensions at the rear of the patio have opened up the building, revealing another angle on the Roman tower and part of the first city wall, dating from the 1st century BC. The outer wall, with square towers and the remains of two aqueducts (which can be seen from Avinguda de la Catedral) is from the 4th century AD.

Enter the **Catedral ❷** (open daily 8am–1.30pm, 4–7.30pm) by the main door. Its glowing darkness and slightly scented air from the myriad candles are a marked but soothing contrast after the bright Mediterranean skies outside. Its traditional, ornate chapels are a far cry from the simple majesty of Santa Maria del Mar (*see page 158*). For any kind of spiritual peace it is essential to visit in off-peak hours, such as first thing in the morning, to avoid herded groups and the inevitable accumulation of human traffic; attending mass is no solution, as the congregation chatters loudly and moves in and out at will.

The construction of the cathedral began in 1298 under the patronage of Jaume II, on the spot where an early Christian church had been destroyed by the pillaging of Al-Mansur, the vizier of Córdoba, in 925. Some signs of it can be seen in the remarkable subterranean world beneath the present Cathedral, which can be visited from the City History Museum (*see page 149*).

The main area consists of three naves and an apse with an ambulatory beneath an octagonal dome. Two 14th- and 15th-century towers rise at each end of the transept. Beneath the main altar is the crypt of Santa Eulàlia, and of particular note are the dome's multi-coloured keystones. Some say that this is one of Catalonia's three "magnetic" points. The tomb of Santa Eulàlia, behind the altar, is an important 14th-century work of art, executed in alabaster by a disciple of Giovanni Pisano during the same period as the episcopal cathedral. The most outstanding altarpiece is that of the Transfiguration, designed by Bernat Martorell in the chapel dedicated to Sant Salvador, which was built in 1447.

The high-backed choir pews are by Pere Sanglada (1399), and the lower-backed benches were carved by Maciá Bonafé towards the end of the same century. The retrochoir (the extension behind the high altar) was built at the beginning of the 16th century by the artist Bartolomé Ordoñez. The Capella del Santo Cristo de Lepanto (Chapel of Christ Lepanto) contains the crucifix borne in the Christian flagship against the Ottomans in the battle of Lepanto. It was built between 1405 and 1454 and is considered to be the finest example of Gothic art in the cathedral.

The oldest part is that of the Porta de Sant Ivo (St Ive's Door), where some of the Romanesque windows and archways can still be seen. Although most of the

By the entrance to the Casa de l'Ardiaca is a letterbox, designed by modernista architect Domènech i Montaner. The swallows suggest how fast the post should travel; the tortoise represents the reality.

BELOW: traffic is no longer allowed to enter Cathedral square.

TIP

For a gargoyle's view
of the city, take a lift
to the rooftop of the
cathedral (open from
10.30am to 1pm, 4.30
to 6pm; closed Sat pm
and Sun; entrance
charge).

cathedral's more antique furnishings are now housed in the city museum, there is a small collection in the **Sala Capitular** or Chapter House (open daily 10am–1pm, 4–7pm; entrance charge).

A small pavilion beside the Porta de la Pietat still shelters a 15th-century terracotta statue of St George by Antoni Claperós, and the door that leads to the western end of the transept is made from the marble taken from the earlier Romanesque cathedral.

On one side is the Santa Eulàlia Portal which leads to the **cathedral cloister**, a quiet haven and perhaps the most atmospheric part of the Cathedral, with the sound of running water from the pretty fountain and a romantic garden of elegant palms, medlars and highly perfumed magnolia trees, all enclosed by the 15th-century wrought-iron railings. Thirteen geese are the sole residents, symbolising the age of Santa Eulàlia, co-patron saint of Barcelona, when she died.

Recommended restaurants near the Cathedral include La Cassola, with tasty Catalan home cooking, in Sant Sever, and Portalón in Banys Nous. The latter, a timeless *bodega,* is a good bet in winter, when its wholesome bean stews can best be appreciated.

Devastation of war

Leave the cloister through the side door which gives on to **Plaça Garriga Bachs**. To the left notice the picturesque bridge across the street (another neo Gothic construction), linking two departments of the Generalitat. Cross the square to **Montjuïc del Bisbe**, a narrow street leading into **Plaça Sant Felip Neri ❸**. This small square is a treasure, enclosed by heavy stone buildings and happily neglected, which increases its historic impact.

BELOW: *sardanas* in front of the Cathedral.

Adjoining an 18th-century church here is a school, so if you coincide with laytime the peace will be shattered by shrieking children and stray footballs. he children's cries, echoing around the walls, are a melancholy reminder that large number of children were killed here when a bomb dropped nearby dur- ng the Civil War. The pock-marked church facade tells the tale, and the eccen- ric **Museu del Calçat** (Shoe Museum) shares the story (open Tues–Sun 1am–2pm; entrance charge). The museum was formerly in a street that used to e opposite the Cathedral, **Corríbia**, which has since been cleared to make Avinguda de la Catedral, and was moved to the *plaça*, brick by brick. An enor- nous shoe made to measure for the Columbus statue in La Rambla and a gold tiletto worn by Victoria de los Angeles are among the curiosities.

Take the other exit to **Sant Sever**, turn right past several antique shops then ollow the road down **Baixada Santa Eulàlia** into a world apart, with hidden :ourtyards behind enormous wooden doors and small dark workshops where urniture is polished and restored. At **Banys Nous**, turn right past a shop dis- olaying nightdresses from another era. On the wall opposite, a panel of ceramic iles explains the origin of the street's name.

Life in the squares

Where the street joins Palla (which, to the right, runs back to the Cathedral) turn left towards **Plaça Sant Josep Oriol ❹**. This lively square, dominated by the sought-after terrace of the **Bar del Pi**, is one of the most popular spots in the Old Town. Along with the adjoining Plaça del Pi and Placeta del Pi, it embraces the church of **Santa Maria del Pi**. Begun in 1322 and completed in the 15th century, this is a fine example of Catalan Gothic architecture, fortress-like on the

A giant shoe in the Museu del Calçat, made to fit the Columbus statue.

BELOW: entertainment in the Plaça del Pi.

exterior but ample and welcoming inside. The rose window is magnificent when lit from within. Often, guests in full evening dress attending society weddings at the church can be seen mingling in the square with stall holders who come in from the country to sell goat's cheese and honey at the weekend market (open Sat 10am–8.30pm, Sun 9am–2pm). In the adjacent Plaça Sant Josep Oriol artists display and sell their work.

Live music from buskers became so regular here that local residents campaigned to have it banned, except between 6–8pm on Saturday and noon–2pm on Sunday. Guests of the extremely popular Hotel Jardí no doubt appreciate the ruling. Before leaving the square check out the Roca knife shop, which dates from 1911, and around the corner from it the very pretty street **Petritxol**

The **Palau Fiveller,** at No. 4 in Plaça Sant Josep Oriol, is occupied by an Agricultural Institute with information on rural tourism. Take the narrow street **Ave Maria** that runs down its side and at the end turn right, back into Banys Nous. Even the old *granja* (milk bar) here has had the trendy 1990s treatment. It is well worth having a look in Instinto at No. 5 for well-designed fashion for women. One landmark, the wonderful Obach hat shop, remains unchanged. Turn left here and follow **Call**, the main street in Barcelona's important Jewish quarter until 1401 (*see page 151*), as it winds up to **Plaça Sant Jaume ➎**.

Each year, from early December until after the fiesta of Els Reis on 6 January, the Plaça Sant Jaume is dominated by the largest nativity scene in town – and the queue to visit it.

The political heart of the city

The area that today forms the Plaça Sant Jaume was inaugurated in 1823, at the same time as the streets **Ferran** and **Jaume I**. The square is considered to be the civic heart of the city, and it is from here that the **Ajuntament** (Town Hall) presides over Barcelona from the Casa de la Ciutat, and the Generalitat (autonomous government) presides over Catalonia. Their position, facing each other across the square, has been a potent symbol of political opposition in recent years: the socialist Ajuntament, under the popular mayor Pasqual Maragall and his successor Joan Clos, and the conservative Generalitat led by Jordi Pujol as president and his **Convergencia i Unió** party. Maragall challenged Pujol for the presidency of Catalonia in the October 1999 elections: it was a close-run contest, but the status quo was retained.

Dark grey, German-made cars with plain-clothed escorts sweep in and out of the Palau de la Generalitat under the respectful salutes of the *Mossos d'Esquadra*, the autonomous police force. Opposite, the town councillors travel in blue *Seat* saloons, passing the time of day with the dishevelled *Guardia Urbanas*, as they leave. Demonstrations wind up here, as do festive parades, Barça fans and players after major football and basketball victories and, of course, visiting dignitaries. This is where President Tarradellas was given a clamorous reception on his return from exile to attend the birth of the new democracy.

Both buildings are of Gothic origin and can be visited on key public holidays (such as Sant Jordi, 23 April) or at weekends by prior arrangement (tel: 93 402 4600 for the Generalitat, and 93 402 7364 for the Casa de la Ciutat). Each has some fine elements: the oldest part of the Casa de la Ciutat is the **Saló de**

BELOW: *castellers* at a festival in Plaça Sant Jaume.

ent, created by Pere Llobet in 1373; the Gothic facade tucked down the side treet **Ciutat** is the most delicate. The **Pati dels Tarongers** (a 16th-century ourtyard full of orange trees) is perhaps the most famous part of the Palau de a Generalitat and the scene of many official photographs. From the square you an glimpse the painted ceilings of a large reception room.

There is a tourist information office in the Town Hall, on the corner of La Ciu-at (open Mon–Sat 10am–8pm, Sun 10am–2pm). Take La Ciutat out of the quare and immediately turn left into Hercules, a quiet street leading to **Plaça ant Just ⑥**. This is an interesting, often overlooked corner of the *barri* with strong sense of identity. The *plaça* has all the elements of a village: a church, colmado (grocer's shop), a restaurant, a noble house, and kids playing foot-all. The streets off it are also worth exploring, notably **Palma Sant Just** for the *odega* and its breakfasts with homemade omelettes, and **Lledó** for its neglected medieval houses.

The church of **Sant Just and Sant Pastor** was an ancient royal chapel until he 15th century. According to legend, it is built on the site of Barcelona's first Christian temple. The Café de l'Acadèmia spills out on to the square, serving xcellent Catalan *nouvelle cuisine* at an accessible price.

Follow **Dagueria** past a feminist bookshop, an excellent cheese shop and ver Jaume I turning right into Baixada Llibreteria until you come to the **Museu d'Història de la Ciutat ⑦** on the corner of Veguer (open Tues–Sat 10am–2pm, 4–8pm, all day in summer, Sun 10am–2pm; entrance charge). The museum provides a useful and enlightening perspective on the city's his-ory. Particularly impressive are the well-charted Roman remains that spread ut beneath the streets, running as far as the Cathedral.

Map on page 144

An inscription in the Museu d'Història de la Ciutat.

BELOW: there is still a neighbourhood atmosphere in the Barri Gòtic.

Map
on page
144

Royal palace

The **Plaça del Rei ❽** is a fine medieval square, a living testimony to the nobil-ity of the ancient city of Barcelona, and was a cattle fodder market for three cen-turies. It was here that all the flour brought into the city in payment of taxes was collected. Little seems to have changed since then. The sculpture is by Basque artist Eduardo Chillida.

At one end is the **Palau Reial Major**, with vast vaulted ceilings, 13th-century triple-recess windows and 14th-century rose windows. The silhouette of the box-shaped Renaissance tower of Rei Martí is an outstanding feature of the palace. Built like a dovecote, it has fine views down over the royal complex. The main room of the palace, the great **Saló del Tinell**, whose construction began with Pedro "El Cerimoniós" in 1359, was later converted to a baroque church, only to recover its original appearance after restoration works were carried out during and after the Civil War. During the 15th century this was where the Inquisition held court. Legend has it that the walls of the tribunal cannot bear a lie to be told and that, when this occurred, the ceiling stones would move, adding further to the terror of the unfortunate victims. Today, the salon functions as an exhibition area. Adjacent to it is the **Capella de Santa Àgata**, which houses the stone on which the saint's breasts were mutilated. Construction of the chapel started at the beginning of the 14th century. Inside is the *Condestable* altarpiece by Jaume Huguet.

Opposite the chapel is the **Palau del Lloctinent**. When the kingdoms of Catalonia and Aragón were joined with that of Castile, Carlos V created the office of Deputy (*Lloctinent*) for the court's representative, and this palace, the official residence, was built in 1549 by Antoni Carbonell. The facade is Catalan-Gothic; however, the inner courtyard is one of the few extant examples of Renaissance architec-ture left in the city. Until recently the palace was the headquarters of the **Arxiu de la Corona d'Aragó** (Archive of the Crown of Aragon).

Feeding the masses

The Baixada de Santa Clara leads up behind the cathe-dral's transept. Return to Comtes and follow the side of the Cathedral to a tiny square, **Sant Iu**, which leads into the lovely courtyard of the **Museu Frederic Marès ❾** (open Tues–Sat 10am–7pm, Sun 10am–3pm; entrance charge). This private collection, donated by the sculptor, Marès, in 1946, includes one of the most important displays of Spanish sculpture including medieval pieces in the newly opened crypt. The **Museu Sentimental**, on the upper floors, gives an insight into daily life in Barcelona in the 18th and 19th century. The summer café is even more enticing.

Comtes comes out into the **Pla de la Seu**, the small space immediately in front of the Cathedral. On the right is a simple but very beautiful Gothic building, recently restored, the **Pia Almoina**. Once the place where 100 meals were given out to the poor daily, it now houses the **Museu Diocesà ❿** (open Tues–Sat 10am–2pm, 5–8pm, Sun 11am–2pm; entrance charge), which has a small but varied collection of religious objects and paintings. ❏

BELOW: the Palau del Lloctinent and Rei Martí tower.

The Jewish City

Throughout Catalonia the Jewish quarter of a town or city is known as the *call*, from the Hebrew *qahqal* which means "meeting". The most important *call* was in Barcelona. Situated west of the Roman metropolis in what is now the Gothic Quarter, it reached its peak of importance during the Middle Ages and had a remarkable cultural reputation. Many famous philosophers, writers, astronomers and intellectuals lived here between the 9th and 12th centuries, including the poet Ben Ruben Izahac, philosophers Abraham Ben Samuel Hasdai, Rabbi Salomon Arisba and the Biblical scholar Joseph Ben Caspí.

For centuries the only university institution in Catalonia was the "Universidad Judía" or "Escuela Mayor". This thriving community also had a talent for finance and monarchs were known to apply for loans. Their knowledge was so advanced that they were made ambassadors at court. But their display of wealth and their superior lifestyle created great jealousy.

The fortunes of the Jews began a slow decline in 1243 when Jaume I ordered the separation of the Jewish quarter from the rest of the city and made Jews wear long hooded capes with distinguishing red or yellow circles. Fights began to break out, and became worse when a rumour spread that the Jews were responsible for bringing the Black Death to Spain. Full-scale rioting erupted in several cities in 1391, provoked mainly by a group from Seville who encouraged the population to storm houses in the Jewish quarter and murder their occupants.

These riots began in Valencia in July 1391 and spread to Mallorca, Barcelona, Girona, Lléida and Perpignan. But those in Barcelona were by far the most violent; the *qahqal* was virtually destroyed and about 1,000 Jews died. The survivors were forced either to convert to Christianity or flee, despite the efforts of the national guard who defended the lives and properties of the persecuted as best they could.

Joan I ordered the arrest and execution of 15 Castilians responsible for the uprising but despite the monarch's good intentions the *call* was never rebuilt. By 1395 the flow of anti-semitism had reached such proportions that the synagogue on the street then called "Sanahuja" was converted into a church (today the Església de Sant Jaume, in the Carrer de Ferran). In 1396, the principal synagogue was rented to a pottery maker.

The *call* finally disappeared in 1401 when the synagogues were abolished and Jewish cemeteries destroyed. It was not until 1931 that the first new Spanish synagogue was established, at the corner of Balmes and Provença streets. It was shut down at the beginning of the Civil War, and reopened in 1948, in the Avinguda de Roma. It later moved to its present site in Carrer d'Avenir.

Today the only evidence of the prosperous era of the *call* are certain stretches of the Carrer de Banys Nous and the Carrer del Call, the Jewish quarter's main street. To a lesser extent, Carrer de Sant Domènec del Call preserves some historic buildings. ❑

RIGHT: Hebrew inscription on a 14th-century memorial stone in the Carrer de Marlet.

LA RIBERA

The narrow streets and grand mansions of La Ribera resound with reminders of medieval commerce, but the focus is switching to a lively bar and restaurant scene

Map on page 156

The *barri* of La Ribera is loosely defined as that part of the Old Town which is separated from the Barri Gòtic by Via Laietana. There is a very beaten track to the door of its star museum, the Museu Picasso. The most visited museum in Barcelona, the Picasso is a must, but the area has many other charms which should not be overlooked. Technically speaking, La Ribera lies between Princesa and the waterfront, but extending the definition slightly we'll take the long way round to get there and enjoy discovering this district with its many contrasts, from the present-day rag trade to medieval merchants' houses, from new social and urban developments to the most beautiful church in Barcelona, from contemporary artists' studios to carpenters' workshops.

Like so many of the city's *barris*, La Ribera is a richly woven texture of contrasts. What could be more representative of this than the **Palau de la Música Catalana ❶** (guided tours daily 10.30am–3.30pm; entrance charge), an extravaganza of a concert hall designed by leading *modernista* architect Domènech i Montaner in 1908, and declared a World Heritage building by UNESCO. The only concert hall in Europe to be naturally lit, it was cramped uncomfortably in all its ornate splendour between dull neighbours. However, in a major renovation plan by Oscar Tusquets, architect of an earlier extension, it has been liberated and a new *plaça* and underground rehearsal space are being created.

PRECEDING PAGES: the Palau de la Música Catalana. **LEFT:** Santa Maria del Mar. **BELOW:** the first modern addition to the Palau de la Música.

Locals rush past dismissively, busy about their day-to-day routine, while visitors queue patiently for a tour of the building. Tours are often accompanied by the sounds of a soprano in an upstairs rehearsal room practising her scales. Visits are now possible since the resident orchestra, the Orquestra Simfònica de Barcelona i Nacional de Catalunya (OBC), moved to the grand new **Auditori**, near Glòries. Don't miss the chance to see inside the Palau de la Música, though perhaps the best way is to attend one of the concerts in its busy classical season, or even a jazz concert during the International Jazz Festival.

Rags to riches

Keeping the colourful kaleidoscope of stained glass and mosaics in mind, continue along the street Sant Pere Més Alt through the heart of today's rag trade district. This is the wholesale end of Catalonia's once great textile industry. On weekdays it is buzzing with commercial activity, particularly around the 19th-century arcades, like the Passeig Sert, birthplace of the painter Josep Maria Sert (1876–1945).

The street emerges into the comparative tranquillity of **Plaça Sant Pere ❷**, with the much renovated 10th-century church, **Sant Pere de les Puel.les**, a former Benedictine monastery. In the middle of this triangu-

Street theatre is endemic in the old quarter of Barcelona: a puppeteer attracts an audience.

BELOW: dancing in the street at a local fiesta.

lar square is a delicate *modernista* drinking fountain, designed by Pere Falqués, famed for his bench-cum-lampposts on Passeig de Gràcia. Follow Basses Sant Pere down past stray dogs, drunks and local bars with a firm grip on rucksacks and cameras to **Plaça Sant Agustí Vell ❸**. Signs of urban cleansing are evident, but thankfully new social housing and created *plaças* have not wiped out local colour altogether. There are several terrace bars, but hold out for the Bar Mundial, a 1950s time warp famed for its seafood *tapas*.

From here, one option is to take Carders, rapidly becoming Dominican territory (there is a great musical atmosphere on Saturday and Sunday evenings), to the delightful Romanesque chapel of **Marcús**, where post horses were blessed on the main route out, being just beyond the city walls and the Portal Major. Turn left into Montcada for the Museu Picasso. Another option is to meander a little longer down Tantarantana, passing more urban rehabilitation to the former **Convent de Sant Agustí ❹**. Now a civic centre, and highlighted by the Ruta del Gòtic as a 14th-century building, it also houses the new **Museu de la Xocolata** (Mon–Sat 10am–7pm, Sun 10am–3pm; closed Tues; entrance charge), mildly interesting for kids and chocolate buffs.

Just before Princesa, turn right into **Assaonadors**, which immediately on the right opens up into a long *plaça*, **Allada-Vermell**, a typical Barcelona "hard" square. Created by the demolition of a row of housing on one side of Carrer de l'Allada and a row from Carrer Vermell, it brings light and space into the dense *barri*, and provides a recreation area for local residents. The **Espai Escènic Joan Brossa**, an alternative theatre with its own company, whose productions tend to be in line with artist-poet Brossa's thinking and interests (*see page 75*) is well worth checking out. One of Brossa's visual poems sets the scene: the

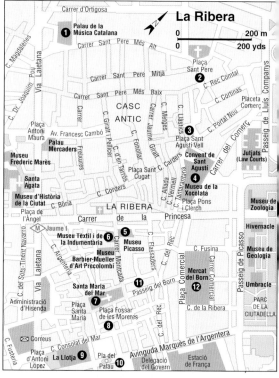

horizontal B (for Brossa) on the roof has "lost" one of its curved pieces, which is lying on the ground to provide an open-air stage.

Continue along Assaonadors, taking the first left which leads into **Princesa**. The Parc de la Ciutadella (*see page 162*) is at the end of the road, but turn right towards the city centre again. It is a busy, narrow street full of lorries unloading goods "made in China" and taxis unloading tourists by Montcada. Many of the buildings are being restored to a bygone elegance and sold off expensively as studio flats by rich developers. The pavements are crowded with Asian shopkeepers on mobile telephones and tourists looking for the Picasso Museum.

On the corner before turning into Montcada be tempted by a "roque de Montserrat", speciality of the *patisseria* **Brunells**. If these boulders, looking remarkably like meringues, from the sacred mountain of Montserrat don't appeal, there is a wide choice of refreshments in the café behind the shop.

Street of museums

Montcada has become museum street supreme since the local authorities started renovating its medieval palaces in 1957, but it is a lot more besides and can be enjoyed on many levels. Named after the fallen during the conquest of Mallorca, it was the city's most elegant district from the 12th to the 18th centuries. It linked the waterfront with the commercial areas, when Catalonia's trading in the Mediterranean was at its height. The rich merchants' palaces reflect this former prosperity. As you jostle with the crowd in the narrow street, glance up at the menacing gargoyles and elegant medieval arches on top-floor terraces. And pause between exhibitions to sit in one of the peaceful patios, where the past is palpable in the stones and fine masonry.

Map on page 156

BELOW:
Picasso's favourite meeting place, Els Quatre Gats.

The **Museu Picasso** ❺ (open Tues–Sat including public holidays 10am–8pm, Sun 10am–3pm; entrance charge) at Montcada 15–23, opened in 1963, now occupies five palaces: Palau Berenguer d'Aguilar, Baró de Castellet, Meca, Casa Mauri and Finestres. The latter two, opened in October 1999, are for temporary exhibitions; the main entrance is through the 15th-century Aguilar palace. Its beautiful courtyard, with a surrounding first-floor gallery and pointed archways resting on slender columns, was designed by Marc Safont, best known for the inner patio of the **Generalitat** building.

The museum has the most complete collection of Picasso's early works, including sketches in school books and a masterly portrait of his mother done when he was only 16. The Blue Period (1901–4) is also well represented. It is an absorbing collection although there are only a limited number of Picasso's later works, apart from the fascinating studies of *Las Meninas* from the 1950s.

Opposite is the **Museu Tèxtil i de la Indumentària** ❻ (open Tues–Sat 10am–6pm, Sun 10am–3pm; entrance charge) housed in another noble Gothic palace, the Marquès de Lló. The museum has a small collection, with fabrics from the 14th century to the present day, some notable *modernista* and Balenciaga creations and tools from the 19th-century Catalan textile industry. In truth, it is perhaps more visited for the attractive café that spills on to the courtyard, serving snacks until late in the evening, and for its inspired gift shop.

Adjoining it is the **Museu Barbier-Mueller d'Art Precolombí** (open Tues–Sat 10am–6pm, Sun 10am–3pm; entrance charge), which has a small but prestigious collection of pre-Colombian art, representing most styles of pre-Hispanic American civilisations, bequeathed to Barcelona by the Geneva museum. The gift shop has some beautiful contemporary Indian work, albeit at Western prices.

Continuing down the street there is the avant-garde **Sala Montcada** at No. 14, run by the highly regarded prosperous cultural foundation of La Caixa, the affluent Catalan savings bank. On the other side in the Palau Cervelló, No. 25, is the **Galeria Maeght** (closed lunchtime). Both are guaranteed to have worthwhile exhibitions.

Reeling from these cultural riches, pop into the marble-and-tile haven **El Xampanyet** for a glass of wonderful sparkling wine and some anchovies. Here the street opens into **Plaçeta Montcada**, which contains an exotic palm tree, and **Euskaletxea**, one of the most authentic Basque bars to emerge in the recent trend for Basque bars. You must arrive at aperitif time (around 1pm or 8pm) to catch the best *tapas*, or else you'll have to go for a full meal in the restaurant.

Souvenir and "arty" shops abound here, and are beginning to eclipse the originals selling blue overalls and such like. Wander through the labyrinth of streets off Montcada to get closer to the true local atmosphere. There are many attractive new shops, bars and studios, too, worth visiting and useful for gift ideas.

Santa Maria del Mar

One such street is **Sombrerers** on the right (named, like many in the area, after the medieval guilds, in this case the hatters'), just before reaching the Passeig lel Born. Follow its shade, with the towering edifice of Santa Maria del Mar on the left, past an exquisite grocer's specialising in nuts, a local barber's and the gossip of the chicken shop, to reach the Plaça Santa Maria, once the church's graveyard. The Gothic fountain is one of the oldest in the city, dating from 1402. On reaching the square, stand back and take in the Gothic facade of the **Església de Santa Maria del Mar** ❼ (open daily 9.30am–1.30pm, 4.30–8pm; free) considered by many – and justly so – to be the most beautiful church in Barcelona. Its soaring majesty is uplifting, and should not be missed.

The church was built relatively quickly, between 1329 and 1384, resulting in a purity of style which ranks it as the most perfect example of Gothic church architecture in Catalonia. All the local corporations collaborated in the building and it became a symbol of the economic and political power of Catalonia in this period. The facade exhibits all the characteristics of the Catalan Gothic style: "prevalence of horizontal lines; flat terraced roofing; wide open spaces; strong buttresses and octagonal towers ending in terraces", according to Alexandre Cirici, the Catalan art historian. It is a much more down-to-earth style than Northern European Gothic, lacking the decorative filigree and pointed spires of the latter. As the critic Robert Hughes says in his book *Barcelona*: "The mass counts for more than the opening… Catalan architects did not want to imitate the organic profusion of detail in northern Gothic. They liked a wall."

The rose window is 15th century, the original having been lost in the earthquake of 1428. The interior is breathtaking in its simplicity and elegance. The church is built in what is known as the "salon" design, with three lofty and almost identical naves, which contribute to the sense of space. Ironically, the drama of more recent history has also contributed to this purity: fire during the

Map on page 156

Sun streams through a stained-glass window in Santa Maria del Mar.

LEFT: fancy dress costume for sale.
BELOW: candles glow in the church.

TIP

Santa Maria del Mar is a popular venue for concerts (as well as for fashionable weddings), so check local listings for a recommended opportunity to sit back and enjoy this sacred corner of Barcelona.

Civil War destroyed a great deal of the interior, which left it free of over-ornate decoration. The octagonal columns are 13 metres (43 ft) apart, a distance no other medieval structure was able to achieve. Robert Hughes sums up this extraordinary beauty: "There is no grander or more solemn architectural space in Spain than Santa Maria del Mar."

The old commercial district

Leave through the side door of the church, which gives on to the **Plaça Fossar de les Moreres** ❽, a memorial to the fallen in the 1714 siege of Barcelona (*see page 32*), who are buried here in the former cemetery. Restored in 1986 by Carme Fiol, one of the leading architects in Barcelona's urban space programme, it is a favourite venue for Catalan nationalists to meet on 11 September, La Diada, the day the siege ended.

Return to Plaça Santa Maria, passing a shop selling the most creative *botifarras* (sausages) imaginable, and turn left into **Canvis Vells**. If you want to be sidetracked, one of the widest selections of Catalan and Spanish wines is just down **Agullers** in the Viniteca. If not, continue to Consolat del Mar, and the large volume of **La Llotja** ❾, the former stock exchange (now in Passeig de Gràcia). Its core is from the 14th century, but the outer shell was completed in 1802. The Chamber of Commerce occupies most of the building and organises occasional visits (tel: 93 319 2412), although part of the Acadèmia de Bellas Artes, where Picasso and Miró studied, is still on an upper floor.

The main facade of La Llotja (not used as an entrance), gives on to **Pla del Palau** ❿ where a royal palace once stood. Now devoted mostly to restaurants, it was the political centre of town for a period during the 18th and 19th centuries

BELOW:
the courtyard
of La Llotja.

MEDIEVAL GUILDS

Wandering around the *barri* of La Ribera, you get a real sense of pervading history from the evocative names of its narrow streets. Particularly noticeable are the streets named after trades, a throwback to the medieval boom when many guilds were formed to look after the interests of the different craftsmen.

At their height, between the 13th and 15th centuries, there were 135 *gremis* (guilds), and 52 streets still carry their names. Watch out for Sombrerers (hatters), Flassaders (blanket weavers), Mirallers (mirror makers), Argenteria (silversmiths), Assaonadors (tanners), Agullers (needle makers) and Semoleres (pasta makers). A few medieval *tallers* (workshops) also remain.

In some streets a niche in the wall indicates where the devoted saint of the respective guild, usually dedicated to its patrons, would stand. The Museu d'Història de la Ciutat (*see page 149*) has a room dedicated to the guilds, with documents and paintings pertaining to the craftsmen and their work. The Museu del Calçat (Shoe Museum) in Plaça Sant Felip Neri is housed in the guildhall of the Shoemakers, the first guild to be formed and the last to be disbanded – not until the 20th century, in fact, when Civil War broke out.

Map on page 156

under the dominant viceroy. There are several good restaurants to choose from, but you could walk past the most famous without even knowing it, **Passadís d'en Pep** at No. 2, hidden away down a private-looking corridor.

Keeping on the same pavement, walk through to **Plaça de les Olles** (Square of the Cooking Pots), a charming little square with pleasant terrace cafés. In the far corner turn into Vidrieria. Anna Povo is a stylish shop on the corner of Esparteria selling its own label clothes. An ancient glass shop at No. 8 befits this street of "glaziers", selling all manner of glassware and run by the twelfth generation of the same family.

Glass and tin fairs used to be held in the **Passeig del Born** ⓫ at the end of the road, as well as jousts and tournaments from the 13th to the 17th century. Take time to wander along this boulevard and its adjoining streets, where the bars, shops and art galleries change hands and style with remarkable frequency, but where a few stalwarts remain, like the *colmado* selling *legumbres*, delicious ready-cooked lentils and beans.

At the end, in Plaça Comercial, there are several good cafés and restaurants, any of which would make a good stopping point and a fine place to contemplate the magnificent wrought-iron **Mercat del Born** ⓬, designed by Fontseré and Cornet in 1873. The building functioned as Barcelona's central wholesale fruit and vegetable market from 1876 until 1971, and is now being converted into what will be the largest library in the city.

The whole area takes on a different atmosphere at night when the many small bars and hidden restaurants come to life. International and Catalan cuisines abound, with a range to please all tastes, from Brazilian cocktails to cuban *frijoles* (beans) and, of course, Catalan *pa amb tomaquet* (bread with tomato). ❑

Dried and salted anchovies are a popular tapes.

BELOW: daily life in the Passeig del Born.

Map on page 163

PARC DE LA CIUTADELLA

Despite inauspicious beginnings as the site of an oppressive fortress, this verdant park offers old world charm and a refreshing respite from the rigours of city life

Barcelona's oldest and most visited park, the Parc de la Ciutadella is also one of its most attractive. It is easy (and therapeutic) to while away half a day here, simply walking in the fresher air, or enjoying some of the diverse activities on offer. Located between the Old Town and the new Vila Olímpica, it lies on the eastern side of the Mercat del Born, just across the Passeig de Picasso, where there are two entrances.

However, one of the most interesting approaches, which also gives the park its historical perspective, is from the northern end of Passeig de Lluís Companys, next to the **Arc de Triomf ❶** (easily reached by the metro of the same name, or by bus). This enormous brick arch served as the entrance to the 1888 World Exposition site (*see page 40*), which was held on the redeveloped land previously occupied by the fortress. From the top of Passeig de Lluís Companys you can look down towards the park or up along **Passeig Sant Joan** – a typical Eixample street with architectural echoes of Passeig de Gràcia, including some fine *modernista* houses – towards the Collserola range.

The clear light and sense of space around the Arc de Triomf are truly representative of Barcelona. Designed by Josep Vilaseca, the arch includes sculptures by Josep Llimona, among others. It is easy to imagine visitors to the Exposition sweeping down this elegant route to the showground, past the magnificent street lamps. Today's palms are some of the most attractive of the many species growing in the city. In front of the monumental Law Courts on the left, old men play *petanca* (a southern European bowls), while roller bladers vie for space with retired couples who sit on pieces of cardboard playing card games. A large tent on this promenade is the temporary home (for several years) of the Santa Catarina market, until the new market in La Ribera is completed. Just behind this is the main entrance to the **Parc de la Ciutadella ❷** (open daily 8am–9pm in summer, 8am–8pm in winter; free).

A turbulent history

The name, La Ciutadella (which means citadel, or fortress), has its origins in the use to which Felipe V put this land. After the fall of Barcelona in 1714, following a siege by Franco-Spanish troops, he ordered a fortress to be built that was capable of housing 8,000 soldiers, with the intention that they would control the city in his name. To do this it was necessary to demolish 40 streets and 1,262 buildings. Barceloneta was built to accommodate the evicted residents. For many years after the Civil War the citadel was used as a political prison.

In 1869 General Prim ceded the land to the city for conversion into a public park; the town hall issued a

BELOW: a detail on the Arc de Triomf.

public tender for the landscaping and construction of the gardens, which went to Josep Fontseré. His plan was approved in 1873 but it was not until 1888, the year of the World Exposition, that the park began to be a reality, emerging in a shape later to be damaged by bombing in the Civil War.

Interesting buildings remain from its military past, and from its glorious time as the Exposition showground, but the most remarkable aspect of the park is its refreshing tranquillity. It is a real city park, full of skateboards and footballs, prams and toddlers. There are bicycles made for six for hire, as well as rowing boats on the lake. On Sunday large families parade in their best outfits before lunch. Yet it is still peaceful. Constantly tended by municipal gardeners, it is verdant, scented and shady, a soothing place to walk in all seasons.

Old-fashioned charm

On the right as you enter is the **Museu de Zoologia** ❸ (open Tues–Sun 10am–2pm, Thurs 10am–6.30pm; entrance charge; combined ticket with Museu de Geologia available) in a building designed by Domènech i Montaner, the Castell dels Tres Dragons (Castle of the Three Dragons).

It was intended to be the restaurant of the 1888 Exposition, though it never opened as such. However, it was one of the first *modernista* projects in Barcelona and the architect's studio for years. Its collections of zoological specimens and impressive skeletons are well-housed amid the 19th-century marble and polished floors.

Behind is the beautiful **Hivernacle**, an elegant greenhouse bursting with tropical plants, which has been well restored to include a restaurant. Jazz and classical concerts are held here on summer evenings. In line with these two buildings is a more classical-looking structure built to be a museum in 1878, the first public one in Barcelona. Now the **Museu de Geologia** ❹ (opening times are as for the Museu de Zoologia), it has collections of rocks,

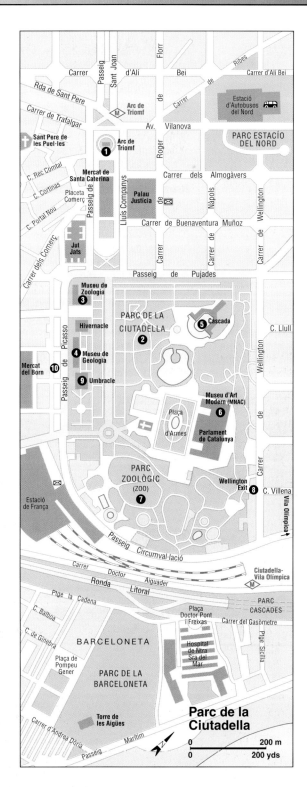

Parc de la Ciutadella

0   200 m
0   200 yds

minerals and fossils, notably from Catalonia and the rest of Spain, and the same old world charm as the Museu de Zoologia. These are a different breed from the new generation, state-of-the-art museums in other parts of the city.

Cross over the inner road and follow signs to the **Cascada** ❺, the monumental fountain and artificial lake designed by Fontseré in 1875; both the cascade and the lake were intended to camouflage a huge water deposit in the central section of the waterfall, which can be reached by two flanking, symmetrical stairways. Curiously, Gaudí worked on this project as a young architectural student. Something of a landmark and meeting place, its esplanade is often used for concerts, shows or fairs.

Reminders of the citadel

With your back to the Cascada, follow the boating lake round either way to the **Plaça d'Armes**, where there is a serene, oval formal garden designed by French landscape architect, J.C.N. Forestier. The statue in the lake is "El Desconsol", one of Catalan sculptor Josep Llimona's most highly regarded pieces. This square is bordered by the remnants of the citadel era: the Governor's Palace, now a secondary school, the chapel and the arsenal.

The latter is now where the Catalan Parliament sits. Part of the building is also occupied by the **Museu d'Art Modern** ❻ (open Tues–Sat 10am–7pm, Sun 10am–2.30pm; entrance charge). The museum contains a large collection of Catalan painting, drawing, sculpture and decorative art, including furniture from the 19th and early 20th centuries. It is an attractive collection, in which work by Casas, Rusiñol, Nonell and Fortuny successfully evokes the atmosphere of Barcelona at the turn of the century.

BELOW: a Ramon Casas painting in the Museu d'Art Modern.

Next to the Parliament is the entrance to the **Parc Zoologic** (Zoo) **❼**, which remains as popular as ever (open daily May–Aug: 9.30am–7.30pm; Sept–Apr: 10am–5pm; entrance charge). Founded in 1892, its most famous inmate is the only albino gorilla in captivity, with the unlikely name of **Floquet de Neu** (Snowflake). Other highlights include the Aquarama dolphin show and the adventure playground.

From within the zoo the **Wellington Exit ❽**, which gives on to the street of the same name, leads to the **Vila Olímpica** and its beaches (*see page 187*). The metro is close by, but for further exploration take **Avinguda Icària** into the Olympic Village, or head for the Hotel Arts (the right-hand skyscraper) passing through a small, modern park, **Parc Cascades**, above the Ronda Litoral. Complete your day with a swim on Barceloneta beach and dinner in the Olympic port. If this sounds appealing, but the zoo doesn't, there is another exit from the park on Pujades, behind the Cascade. Turn right and follow Wellington past the haunting brick structure, the **Diposit de les Aigües**, which stored water on its roof. Part of this building has been impressively restored as the library of the nearby University Pompeu Fabra. This street links up with the zoo exit.

However, if you prefer to do full justice to the Ciutadella, from the main entrance to the zoo (inside the park), take the road that leads past the Plaça d'Armes on the right and meander through to the **Umbracle ❾** on the far side of the park. This is a beautiful arched building of brick and wood, with fine iron columns, also designed by Fontseré. It offers much-needed shade for the more delicate species in the park. The dim light inside is reminiscent of a jungle.

Homage to Picasso

A small gate by the Umbracle leads out of the park on to the **Passeig de Picasso ❿**. The handsome arcaded apartment blocks that line this side of the park were designed by Fontseré as an integral part of his plans for redevelopment of the site. Some good bars and a useful bike rental shop are located under the arches at this end. A large modern sculpture in a transparent cube on the boundary of the park is by leading Catalan artist Antoni Tàpies and was designed as a homage to Picasso (*Homenatge a Picasso*). Old men in berets play *petanca* alongside it, seemingly oblivious.

The heavy traffic thunders past here on its way to the port, turning the corner into **Marquès de L'Argentera**. Spain's first railway line was inaugurated here in 1848 with a route that ran from Barcelona to Mataró. The railway station was little more than a shack near today's **Estació de França** (halfway down the avenue) which, at the time of its opening in September 1929, was the largest station in Europe. It was closed for several years while the tracks were buried underground to make way for the Olympic Village. The station has now been restored to formidable splendour, and looks more like a Grand Hotel than an international railway station. Occasionally, exhibitions are held here in its marble, polished expanse. Whether it forms part of your journey or not, be sure to visit it to capture the romance of train journeys from an earlier epoch. ❑

Map on page 163

The Aquarama show takes place three times a day in the Parc Zoologic.

BELOW: Snowflake, the Zoo's oldest resident.

TREASURES AND TREATS IN THE CITY'S MARKETS

Even if you have no intention of buying, it's fun to visit a market or two, to enjoy the energy and colour of this age-old tradition of trading

Whether you are in search of a rare stamp or a 1960s comic, an antique oil painting or a contemporary water-colour, a garden gnome or a Christmas tree, somewhere in Barcelona you'll find a market that will have just the thing you need.

Forty municipal food markets, full of Mediterranean goodness, still thrive despite the increase in the number of out-of-town hypermarkets. The morning bustle is the best. Apart from the famed La Boqueria, the 19th-century Mercat Sant Antoni (the only market in the Eixample built according to Cerdà's ideal plan) or the renovated Concepció, also in the Eixample, whose slick modern interior enhances the 1880s ironwork, are interesting.

THEMES AND SEASONS

There are thematic and seasonal markets, notably the Fira de Santa Llúcia at Christmas time. New, small street markets appear regularly, but the best established are Mercat Sant Antoni (second-hand books) and the Plaça Reial stamp and coin market (both on Sunday morning), the antiques market in the Cathedral square (Thursday), the art market in Plaça Sant Josep Oriol (weekends) and Els Encants flea market, held in Plaça de les Glòries (Monday, Wednesday, Friday and Saturday).

▷ **FIRA DE SANTA LLUCIA**
Festive stalls in the Cathedral square sell *pessebres* (nativity scenes), Christmas trees, and *tiós* (a jolly-faced log that "excretes" presents.)

△ **A SENSUAL FEAST**
Walking through any of Barcelona's dazzling food markets is a feast for the senses and an insight into daily life.

△ **BARGAIN HUNT**
You should arrive early to find good deals amid the mounds of bric-à-brac in Els Encants market.

◁ **MISSING PARTS**
You never know what you may find in Els Encants flea market – maybe more than you bargained for.

THE MOTHER OF ALL MARKETS

La Boqueria in La Rambla, the hub of Barcelona's culinary world, is as much a symbol of the city as Gaudí's Sagrada Família. Officially Mercat de Sant Josep, after the ravaged convent on whose ground it was built, it rivals Mercat Santa Caterina for the title of oldest, both having celebrated their 150th anniversary.

Within its iron frame some 300 stalls overflow with luscious fruit and vegetables, fish on beds of ice, salt cod in marble sinks, cured meats and cheese, garlic-marinaded olives the size of plums, herbs and spices, dried fruit and nuts and in the autumn kilos of wild mushrooms. Outside, *pagesos* (farmers) sell freshly-picked products.

Pull up a stool at one of the steel counters and absorb the kaleidoscope of sights and sounds over a glass of *cava*. Here the best chefs select their ingredients, pensioners haggle over a couple of chicken wings, and one of Barcelona's greatest restaurateurs chose to commit suicide, as it was the place where he had been happiest.

HIDDEN TREASURES
Hunting for rare stamps and ancient coins is a Sunday morning pastime in the majestic Plaça Reial.

◁ **ART AL FRESCO**
A wide selection of paintings are on sale every weekend in Plaça Sant Josep Oriol, one of the Barri Gòtic's most picturesque squares.

△ **ARTS AND CRAFTS**
A strong Catalan arts and crafts tradition is well represented by weekend markets, Christmas fairs, and at diverse fiestas throughout the year.

EL RAVAL

*Contemporary art, music, design and cultural centres plus
a new Rambla are rejuvenating the historic but long
neglected quarter of El Raval*

Map on page 173

Walking down **La Rambla** from **Plaça Catalunya**, the section of the Old Town to the right-hand side is known as El Raval. Enclosed by **Ronda Sant Antoni** and **Ronda Sant Pau**, in the 1930s this area was one of the most densely populated urban areas in the world, when it became derogatively known as the Barri Xino (Chinese Quarter). It is still given a wide berth by many of Barcelona's inhabitants. However, it is one of the districts of the city with the most potential, and a stimulating area in which to wander and observe. Although some areas are still run-down and at times menacing, some of the most interesting cultural activities in the city are now taking place here.

Religious past

In its medieval past the area was heavily populated by convents and religious institutions. With the advent of industrialisation in the late 18th century the emphasis switched to factories, and dense urbanisation began. Relics of the religious past still stand out in today's bustling Raval. From La Rambla, turn down the second road on the right, Bonsuccés, which opens into the **Plaça Bonsuccés**. The large, handsome building dominating the square is a former convent dating from 1635, now used as district council offices. The adjoining modern archway leads into **Plaça Vicenç Martorell**, a newly created square where the convent cloisters would have been. In the far corner in the arches, the popular bar, **Kasparo**, provides delicious alternative snacks; relax on its shady terrace and watch children playing in the central park. Behind the newspaper kiosk the long-neglected **Casa de la Misericòrdia** (1583), formerly a hospice for abandoned children, has been cleverly restored, complete with interior palm tree, to make more council offices. If you look closely you will see a small wooden circle in the wall, where babies were pushed through and received by nuns on the other side until as recently as 1931.

Return to Plaça Bonsuccés and turn into **Elisabets**, by the restaurant of the same name (good for hearty winter dishes and atmosphere), heading towards the **Convent dels Angels**, which forms an evocative backdrop at the end of the street. There is a good bookshop in the lofty space of the Misericòrdia chapel and some wonderful tall palms in a secret garden bounded by lush wisteria. **Doctor Dou** on the left has some interesting bars, good value restaurants and modern art galleries. Just past a fashion designer's shop on Elisabets is another well-renovated chapel, part of an orphanage dating back to 1370.

At this point you emerge into the **Plaça dels Angels**, which opens up into the unexpected space dominated by the breathtaking **Museu d'Art**

PRECEDING PAGES: Centre de Cultura Contemporània. **LEFT:** a Barri Xino restaurant. **BELOW:** trendy second-hand shop.

TIP

For a different perspective on the city, don't miss the view from the Sala de Mirador in the Centre de Cultura Contemporània.

Contemporani de Barcelona (MACBA) ❶ (open 11am–7.30pm, Sat 10am–8pm, Sun 10am–3pm, closed Tues; entrance charge). Designed by US architect Richard Meier and opened in 1995, the building is dazzling against the Mediterranean blue sky and gigantic within the context of the humble buildings beyond. The social and urban significance of the architecture in this once declining area have been almost more of a talking point than the collection inside, which comprises Catalan, Spanish and some international art, mostly from the second half of the 20th century. The museum also hosts temporary exhibitions. Its large forecourt has evolved into a popular public space for skate-boarding and football matches. Filipino families who live in the narrow streets around **Joaquín Costa** often gather here with picnic suppers on warm evenings: the square is a fascinating melting pot of local residents and cosmopolitan visitors.

Symbol of urban renewal

The museum was built in the grounds of the enormous Casa de la Caritat (poorhouse), which once provided a home for thousands of children and part of which still stands around the corner in Montalegre. The former 18th-century hospice has been transformed into the **Centre de Cultura Contemporània de Barcelona** (CCCB) ❷ (open Tues, Thur, Fri 11am–2pm & 4–8pm, Wed, Sat 11am–8pm, Sun 11am–7pm; entrance charge), a series of exhibition spaces dedicated to the exploration of urban phenomena, through diverse cultural activities including dance, music, film, video and seminars.

The complex – a wonderful renovation by prestigious architects Piñon and Vilaplana – rivals MACBA for its architectural interest. The ripples of urban renewal have spread to the surrounding streets where galleries and designers'

BELOW: Museu d'Art Contemporani de Barcelona.

MUSEU D'ART CONTEMPORANI DE BARCELONA

Map on page 173

tudios are opening. Go through the central Patí de les Dones of the CCCB, past ts excellent bookshop, into the **Plaça Joan Coromines** which links it with the art museum. Part of the Ramon Llull University also gives on to this square. A glass door leads into the older part of the Casa de la Caritat and its ceramic tiled courtyard, Patí Manning, sometimes used as a theatre or dance space, but primarily cultural offices.

Return down Montalegre and continue along as it becomes Angels, a pleasant tree-lined street. When it reaches Carme turn left and cross the road into the **Hospital de la Santa Creu** ❸, a large Gothic complex which was a hospital until the 1920s (open daily). On the left is the 18th-century Academy of Medicine and Surgery, and on the right the **Institut d'Estudis Catalans** in the hospital's **Casa de Convalescència**, which is currently being restored. Wander through the charming and atmospheric cloistered patio, although it is lamentably neglected and a favourite meeting place for lonely down-and-outs. The Biblioteca de Catalunya occupies much of the old hospital, along with the Massana art school.

As you emerge into Hospital, check if there is an exhibition in **La Capella** (open Tues–Sat noon–2pm & 4–8pm, Sun 11am–2pm), once the hospital's chapel, which promotes experimental artists and has fascinating work on display.

A stroll downtown

With your back to La Rambla, follow Hospital deeper into El Raval. This is a busy commercial street, even on Sundays, because of the increasing number of Pakistani shops, a reflection on the most recent immigrant group in the district. Tandoori restaurants jostle side by side with Halal butchers, Arab pastry shops,

BELOW: the Hospital de la Santa Creu.

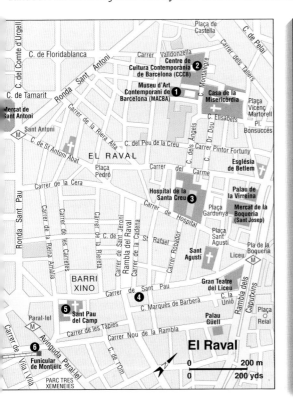

El Raval

100-peseta bazaars and old established tailors selling starched uniforms for the catering business. A sign above a narrow doorway, squeezed between two shops, indicates the entrance to a *mezquita*, the main city mosque, though a new one is now being built. An arcade on the left, **Passatge Bernardí Martorell**, leads to one of Barcelona's most traditional and recommendable fish restaurants, Casa Leopoldo, run by Rosa, the charming and welcoming granddaughter of the founder, in the dubious-looking street **Sant Rafael** where soon a hotel is to be built. Trendy second-hand clothes shops are another new thread in this multi-coloured fabric. **Riera Baixa**, a short pedestrian street on the right, has some wacky shops and an outdoor market on Saturday.

Turn left at Cadena and be dazzled by the sunlight in the new broad Rambla that leads down to **Sant Pau** ❹, part of the city council's policy of forging through dense urban areas. Old housing has been demolished and new blocks built to create this Rambla del Raval. Old residents and new immigrants are finally coming out into the sunshine to enjoy the space and gossip on new designer benches. Prostitutes (of questionable gender) and junkies are retreating to the narrower streets behind. The darker side of urban life – sickness decadence and desperation – is on the streets here. An abundance of chemists' shops reflects its state of health.

Green oasis

Turn right in Sant Pau to reach the Romanesque **Església de Sant Pau del Camp** ❺ (open Mon–Sat 5–7.45pm, and sometimes in the morning on a haphazard basis, Sun 10.30am–1.30pm; admission free). Surrounded by greenery, including an olive tree, a cypress and a palm, as well as a modern park which

sweeps around it protectively, it is a true survivor in this beleaguered area. Much of the former industrial activity was in this lower part of the Raval – the new park was recently created after a fire burned down a factory – and the tall chimney is a fitting memorial to the area's industrial past. Another old factory, now **Can Xatarra**, is a training centre for young people.

Considered the oldest church in Barcelona, Sant Pau del Camp is a fine example of Romanesque architecture, quite rare in the city. The present building is 12th century but it incorporates elements of an earlier church built in 912. Its small cloister, with unusual carvings, is a spiritual gem and exquisitely peaceful. On the exterior above the main door is a simple carving of the Hand of God and a winged creature, a symbolic representation of one of the evangelists.

Continue along the last block in Sant Pau, which brings you right back into the late 19th–early 20th century: decorative mirrored shop fronts proclaim an old grocers' shop, **Ultramarinos Casa Victor**, or **La Confiteria**, a pastry shop turned stylish restaurant; an old bodega is straight out of the 1950s.

Variety theatreland

A string of theatres runs mainly along the **Avinguda Paral.lel**, showing musicals and comedy shows which attract coachloads of pensioners from outside Barcelona. The famed music hall tradition of the area seems to be fading fast, however, especially with the demise of the much-loved **El Molino**. From this point walk up to Poble Sec metro or on to **Plaça d'Espanya** for more metro lines, or an approach to Montjuïc. Alternatively, catch the metro in nearby Paral.lel station or its **funicular ❻** which goes up to Montjuïc and links with the cable car for Montjuïc castle (*see page 202*). ❑

Map on page 173

The magnificent Romanesque doorway of Sant Pau del Camp.

BELOW: a neighbourhood restaruant.

THE WATERFRONT

Since the Barcelona Olympics in 1992, the rejuvenated waterfront area has added an exciting new dimension to the city, transforming the district where the city meets the sea

Map on pages 180–1

It is perhaps ironic that Barcelona, a city on the shores of the Mediterranean with a large industrial port and strong maritime tradition, gained a "waterfront" only in the last decade of the 20th century. As the popular saying goes, Barcelona lived with its back to the sea, which meant that although a great deal of the city's trade depended upon the water, the attitude of its residents was directed inland.

Inevitably, because of the geographical limitation of the sea, the residential and commercial areas expanded inland, first with the construction of the 19th-century Eixample and then by moving further up the hill towards Collserola during the next century. Investment tended to be linked with this movement, and as a result the Old Town and Barceloneta were neglected. Factories mushroomed in the 19th century along the shoreline going north to the River Besòs, with only humble housing provided for the workers.

Impetus for change

The rediscovery of the waterfront began in the 1980s as part of the socialist city council's vision, but the 1992 Olympics were the vital catalyst. The development, perhaps the most radical transformation of any city in Europe, represented an investment of some 400 billion pesetas (£2 billion/US$3 billion). Some 5 km (8 miles) of beaches were renovated or newly created, landscaped and equipped with facilities. The Vila Olímpica was built and is now a new residential district. The old city wharves, once hidden under tumble-down sheds, emerged, blinking, into the sun. Barceloneta was transformed. And since 1992, despite a slight economic hiccup with the recession in 1993–94, the momentum has been sustained: more developments have been completed and, for better or worse, there are more to come.

For energetic walkers or those on bicycles, this route could be one long itinerary right along the walkable parts of the front. However, to be able to enjoy the walk and fully appreciate the extensive renovations, to take in the many colourful details and have time to pause in the right places (such as the fish restaurants in Barceloneta), the route should be split into two (or more) days. What's on offer on Barcelona's waterfront is something quite extraordinary for a large cosmopolitan European city.

What could be a better place to begin than the maritime museum, a pleasing museum that appeals to all ages and gives a vivid sense of Catalonia's seafaring past. The **Museu Marítim** ❶ (open daily 10am–7pm; entrance charge) is housed in the **Reials Drassanes** (Royal Shipyards), at the foot of La Rambla just before it meets the port. It is half a minute from the

PRECEDING PAGES: the Vila Olímpica. **LEFT:** old visitor to a new quay. **BELOW:** ship in the Museu Marítim.

metro Drassanes. One of the most imposing aspects of the museum is the building itself – the magnificent Gothic shipyards dating from the 13th century are a fine and rare example of civil architecture from that period. There is something quite breathtaking about their lines and structure, which as art critic Robert Hughes says in his book *Barcelona* is "perhaps the most stirring ancient industrial space of any kind that has survived from the Middle Ages: a masterpiece of civil engineering."

Enter the museum from the side where, adjacent to the restaurant, an inviting terrace café in a shady garden with a lily pond is bound to tempt you after your visit. The collection includes real fishing boats from the Catalan coast, representing the importance of both fishing and boat-building in the country's history, as well as models of vessels from all ages. Also on display is a modern Olympic winner, and maps, instruments, paintings and more are well presented. The highlight is the *son et lumière* show known as *La Gran Aventura del Mar* (the Great Sea Adventure), which charts Catalonia's maritime history and includes a tour around the full-scale replica of the 16th-century galley in which Don Juan of Austria led the Christian fleet to defeat the Turks in the Battle of Lepanto in 1571. Like so many vessels over the centuries, it was built in Barcelona in one of the slipways on the water's edge.

The port of Barcelona

Today you have to cross a wide road, full of traffic leading to the Ronda Litoral, before reaching the water. Leaving the Monument a Colom to your left, go down the side of a rather overbearing building that is the **Duana Nova** (New Customs House), built between 1895 and 1902 from a project drawn up by Enric Sagnier and Pere García. Crowned by a massive winged sphinx and other mythical flying beasts (Barcelona's port buildings seem to specialise in fine roof-top silhouettes), the Duana Nova is designed in the form of the letter "H", the most practical design for processing cargoes.

To the left of the Columbus statue is the **Junta d'Obres del Port** (Port Authority Building), designed by the engineer Julio Valdés and built in 1907. Its

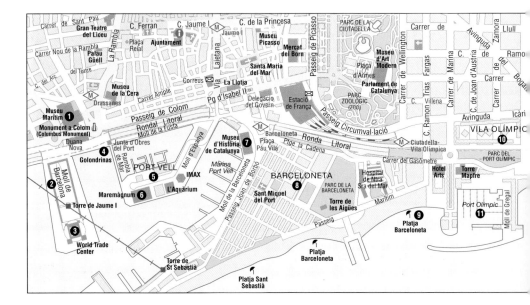

original use was as the reception for passengers arriving in the city from the sea. The interior is somewhat eclectic in style, and rather ornamental for its present mundane function. A recent external facelift has much improved the outward appearance of the building.

To the right, the **Moll de Barcelona ❷** and, beyond it, the **Moll de Sant Bertran** are the centre for ferry services to the Balearic Islands, including a new high-speed space-age catamaran, the so-called Buquebus, which reaches Palma in 2½ hours. The jetty also has the 390-ft (119-metre) **Torre de Jaume I** link for the cross-harbour cable car, which comes from Montjüic and goes to the tower on the other side of the harbour, the **Torre de Sant Sebastià** (an alternative route to the beach). The cable car has hardly changed since its introduction in 1931 – unlike the spectacular views it affords of the city and port, which are constantly changing.

After years of discussion, financial crises and local resistance, the **World Trade Center ❸** has now been completed at the end of the Moll de Barcelona. Designed by the world-famous architect I.M. Pei, it makes a loud statement in the middle of the port, looking remarkably like the luxury cruisers regularly moored alongside it. Unlike most new developments on the waterfront, this building is not used for social or leisure activities by the citizens of Barcelona: it is a commercial centre with offices and a hotel.

The controversial World Trade Center, designed by architect I.M. Pei.

Of course, the port of Barcelona plays an important commercial role: it covers a huge expanse, winding south below Montjüic towards the airport, and it is undergoing further enlargement. The authorities' much vaunted aim is to establish it as "Europe's southern port", tying in with the city's aspiration to be regarded as the "capital of the Mediterranean". During the summer months enormous white cruisers are a daily sight, moored against the far sea wall, the **Moll Adossat**, from where coach loads of passengers are disgorged into La Rambla for a day on shore.

The serious business of large cargo ships and containers goes on in an area where no visitors are welcomed. A glimpse of the industrial port is possible, however, if you take a trip around the harbour in one of the historic pleasure

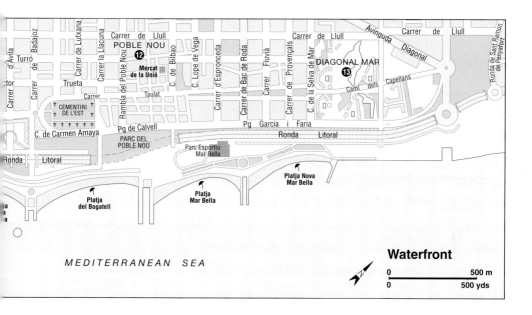

Waterfront

MEDITERRANEAN SEA

0   500 m
0   500 yds

The Golondrinas wait to take passengers around the harbour. Their name means "swallows".

BELOW: Port Vell and Maremàgnum.

boats, the "**Golondrinas" (Ferries)** ❹ which, apart from a pause during the Civil War, have been plying these waters since the 1888 Exposition. The ferries wait patiently in the **Moll de Drassanes**, the jetty opposite the Columbus monument. Half-hour trips take you out to the sea wall and back again, although you can disembark there and have a drink before catching a return boat. Be sure to choose one of the older, more elegant Golondrinas with names like *Mercedes*, *Lolita* and *Encarnación*.

As the ferry chugs through the working port you get a different perspective on the waterfront, seeing the enormity of the surrounding vessels and the battering they take in high seas. The same company also offers a longer trip as far as the **Port Olímpic** beyond Barceloneta beach, in a slick catamaran.

Waterfront leisure complex

The Golondrinas mark a divide between the industrial port and the leisure areas encompassed in **Port Vell** ❺, the old port. If you visit this area at the weekend, or on summer evenings, you will see from the noisy crowds that the Barcelonans are enjoying their newfound waterfront. An architect-designed walkway and footbridge, the **Rambla de Mar**, leads across the water to the large commercial complex in the middle of the harbour on the **Moll d'Espanya**.

Alternatively, you can continue on the mainland along the **Moll de la Fusta**, a promenade built in the 1980s on the site of the old wooden cargo sheds already being redesigned as its brief life offering restaurants and nightlife was not entirely successful.

Better to look to the sea, where an exhibit from the **Maritime Museum** (Tues–Fri noon–5.30pm, weekend 10am–5.30pm) can be visited. The *Santa*

Eulàlia is an old sailing boat, restored by the museum to its original glory from the beginning of the 20th century when it took cargo to the Americas.

Inevitably the crowds head over the Rambla de Mar to **Maremàgnum ⑥**, **L'Aquàrium** and the **Imax** cinema. Take heed of the warning signs to mind your step at the start of the walkway, as the designers take no responsibility for sprained ankles. The undulating design of the Rambla de Mar fits in well with the maritime environment, and is a great concept for crossing the harbour, but the subtle "waves" and changes in level can sometimes catch you out.

Cross over above yachts and yacht clubs to the Maremàgnum shopping and eating emporium, where you can shop until 11pm every day of the year. A selection of bars and restaurants seems to be dominated by fast food outlets – a new phenomenon in Barcelona – but there are some old favourites like **El Salmonete**, a fish restaurant that used to be located on Barceloneta beach before the redevelopment. Despite the commercial context, a few *tapas* in the spring sunshine while watching the maritime traffic or looking across the harbour at Barcelona's Gothic towers and 19th-century chimneys takes some beating. The place throbs at night with salsa music and tacky discotheques.

Map on pages 180–1

TIP

The Maremàgnum shopping complex, selling a range of goods from designer fashions to trendy souvenirs, is a useful place to shop for presents.

Ultra-modern aquarium

Wander through Maremàgnum towards **L'Aquàrium** (open daily 9.30am–11pm in summer 9.30am–9pm in winter; entrance charge). Not long ago this area was taken up by disused warehouses. Old-timer tenants include the Reial Club Nautic and the Reial Club Marítim, two of the city's most elite sports clubs. The wharf has now been landscaped in the best tradition of Barcelona's new urban spaces, and leisure opportunities abound: the Cines Maremàgnum, with eight screens, rooftop mini-golf, the Imax cinema (with a semi-circular screen) and, of course, the spectacular aquarium. Holding over 5 million litres of water, this is the largest aquarium in Europe. Since opening in 1995 it has become the largest crowd-puller in Barcelona, beating the Sagrada Família into second place. The much vaunted shark tunnel is a disappointment, however.

BELOW:
the unmissable creation of Roy Lichtenstein.

Pass the historic submarine and follow the path that leads up to the **Mirador del Port Vell** (a slightly raised lookout point) and down towards the "Barcelona Head", an unmistakable Roy Lichtenstein sculpture. Inland from the sculpture, on the corner of Via Laietana, is the headquarters of Correus (the Post Office), a rather pompously grand building completed in 1927. The enormous vestibule was decorated by the prestigious *noucentiste* artists (from the 1900s) Canyellas, Obiols, Galí and Labarta. It is easier to buy stamps in an *estanc*, but not nearly as interesting. It is not hard to see why the facade has been used by filmmakers as a stand-in for American law courts.

On the sea side of **Passeig d'Isabel II** is a neoclassic arcade known as the **Porxos d'en Xifré**, built by the "Indiano" (a name given to anyone who left Spain to make their fortune in the Americas) Josep Xifré between 1836 and 1840. One of these apartments was the first home of the Picasso family in 1895 when they arrived in Barcelona from Málaga.

There's a plethora of open-air restaurants in which to have dinner by the harbour.

BELOW: Port Vell and the Museu d'Història de Catalunya.

A chance to refuel

The arcade is also the site of one of Barcelona's most historic restaurants, the **Set Portes**, first established in 1838 by Josep Cuyás. Set Portes was the first bar in Barcelona to have an outdoor terrace set with tables and chairs and was among the city's leading café-theatres. Both features now form part of its long history, but its elegance and atmosphere remain. Specialising in rice dishes, a different one for each day of the week, it is the kind of place every first-time visitor to Barcelona should try. On the other side of Pla del Palau is the **Delegació del Govern**, Madrid's central government foothold in Catalonia. It was built in the 18th century as a customs house.

Return to the harbour by **Reina Cristina**, a street full of bazaars behind the Set Portes restaurant. Towards the end, beware of the popular *cava* bar on the right, which sells sparkling wine at a price that can't be good for you and is much frequented by English-language teachers clutching bottles of the stuff and *chorizo* sandwiches. Just beyond it is the first Galician seafood restaurant to open in Barcelona, **Carballeira**. If you are passing when the *arròs a la banda* (a delicious rice and seafood dish) is coming out of the kitchen, cancel all other plans: stand at the bar, request a *tapa* of it with *allioli* (garlic mayonnaise) and a glass of Galician *vino turbio*.

Back on the quayside, the promenade sweeps on round, past a floating bar, to the **Moll Dipòsit** and the **Moll de la Barceloneta**. These once busy working quays now shelter the **Marina Port Vell**, where some of the most exclusive motor and sailing yachts in the Mediterranean winter or pass through on their way to the Balearics or the Caribbean. In 1992 the former warehouse complex, the Magatzem General de Comerç (1878) by Elias Rogent, was transformed

into the Palau de Mar. This is a handsome building, very well renovated, and part of it now houses the fascinating **Museu d'Història de Catalunya ❼** (open Tues–Sat 10am–7pm, Wed till 8pm, Sun 10am–2.30pm, slightly extended opening times in summer; entrance charge). True to its name, it elucidates Catalan history but also serves as a generic history museum with various bits of technical wizardry and plenty of interactive spaces – try walking in a suit of armour, or building a Roman arch – which kids of all ages love.

There are a couple of government offices in the back of the building, but the main focus here is on the restaurants that line the front. Sunday lunch in the Palau de Mar has become an institution for those who can afford it. This is an attractive place to sit and watch the world go by, and sheltered even in winter. The restaurants are new and glossy, not famed establishments, but the charms of outdoor eating often outweigh the gastronomic shortcomings. As long as you don't expect *haute cuisine* you will be spoilt for choice along here, from Palau de Mar along the whole length of **Passeig Joan de Borbó**. Even for Barcelona residents it is a thrill to eat on a pavement in the December sun. Serious eaters, however, tend to go into the back streets of **Barceloneta ❽** that form a grid between Marina Port Vell and the open sea.

Above the Moll de la Barceloneta is another landscaped, broad promenade with benches and palm trees. A favourite spot for roller-bladers, cyclists and dog-walkers, it was until comparatively recently covered in crumbling *tinglados* (sheds), and the decision to knock them down to bring this area into line with the new-look Barcelona of the 1990s was met with outrage. However, people are evidently making the most of the vacated space, and the seafood restaurants on Joan de Borbó are happy to have been given their own view of the harbour.

Map
on pages
180–1

BELOW: feeding
the pigeons in
Barceloneta.

At the end of the promenade is an expensive but excellent fish restaurant called Barceloneta, with great harbour views, and just beyond are glimpses of the hard-working fishing boats moored up against the Moll de Pescadors (Fishermen's Wharf). The distinctive clock tower, **Torre del Rellotge**, started life as a lighthouse. Close by is the fish market (first opened in 1924), where auctions are held twice a day on weekdays.

Towering above the scene is the **Torre de Sant Sebastià** whose 78-metre (257-ft) height marks the end, or the beginning, of the cable car's route which completes its 1,292-metre (4,200-ft) journey at Miramar, on Montjuïc. At the foot of the Torre is an excellent swimming club which is open to the public and overlooks the beach of Sant Sebastià. Beyond the beach, major building works have begun: the sea wall is being extended to make way for a new entrance to the port. Further large-scale development of the area, including a gigantic hotel designed by Ricardo Bofill, are under discussion. Meanwhile, there are worries that the city is losing sight of the intelligent town planning of the 1980s for which Barcelona has been justly renowned.

Origins of Barceloneta

Town planning in the 18th century was also of questionable merit. The rigidity of Barceloneta's street plan gives a clue to its origin. Misleadingly called the fishermen's quarter, this area was in fact born of a political, military decision. It was to this area that the inhabitants of La Ribera were relocated when their homes were demolished to make way for the building of the fortress, La Ciutadella, after the siege and conquest of Barcelona by Felipe V. The plans for Barceloneta were based on the construction of 15 short identical streets giving

BELOW: the fleet's in port again.

rise to a series of narrow, rectangular blocks all facing in the same direction (towards Ciutadella), facilitating easy military control.

During the second half of the 19th century the lack of living accommodation in the city and pressure from the local proprietors resulted in the buildings of Barceloneta being raised to three storeys. The first inhabitants of the district were therefore refugees under careful military control.

Map on pages 180–1

New beach development

By cutting through the streets of Barceloneta to the **Passeig Marítim**, or wandering along from Platja Sant Sebastià, you get to **Platja Barceloneta ❾**. The wooden walkways, palms and designer showers of the post-Olympic sea front were ravaged by storms in 2001, but are being replaced at vast expense. The six beaches along this stretch are easily accessible by public transport, and both the sand and the water's surface are cleaned daily, with weekly sanitary checks on top of that. Many fondly remember the *chiringuitos*, colourful restaurants which were no more than huts on the beach here where you could eat good fish with your toes in the sand. They were swept away in the early 1990s under a cloud of controversy but reputedly because of a ruling by the national coastal authority.

No one can deny the obvious pleasure the people of Barcelona now derive from these wide open beaches. Every morning, the chestnut-brown locals from Barceloneta come down in their towelling dressing gowns to swim in all weathers, play cards, gossip and get fit. In summer the beaches get very crowded and noisy by midday, then comes the lunchtime exodus. If you can't make it for the silvery early morning, wait until the golden evening sun brings a new tranquillity – an eight o'clock swim here is sheer bliss.

Walk towards the unmistakable **Vila Olímpica ❿**, distinctive by virtue of its two skyscrapers and the copper fish sculpture (*Pez y Esfera* by Frank Gehry) rippling in the sun. A new park just before the Hospital del Mar does justice to the *modernista* Watertower (1905) by Jose Domènech i Estapà, virtually the only original industrial building left in this area. The formerly gloomy hospital underwent a metamorphosis for the Olympics and is now more reminiscent of an international airport than a major public hospital. At beach level is a bike-rental shop.

Nearing the Olympic village, the bars and restaurants begin, with entrances on the promenade above: both here and in the **Port Olímpic ⓫**, just beyond, a tacky element has crept in since 1992 when gold medallists lived in the village and the Spanish royal family supported the yachtsmen in the port. Inevitably, brash commercialism has played a part – the overpowering smell of fried fish and the ubiquitous electronic Andean flutes detract from the glamorous yachts in the port and the few good restaurants on the quayside. You can wander beneath Frank Gehry's awesome fish and imagine the heady view from the exclusive rooms in the Hotel Arts that towers above, but the canned music filling the air will bring you safely down to earth. Down at ground level, what was once an exclusive shopping area is now the home of the Barcelona Casino (against many wishes).

An evocative sculpture by Rebecca Horn marks the spot where Barceloneta's beach restaurants once stood.

BELOW: having a drink in one of the new beachside cafés.

The strikingly designed Port Olímpic is a pleasant place to walk, particularly out of season. At the end of the **Moll de Gregal**, jutting out to sea, is the municipal sailing school, offering courses to the public.

Architect-designed village

It is worth taking time to go inland a block or two, to see the architectural feats of the Olympic village. Built according to a master plan developed by architects Mackay, Martorell, Bohigas and Puigdomènech, on land formerly occupied by 19th-century ramshackle warehouses and tumbledown factories, the flats accommodated athletes in 1992 and since then have been gradually sold. It was a major undertaking, and a vital part of Barcelona's wider plan of achieving long overdue improvements to the city's infrastructure. In order to assimilate the village into the city, the major railway lines into Estació de França, the international train terminus, had to be buried below ground.

The 200 new buildings cover 183 acres (74 hectares), and are in 200 different designs. The area has not become a new neighbourhood of Barcelona overnight, but with the help of the many new parks and gardens it is now looking more established, and even beginning to merge with the remaining buildings of **Poble Nou** ⑫ that surround its outer limits. In the midst of a clinical, totally un-Spanish shopping mall is one of the few magnetic points that attracts people in the evenings: the 15-screen cinema complex, Icaria Yelmo, which specialises in *v.o.* (original language) films.

Return to the front to walk along the series of new beaches that begins after the Port Olímpic. Tons of sand were brought in to create **Platja Nova Icària** (named after the original industrial neighbourhood), **Bogatell**, **Mar Bella** and

BELOW: the beach at Poble Nou.

Map
on pages
180–1

finally **Nova Mar Bella**, reclaiming a sea front that had become inaccessible because of railway lines, yards and warehouses. The strategic Ronda Litoral (ring road) runs all along here but at a lower level and is cleverly hidden beneath parks, playgrounds and bridges that connect with the residential areas behind.

Just after the cemetery behind Bogatell beach, make a detour inland to visit the centre of Poble Nou and have a drink on its Rambla. It was the "new village" in the mid-19th century, built to accommodate the factory workers of what was known as the "Catalan Manchester". Little industry remains and many of the old factories have been converted into lofts or artists' studios. The predicted metamorphosis of Poble Nou into a trendy place to live is slowly evolving. Much of its original character and charm has been retained and a village atmosphere prevails. A good time to visit is during the *Festa Major* in mid-September. It is to be hoped that the remnants of its industrial past continue to be resurrected as studios or civic centres, like the impressive Can Felipa (an old textile factory converted in 1978, which has a swimming pool) near the metro in Pallars.

Beyond the new millennium

Moving on towards **Selva de Mar**, many old buildings are falling prey to Barcelona's latest enormous development, **Diagonal Mar ⓭**. This is a project to bring Avinguda Diagonal all the way down to the sea, and has created a new district within the city's bounds. The landscape here changes daily: old buildings and areas of wasteland are being transformed into vast square apartment blocks. Several hotels and a vast shopping centre are already open. This is serious investment and seems unstoppable. On the positive side, it links up with Barcelona's latest brainchild: the **Forum 2004** *(see below)*. ❑

BELOW: taking a trip
around the harbour.

BARCELONA'S FORUM 2004

Yet again, Barcelona has come up with an ingenious idea to project itself forward internationally, solve some fundamental domestic needs, and dazzle the world. The Universal Forum of Cultures, to be held in Barcelona from 23 April (Sant Jordi) to 24 September (La Mercè) 2004, is a totally original idea proposing three main themes – to promote cultural diversity, world peace and a sustainable urban environment.

The Forum will involve debates, exhibitions and a world festival of the arts. All the events in Barcelona will simultaneously reach every corner of the world via a Virtual Forum, in keeping with one of the key aims which is to transcend the limitations of nationality.

Where Avinguda Diagonal meets the sea a huge showground is under construction, comprising a New Age zoological park, exhibition areas and a port. Already, plans are being made to convert the Forum's buildings for use after the event – for example, conference centres and a solar park will be set up on land reclaimed from the sea.

It is an impressive and hugely ambitious project, and a totally fitting way for Barcelona to throw itself into the new millennium. So take the opportunity to wander to the end of the waterfront and watch that space.

MONTJUÏC

*The lofty setting for the 1992 Olympic Games has superb
views of the city, two world-class museums, a brand new
cultural centre and the Poble Espanyol*

Map
on page
194

The small hill of Montjuïc is only 213 metres (699 ft) high, but has an undeniable physical presence that is noticeable from most parts of the city: from along the waterfront it marks the end of the port, and from the Ronda Litoral it acts like a barrier between the inner residential area of the city and the industrial sprawl of the Zona Franca, the gateway to the south. From high points around Barcelona you can see how densely packed a city it is – the result of its growth having been contained within the natural limits of the River Besòs, the Collserola range and Montjuïc.

Past and present

The rocky promontory of Montjuïc has also featured in some of the key events in Barcelona's history. A pre-Roman civilisation made a settlement here, preferring its rough heights to the humid plain that the Romans later opted for. The Romans did, however, build a temple to Jupiter here, which is thought to explain the origin of the name: Mons Iovis eventually evolved into Montjuïc. In 1929 the hill was landscaped and used as the grounds of the Universal Exposition. More recently, it was seen by millions of people worldwide as it hosted the opening and closing ceremonies and core events of the 1992 Olympic Games. It was regarded as the "nerve centre" of the Games.

PRECEDING PAGES:
romance in
the park.
LEFT: the Torre
de Calatrava.
BELOW:
gateway
to Montjuïc.

Today it is a large city park offering a wide range of cultural, leisure and sporting activities – a playground used by both residents and tourists. It is a wonderful space for walking dogs and allowing children to run wild, or just for clearing the head and getting a bird's eye view of Barcelona, especially its maritime area. Apart from the cable car that crosses the harbour, this is the only place where you can piece together the waterfront at a glance, and watch the comings and goings of the busy industrial port.

One of the best approaches to Montjuïc is from **Plaça d'Espanya ❶**, which has good metro and bus connections with the rest of the city. (If you are heading for a specific destination, such as the Fundació Joan Miró or the Castle, the funicular from Paral.lel metro station is a better option.) Plaça d'Espanya is a large, noisy junction at the southern end of town. It is glaring and hot, surrounded by an incoherent mixture of buildings and with little or no shade, and so is not a place to linger.

Spare a brief moment, however, to look at the statue to Spain in the middle of the square's roundabout, commissioned for the 1929 Universal Exposition. The most intriguing thing about the statue is that Josep Jujol was the sculptor: it is difficult to reconcile this monumental piece with the same artist's brilliant ceramic serpentine bench in Parc Güell (*see page*

221), built at least 15 years earlier. The explanation for the two opposing styles was that the Primo de Rivera dictatorship in Madrid controlled the design of Jujol's monument to Spain.

The disused bullring, **Las Arenas**, on the other side of the square opened in 1900 with a capacity for 15,000 spectators. Weeds now push through the ground where bulls once stamped, but there are plans in the pipeline to convert the bullring into a commercial centre.

The 1929 Universal Exposition

Turning your back on the roundabout, head past the twin Venetian-style towers, designed by Ramon Reventós, that formed the main entrance to the Universal Exposition of 1929. The basic structure of the buildings (most of which are still present on Montjuïc) was designed for this event, with a sweeping vista up to the **Palau Nacional**, the enormous, rather overbearing, building at the top of the steps. The Exposition, opened by King Alfonso XIII, had as its themes

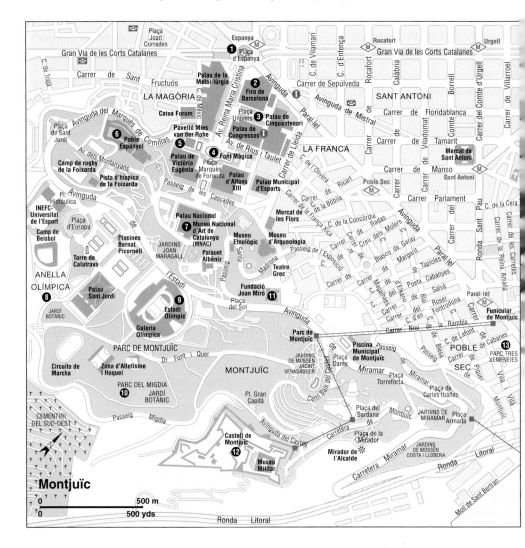

industry, art and sport, and was a political *tour de force* for the Primo de Rivera dictatorship. The mountainside was landscaped in accordance with a plan drawn up by Forestier and Nicolau Maria Rubió i Tudurí. Some 15 palaces were built, as well as national and commercial pavilions, a stadium, a swimming pool, the Poble Espanyol (Spanish Village), ornamental fountains, the Greek Theatre, several towers and the access avenue.

It still looks very much like a showground, and today acts as the main headquarters of the Barcelona Trade Fair organisation, the **Fira de Barcelona ❷**, a complex with 180,000 sq metres (2 million sq ft) of exhibition space and 2 million visitors a year. If a trade fair is being held you will be swept through the gates with the crowds.

The exhibits, mostly in the pavilions lining Avinguda Maria Cristina, are sometimes displayed in the open air, notably in the **Plaça Univers ❸**, a large square created between the main pavilions on the left. The statue in the middle is by Josep Llimona.

Ascending the hill

The upper esplanades are reached by escalator; the system of escalators that covers Montjuïc was created for the 1992 Olympics, the next major event to bring enormous change to this district. The imposing **Font Màgica ❹**, designed by Carlos Buigas in 1929, has recently been restored; the dancing fountain, which is very creatively lit, still delights thousands of visitors several times a week during the *son et lumière* shows (June–Sept: Thurs–Sun 8pm–midnight, Fri & Sat 7–9pm winter). The hill is floodlit at night when, with art-deco beams reaching into the sky, the whole area is at its most impressive.

The spectacular son et lumière *shows at the Font Màgica take place every half hour on summer evenings and last around 15 minutes.*

Below: the Font Màgica in front of the Palau Nacional.

TIP

There is no charge for entry to the Poble Espanyol after 9pm from Sunday to Thursday. In the evenings, this part of Barcelona is a lively entertainment hotspot, with bars, discos and restaurants.

Before going on up, don't miss the **Pavelló Mies van der Rohe ❺** across the esplanade (open daily 10am–8pm; entrance charge). Built by Ludwig Mies van der Rohe as the German pavilion for the 1929 Exposition, it was later dismantled but, at the instigation of some leading architects, rebuilt in 1986 to celebrate the centenary of the architect's birth. Its clean lines and simplicity are quite breathtaking, and help one to understand the beauty of minimalism (*see page 83*). The contrast with some of the other, rather pompously ornate, buildings constructed at the same time is extraordinary. Mies van der Rohe's professor wrote at the time: "This building will one day be remembered as the most beautiful of those built throughout the 20th century."

Across the road is a fascinating former textile factory, **Casaramona**, built by Puig i Cadafalch in 1911. Another gem of *modernista* industrial architecture, it has been overlooked for years but has now been rescued by the Fundació "la Caixa", who have converted it into their new cultural centre the **CaixaForum** (Tues–Sun 10am–8pm; entrance charge). It is a wonderful space with an entrance designed by Isozaki. Apart from their own contemporary collection, it holds temporary exhibitions, concerts, debates and festivals.

Kitsch corner

Just up the road, in the northwest corner of Montjuïc, is the **Poble Espanyol** (Spanish Village) ❻ (open Sun 9am–midnight, Mon 9am–8pm, Tues–Thur 9am–2am, Fri & Sat 9am–4am ; entrance charge), also built for the 1929 Exposition. The shady green of **Avinguda del Marquès de Comillas** is a welcome relief after the exposed areas of the Fira. The Poble Espanyol is pure kitsch, but provides many diversions both day and night, from a *tablao* where you can

BELOW: giants and spectators at a festival in the Poble Espanyol.

watch flamenco dancing to "The Barcelona Experience", an audio-visual show. It is not just "family" entertainment: teenagers flock here for the night scene and retired folk arrive in busloads. The village is one of the most popular venues in Barcelona, welcoming year after year more visitors than even the Sagrada Família or the major museums.

It was built as a showpiece for regional architecture, handicrafts, and cultural and gastronomic styles from all over Spain. It has a Plaza Mayor, typical of many squares you might find in any part of the country, where popular *fiestas* take place. The square is seen in its best light when it stages jazz and rock concerts during the **Grec** summer festival. The entrance is through San Vicente de Ávila Portal; Javier Mariscal, one of Barcelona's most popular designers (he was responsible for the Olympic mascot), put the Poble Espanyol into the limelight in the early 1990s by creating a trendy bar within this stage-set gateway, the **Torres de Ávila**. It was briefly fashionable but has now become a dance club and is only open at weekends.

There are two museums in the village: one, the **Museu d'Arts, Indústries i Tradicions Populars**, is devoted to popular arts and crafts; the other is the **Museu de les Arts Gràfiques**, with exhibits on graphic design since the 19th century (visits by prior arrangement only; tel: 93 426 1999).

Palau Nacional

From here, you can either walk up the hill, following signs to the Palau Nacional, or take a longer walk up Avinguda de l'Estadi straight to the Olympic stadium. The easiest route, however, is to go back down Avinguda del Marquès de Comillas and then take the escalator up. The museum in the Palau Nacional should not be missed.

In some lights, or at a distance, this massive building can look imposing and quite dramatic, but on the whole it looks somewhat out of place in Barcelona. The front steps are full of tourists trying to spot their hotels in the panorama in front of them.

Since 1934 the Palau Nacional has housed the **Museu Nacional d'Art de Catalunya** (MNAC) ❼ (open Tues –Sat 10am–7pm, Sun 10am–2.30pm, entrance charge), which has the most important Romanesque art collection in the world, including murals peeled off the walls of tiny churches in the Pyrenees in the province of Lleida and brought down by donkey. There is also a good Gothic collection and a small selection of Renaissance and Baroque art. The interior, partly remodelled by Italian architect Gae Aulenti, is being renovated to house other collections, including the Museu d'Art Modern, currently in the Parc de la Ciutadella (*see page 164*). Eventually, the plan is to house the whole range of Catalan art under one roof.

From the front steps of the Palau turn right if you want a detour to the museums of archaeology and ethnology on Passeig Santa Madrona. The **Museu Etnològic** (open Tues–Sun 10am–2pm; entrance charge) has collections from all over the world, notably Latin America and the Philippines. A section on Japan, the *Espai Japó*, is an indication of the new cultural (and commercial) exchange between Catalonia and Japan.

Map on page 194

BELOW: a depiction of the 13th-century *Assault on the City of Mallorca*, in the Museu Nacional d'Art de Catalunya.

Further down the hill is the **Teatre Grec**, also built for the 1929 Exposition. Inspired by a model of Epidaurus, the theatre's backdrop is a solid wall of rock which was part of an old abandoned quarry. During the Grec summer festival it is an important venue for plays and concerts. Just beyond it is the **Museu d'Arqueologia de Catalunya** (open Tues–Sat 10am–7pm, Sun 10am–2.30pm entrance charge), with interesting discoveries from the first inhabitants of Catalonia, including the Greek and Roman period.

This route will bring you down the hill as far as the **Mercat de les Flors** on **Lleida**, a complex being renovated to become the **Ciutat del Teatre**, which will be the home of several new municipal theatres including the Teatre Lliure. Productions that take place here are generally interesting and of a good standard. However, if your main goal is to check out the Olympic legacy on Montjuïc, this detour should be left for another day as it takes you a long way down the hill.

Sporting Barcelona

The **Anella Olímpica** (Olympic Ring) ❽ is spread across the hillside behind the Palau Nacional and easily accessible from there by escalator. The buildings here appear to be sculpted on to the ridge, with wide open views to the south dropping down behind them. Despite the passage of time since their moment of glory in 1992, they are still glossy-looking and glamorous, and quite dazzling in the abundant light of Montjuïc.

BELOW: outside the Palau Sant Jordi. **RIGHT:** detail on the exterior of the Museu Etnològic.

There are eight Olympic-standard sports centres and three athletics tracks in the area, but if you stick to the road you will see only a fraction of what was created: fortunately, a walkway on the inland (downhill) side of the main stadium gives access to the central square.

The **Estadi Olímpic** ❾ (open daily 10am–8pm in summer, 10am–6pm in winter; free) was actually built for the 1929 Universal Exposition, following a design by Pere Domènech. Its opening football match was a victory for the Catalan side against Bolton Wanderers – a little known fact. It remained open until the Mediterranean Games in 1955, then fell into disrepair. Extensive works for the 1992 Olympics involved lowering the arena by 11 metres (36 ft) to create the extra seating needed for 55,000 spectators. Most of the track events and the opening and closing ceremonies were held here. You can relive the excitement of Barcelona's glory in the **Galeria Olímpica**, an exhibition space at the rear of the stadium (open Tues–Sat 10am–2pm, 4–8pm, Sun 10am–2pm in summer, Tues–Fri 10am–1pm, 4–6pm in winter; entrance charge).

Below and west of the stadium stretches the immense **Olympic Terrace**, lined with pillars. In the middle of the main terrace is a lawn with an artificial stream flowing through it; on the left is a small forest of identical sculptures. The terrace drops down to a second level in the middle distance, and then to a third – the **Plaça d'Europa** – which is a circular colonnaded area built on top of a massive water tank containing 60,000 cubic metres of drinking water for the city. The whole has the atmosphere of a re-created Roman forum.

Olympic installations

On each side of the terrace are key installations: to the left is the **Palau Sant Jordi**, to the right the **Piscines Bernat Piccornell**, and in the far distance the INEFC **Universitat de l'Esport**. All this is as planned, but there is one highly visible landmark in the whole which caused great controversy at the time, not least with the architects who created the whole Olympic ring: the great white **Torre**

Map on page 194

A cable car is a great way to reach the top of the hill if you have a head for heights.

BELOW: the Estadi Olímpic.

BELOW:
sardana dancers
statue on the hill.

de Calatrava communications tower (188 metres/616 ft), designed by Spanish architect Santiago Calatrava, known for his elegantly engineered bridges. Olympic architects Frederic Correa, Alfonso Milá, Joan Margarit and Carles Buxadé hated the tower project, and rallied dozens of intellectuals to their cause. Nevertheless the Telefònica tower went ahead, and the result is quite stunning.

Other than the stadium itself, the installation most in the public eye is the **Palau Sant Jordi** (open Sat and Sun 10am–6pm, except when hosting an event), an indoor stadium designed by Japanese architect Arata Isozaki. The ultra-modern design in sleek steel and glass can seat 15,000, with not a pillar in sight. Since the Olympics, the Palau has proved popular for concerts and exhibitions as well as sporting events.

Green spaces

Just beyond the stadium is a road which winds behind it. This expanse of hillside is known as the **Parc del Migdia** ❿. Here, after many years of expectancy among the local population, the new botanical garden has opened, the **Jardí Botànic** (daily 10am–3pm, entrance charge), a sustainable garden in keeping with Barcelona's aspirations for the new century. The many new plants and trees are slowly becoming established. Looking to the top of the hill, you can see how the niches from the enormous cemetery, which drops down to the sea on the other side, are beginning to creep over the ridge.

Returning to the Avinguda de l'Estadi, opposite the stadium are the smaller, more peaceful and elegant gardens of Joan Maragall surrounding the **Palauet Albéniz**. This *palauet* or "little palace" is now the official residence of visiting dignitaries to Barcelona. It was built as a Royal Pavilion for the 1929 Exposi-

tion and during the years of self-government in Catalonia – from 1931 until the end of the Civil War – it was used as a music museum.

Surrealist showcase

With the stadium on your right follow the main road until it becomes **Avinguda de Miramar**. On the left is the **Fundació Joan Miró** ⑪ (open Tues, Wed, Fri and Sat 10am–7pm, Thur 10am–9.30pm, Sun 10am–2.30pm; entrance charge), an understated yet powerfully impressive gem on this sporting hill. Designed by Josep Lluís Sert, eminent architect and friend of Miró, the gallery has been open since 1974.

A Mediterranean luminosity floods the striking building and shows Miró's work in its best light. One of the largest collections in the world of Miró's work, it includes paintings, drawings, sculptures and tapestries as well as his complete graphic work. It also contains the mercury fountain designed by Alexander Calder for the Spanish Republic's pavilion in the 1937 Paris Exhibition. It seems fitting that this should be here now: the Spanish pavilion was intended as a political statement, coinciding as it did with the Civil War, and was designed by Sert and included Miró's work and Picasso's *Guernica*. Contemporary exhibitions and concerts are also held here regularly.

The Fundació Joan Miró has one of the largest collections of the artist's work.

Just before the municipal swimming pool on the left, scene of Olympic diving in 1992, is the funicular station, Parc de Montjuïc. Continue along the road for magnificent views of the port from the **Jardins de Miramar**, where there are bars serving food and refreshments and the impressive **Jardins Mossèn Costa i Llobera**. A new hotel is to be built up here, part of a major plan for redeveloping and landscaping Montjuïc. Alternatively, catch the funicular back

BELOW: the Fundació Joan Miró.

Map on page 194

down to Paral.lel metro station, or complete the Montjuïc experience and catch the cable car up to the **Castell de Montjuïc** ⑫ (open Tues–Sun 9.30am–7.30pm, winter 4.30pm; entrance charge) for an even better view.

Place of torture

The castle was built in the 17th century during the battle between Catalonia and Spain's Felipe IV, known as the "War of the Reapers". At the beginning of the 18th century Bourbon troops ransacked the castle; it was rebuilt between 1751 and 1779. The new fortress was in the form of a starred pentagon, with enormous moats, bastions and buttresses. It has little appeal for Catalans, as it represents hated oppression from the central government in Madrid, and is a place where torture and executions took place over many years. It was here that beloved leader **Lluís Companys**, president of the Generalitat, was shot in 1940 (see page 42). Today the castle houses the **Museu Militar**, with a collection of weapons, lead soldiers and military uniforms. Keen climbers spend their weekends abseiling down the castle walls.

The route down

You can descend the hill on foot or take the cable car down. Alternatively, try catching the *transbordador aeri* which leaves Montjuïc and crosses the port. It leaves from the Plaça Armada in the area known as Miramar. Downward travellers who opt for the funicular from near Plaça Dante are using yet another relic of the 1929 exhibition, though greatly refurbished. The rail descends a distance of 760 metres (2,500 ft) and disembarks at **Avinguda Paral.lel**. Avinguda Paral.lel was originally the Calle Marqués del Duero, in honour of the man himself. Then, in 1794, a Frenchman, Pierre François André Méchain, discovered that the avenue's pathway coincided exactly with the navigational parallel 44°44'N. In honour of this discovery a local cook opened a tavern which she called "El Paralelo". The popularity of the place ensured that the name was adopted as the street name.

This area has always been known as the centre of variety theatre and vaudeville. Its most famous theatre was El Molino, a colourful music hall which, sadly, after several attempts at resuscitation, has been closed down indefinitely. Some large theatres remain, usually showing musicals or farces which attract coachloads of people from out of town.

Parc Tres Xemeneies ⑬, just down the avenue towards the sea, is dominated by three enormous 72-metre (235-ft) chimneys. This is a fine example of a "hard" urban park, with interesting design ideas and deservedly frequented by local residents. The chimneys are the remains of the "Grupo Mata", an electricity-producing plant dating from the turn of the 20th century. They are now integrated into the pristine glass premises of FECSA, the electrical company.

Paral.lel is a good departure point for heading into the Old Town through the Barri Xino, or going down to the Waterfront. However, anyone who has thoroughly explored Montjuïc will be looking forward to putting their feet up for a while. ❑

BELOW:
playful statue in the Jardins de Joan Maragall.

The Olympics

On 17 December 1986, in Lausanne, the president of the International Olympic Committee, Switzerland, Juan Antonio Samaranch, announced that the 25th Olympic Games would be held in his native Barcelona. This much anticipated news was greeted with jubilation in Spain, particularly by Barcelonans and Catalans. It was the fourth time the city had pitched for the Games and the Catalans were quick to recognise that it was a golden opportunity to attract long overdue investment in the city. Neglected infrastructure could be repaired, and it could become, some believed, a major city of the 21st century.

This vision took some battering in the following six years of upheaval, and there were serious doubts about whether too much was being attempted in too short a time. However, when the 25th Olympiad opened on 25 July 1992, the confident Catalans were proved right. The Games were a display of great organisational skills, from the moment a burning arrow taken from the torch was unleashed to light up the Olympic flame in the renovated stadium on Montjuïc to the departure of the last athlete from the reconstructed airport.

It was also, being Barcelona, something of a "designer Olympics". Everything looked good. Key elements of the infrastructure were designed by leading national and international architects – the Communications Tower on Collserola by Sir Norman Foster, the one on Montjuïc by Calatrava, the Palau Sant Jordi indoor stadium by Isozaki, the Vila Olímpica by the Barcelona firm Mackay, Martorell, Bohigas and Puigdomenech. With everything from the starting blocks to the medal bearers' uniforms being designed by Barcelona's top fashion designer Toni Miró, the sporting events were meticulously staged for the maximum visual effect, with an eye on the 3½ million viewers around the world.

The 500,000 people who came to the city saw it spruced up with new roads, renovated squares, freshly painted facades, urban sculptures and newly opened vistas. There were four centres of activity located in the four corners of the city, and 16 subsidiary centres, some out-side the city. The key Olympic area in Barcelona itself was the hill of Montjuïc, where the original stadium, built for the 1929 Universal Exhibition, was renovated to accommodate 55,000 spectators, and the Palau Sant Jordi indoor stadium, the INEF (University of Physical Education) and the Picornell swimming pools were constructed. The hill was landscaped and a system of escalators was installed to make access easier. The Olympic Gallery in the stadium today recaptures the atmosphere and excitement of the Games through thousands of photographs, sound recordings and videos.

The other areas of Barcelona to benefit were around the football club on Diagonal, the Vall d'Hebron and, most spectacular of all, the Parc de Mar, built on former industrial land by the sea. This incorporated the Olympic Village (now a desirable area of seaside apartments) and the Olympic port, where dozens of new restaurants buzz every evening and at weekends.

At the closing ceremony on 9 August it was an even prouder Juan Antonio Samaranch who declared that Barcelona had hosted one of the most successful Olympic Games ever. ❏

RIGHT: the Olympic arrow opens the games.

THE EIXAMPLE

*Cerdà's 19th-century grid system of streets allowed the
city's wealthy élite to commission some of the most innovative
buildings of the age, including Gaudí's fabulous Sagrada Família*

Map
on page
208

The **Eixample** is one of the most characteristic districts of Barcelona, and
has some of its most distinctive elements, such as the Sagrada Família and
much of its famed *modernista* architecture. It stands as a symbol of the
19th-century boom that initiated the city's modern era, and today is the most
populated district in the city. After the narrow, irregular streets of the Old
Town, where history has left layer upon layer of building styles, the Eixample
can feel like a new town. Its rigid, regular structure forms a repeated pattern
from its southern boundary by **Plaça d'Espanya** to its northern limit leading
up from **Plaça de les Glòries**. The traffic roars down one street and up another
in a well-structured one-way system.

An expanding city

In a sense it *was* a "new town": it grew from the need to expand out of the old
city in the middle of the 19th century. *Eixample* means "enlargement"
(*ensanche,* the Castilian word, is still often used) and was to extend over the
areas between the old city centre and the equally historic municipalities of
Sants, Sarrià, Sant Gervasi de Cassoles and Gràcia. Although criticised by some,
this exceptional piece of town planning is deeply admired by architects, who still
come from far and wide to see it.

Its designer, Ildefons Cerdà i Sunyer, was a liberal-
minded civil engineer. He planned a garden city in
which only two of the four sides of each block would
be built on. The other sides, together with the central
open space, were to have been attractive, shady
squares and the *xamfrans* (angled street corners) were
meant to be open spaces, not packed with double-
parked vehicles as they are today. Work began in 1859
but Cerdà's plan was not adopted in its entirety for a
number of different reasons. His "utopian socialism"
did not appeal to the more conservative elements in
the city, causing widespread controversy.

The Eixample is broken into two halves, *la dreta*
(right) and *l'esquerra* (left) on either side of **Balmes**
as you look inland towards the summit of Tibidabo.
Within the two halves are well-defined neighbourhoods, such as those of the **Sagrada Família** and **Fort
Pius** (on the right) and **Sant Antoni** and a *barri* near
the old municipal slaughterhouse called **L'Escorxador** (on the left).

Most of Barcelona's *modernista* landmarks can be
found in *la dreta,* while *l'esquerra* is more modern
and residential. Since the 1960s *la dreta* has undergone a profound transformation. With the earlier
inhabitants moving to uptown districts, the larger
houses have been converted into offices and flats.

The best way to appreciate the Eixample is to

PRECEDING PAGES:
the "Trade" office
block in the
Diagonal.
LEFT: the roof of
La Pedrera.
BELOW: 19th
century decorative
details in Eixample.

The façade of the
Hotel Majestic in
Passeig de Gràcia.

wander aimlessly, to be led by the green pedestrian lights at junctions, zig-zagging up, across and down these fascinating streets. Peep into doorways to see *modernista* lamps and ceramic tiles, look up at balconies and stained-glass tribunes (enclosed balconies), notice the decorative facades, as well as the plants, washing and other elements of real life that go on inside these museum pieces. Take time to visit the art galleries that abound, to notice old shop signs, to shop in ancient *colmados* where ageless men in overalls attend obsequiously to your every need.

Whenever possible, catch a glimpse of the inner patios of these *illas*, the name of each four-sided block of buildings: sadly not used for the greater good, as Cerdà would have wished, but mostly for car parks, commercial or private use. They still make fascinating viewing, particularly the backs of the elegant houses and some well-established private gardens.

A change of pace

This itinerary will focus on the central area and some key areas leading off it. Using Plaça de Catalunya as a pivotal point, cross over to **Passeig de Gràcia ❶**. This wide, tree-lined avenue originally linked the old city and the outlying neighbourhood of Gràcia even before the ancient walls of the city were torn down. Cerdà increased its width to 60 metres (200 ft), which makes it distinctive from the uniform streets of the rest of the Eixample; more recently, the pavements have been widened. The beautiful wrought-iron street lamps, which are incorporated with mosaic benches, were designed by Pere Falqués in 1906.

As you walk up on the right-hand side, you will immediately be aware of the change of pace. Notice the hexagonal pavement tiles designed by Gaudí

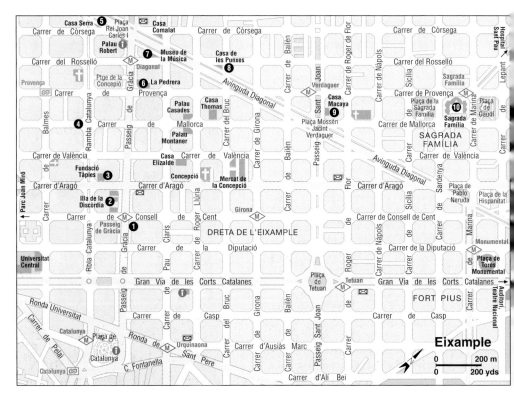

and unique to the Passeig de Gràcia. Everywhere you look there are fascinating buildings to admire and details to observe.

Designer-label shopping

On the *xamfrà* at **Casp** you will find Gonzalo Comella, with designer labels for men and women, and towards **Gran Via**, another classic, Furest, for the well-dressed Catalan man about town (and country). Next comes the flagship premises of **Zara** in the highly desirable building at the very visible junction with **Gran Via**. Galician-based Zara is a recent phenomenon in the fashion world, with shops all over Barcelona, Spain and internationally. Its successful formula seems to be mass production of ever-changing designer-imitations at accessible prices. And the clothes seem to be good enough for the highly style-conscious Catalans.

Gran Via is a broad, busy thoroughfare that brings traffic from the airport and the south right through town to the motorways heading north and up the coast. The fountains in the middle and the impressive buildings around prevent it being merely a major through-road, however. As you cross over and continue up Passeig de Gràcia, don't miss the jeweller's, J. Roca, a fine, subtle example of 1930s architecture by Sert, nor Bel next door, with its universal fashion in the best possible taste.

Consell de Cent, one of the streets cutting across, demands a detour. Cross Passeig de Gràcia and wander a block or two, to see some of the best art galleries as well as **Antonio Miro**, the latest shop of Barcelona's ingenious and always intriguing fashion designer. One of the first designers to bring fame to Catalan fashion in the 1970s, he remains supreme. Apart from his twice-yearly collec-

Map on page 208

TIP

In Casp, on the right-hand side as you begin your walk up Passeig de Gràcia, is one of the best spots in town to have a coffee, Bracafé, which has much the same character as when it opened in 1932.

BELOW: a style-conscious resident in the Eixample.

Distinctive Gaudí balconies on the Casa Batlló.

tions, he is often brought in to advise on important institutional fashion decisions: he designed the uniforms for the *mossos*, the Catalan police force, and various Olympic uniforms. The new Liceu opera house (*see page 139*) also has a Miro label on its velvet designer stage curtain.

Illa de la Discòrdia

The most famous, and no doubt most visited, block on Passeig de Gràcia is between Consell de Cent and Aragó. The block, formerly known as the Mansana de Discòrdia is now called the **Illa de la Discòrdia ❷** (both names means the same – the Block of Discord). It gained its name because of the close juxtaposition of three outstanding buildings, each of which is in a conflicting style, although they are all categorised as modernist.

Casa Lleó Morera, designed by Lluís Domènech i Montaner and decorated with the sculptures of Eusebi Arnau, is on the corner, with an exclusive leather shop occupying the ground floor. Slightly further up is the **Casa Amatller** by Josep Puig i Cadafalch, and next door to it is **Casa Batlló**, which was remodelled by Gaudí in 1906.

Disappointingly, these buildings are no longer open to the public. Casa Lleó Morera is owned by a large publishing company whose plans are uncertain, the Casa Amatller houses a library and offices, and Casa Batlló is also company-owned. But you can still enjoy the splendid facades: peek in to see extraordinary ceramic work (Lleó Morera), stained-glass ceiling and lamp details (Amatller), and amazing Gaudí touches (Batlló), which are also stunning at night.

On sale in the entrance of the Casa Amatller are tickets for the **Ruta del Modernisme**, which takes in a variety of other modernist buildings and arte-

BELOW: the Illa de la Discòrdia.

facts, ranging from the Palau Güell to the Parc Güell. Tickets entitle you to reduced entry to seven buildings and museums along the route, and show you where to find numerous others whose facades can be enjoyed, or whose interiors are accessible because they are shops, cafés, hotel lobbies or restaurants.

Map on page 208

Tàpies showpiece

Around the corner in noisy Aragó is something completely different: **Servicio Estación**, an emporium of a hardware store. Opposite it is another Domènech i Montaner work, built in 1886 for publishers Montaner i Simón and now skilfully converted to become the **Fundació Tàpies ❸** (open Tues–Sun 10am–8pm; entrance charge). Observe the building from this side of the street to get the full perspective, and pick out the chair in the Tàpies sculpture which crowns it, *Núvol i Cadira* ("Cloud and Chair").

Reputedly the first *modernista* building, it seems rather workmanlike after the ornate facade of Casa Batlló. The interior spaces make a good setting for the large collection of work by Antoni Tàpies (*see page 74*), who is considered to be Spain's greatest living artist. Interesting temporary exhibitions of contemporary art are also held here.

After the Tàpies museum continue to the next corner and turn right into **Rambla Catalunya ❹**, which runs parallel with Passeig de Gràcia, one block away. It is like an elongation of the Old Town's La Rambla through the central part of the Eixample. The atmosphere, though, is quite different: the central boulevard is quiet and sedate, very few tourists stroll here and the pavement cafés are patronised by smart, middle-aged Catalans, or their offspring. The shopping is sophisticated – there is not a souvenir in sight – and it's expensive, as are the elegant galleries.

Enjoy the gentle walk up towards Diagonal, pausing at every horizontal crossing to look at the houses on the chamfered corners and the streets leading off, to get into the rhythm of the structure. If you need a break, dive down a few steps into an old wine bar, **La Bodegueta**, at No. 100, welcomingly down to earth in the midst of all this sophistication. Alternatively, go with the flow, and a little further on have a genteel snack in **Mauri** on the corner of **Provença**, with its unusual chocolate hedgehogs and tempting pastries, or a take-away lunch from its mouth-watering delicatessen counter.

BELOW: window-shopping at a *modernista* shop front.

Crossing the Diagonal

At the end of Rambla Catalunya, the Eixample meets the Diagonal and there is another change of gear as a new residential district begins. On the right is **Casa Serra ❺**, built by Puig i Cadafalch in 1908 and controversially adapted to accommodate the **Diputació de Barcelona**, the central government body which occupied the Palau de la Generalitat in Plaça Sant Jaume during the Franco regime, and had to be relocated with the return of democracy. In the Milà and Correa designed complex the new steel building seems like a large shadow of the older one.

There are very few outward signs of the red tape that must proliferate inside, only the presence of some chatting guards suggests anything to do with officialdom. Walk along the short stretch of **Còrsega**, and turn right into the gardens of the **Palau Robert**, a cool haven in mid-summer.

The house was built by a French architect and would not look out of place in a French provincial city. Currently, it houses the Generalitat tourist offices, with information on the whole of Catalonia and occasional exhibitions about the different regions.

Cut through the side entrance to return to Passeig de Gràcia, at the busy junction of **Plaça Rei Joan Carles I**, where a constantly traffic-filled Diagonal runs across the top of the Eixample, up to Plaça Francesc Macià and the upper reaches of the city, and down towards Diagonal Mar, where eventually it will reach the sea; above it the district of Gràcia begins.

Passageways of the Eixample

Heading down towards Plaça de Catalunya on the same pavement, cross **Rosselló** and halfway along the next block you will come to another characteristic feature of the Eixample – a passageway running through the inner part of the block. This one, called the **Passatge de la Concepció**, has decorative iron gates across it, but it is open to the public.

Even if you do not have the time or the budget to eat at **Tragaluz**, one of the chicest and best-looking restaurants in Barcelona, just take a moment to have a look at it. It was designed within one of the typical villas of these passageways, and is extremely attractive. The word *tragaluz* means skylight, and you will see that this makes sense when you go upstairs. Just opposite is its latest branch, a wonderfully minimalist Japanese restaurant called **El Japonés**.

BELOW:
architecture is not
the first thing on
everyone's mind.

La Pedrera

Follow the passage until it comes out into Passeig de Gràcia, and turn right to the end of the block. Pause on this corner to give yourself time to take in the extraordinary spectacle of Gaudí's **Casa Milà**, more often known as **La Pedrera** (The Quarry) ❻ (open daily 10am–8pm; entrance charge) because of its rippling grey stone facade.

This splendid building has been cleaned, refurbished and polished up by its new owners, the foundation of the Caixa de Catalunya.

At the time of its construction in 1910 it was the subject of passionate debate between enthusiasts and denigrators. For many years it was left to fall apart, but UNESCO declared it a monument of world interest and the Caixa de Catalunya stepped in. Take time to visit this exceptional building, which has the *Espai Gaudí*, an enlightening exhibition of the architect's work, in the attic, a spectacular roof where the chimneys have been dubbed the "witch scarers", and *El Pis*, one of the flats now open to the public and decorated as it would have been when the building was first occupied. Major temporary exhibitions are held regularly on the first floor *(principal)* and are open to the public free of charge. A bar and inspiring shop are on the ground floor.

Just up from La Pedrera, at No. 96, is another feast for designer eyes – **Vinçon**. In this widely-famed shop you can buy everything you need (or desire) for the home, and always be confident that the design divas of the day will approve. Based in the former home of 19th-century painter Ramon Casas (*see page 164*), this growing empire is quietly taking over the block, so you can actually cut through the shop to **Pau Claris** or **Provença**. Before leaving, have a look at the inner patio of the block from the *principal*, including a rear

Map on page 208

BELOW: inside the Museu de la Música.

view of La Pedrera. If you don't take the short cut, return to Passeig de Grà-cia and along Provença to Pau Claris, back up to Diagonal.

More modernist creations

An ornate and colourful detail of the still-unfinished Sagrada Família.

At Diagonal No. 373 is Puig i Cadafalch's **Casa Quadras** ❼. Built for the Barón de Quadras in 1904, until recently it housed the Museu de la Música. The museum is to be relocated to the new **Auditorí** but there is a good chance that the house will remain open to the public as it is owned by the city council. Meanwhile enjoy the detailing on the facade, wander into the vestibule and go round the corner to look at its elegant rearside in Rosselló.

Walk down the Diagonal a short way to see another building by Puig i Cadafalch, the magnificent **Casa Terrades** (1903–5) or **Casa de les Punxes** ("House of Spikes") ❽. Sadly, it is not possible to go inside, although the building's outside appearance at a distance is impressive enough. Both of these, and his Casa Serra, show definite influences of Nordic neo-Gothic.

One option here is to continue down Diagonal until it crosses **Passeig de Sant Joan** (a more humble Passeig de Gràcia) to visit an earlier (1901–2) Puig i Cadafalch house at No. 106, the beautiful Casa Macaya. Or take the longer way round to see some more Eixample gems and get to know its atmosphere as a neighbourhood. Go down Bruc and turn right into Mallorca to **Casa Thomas** (No. 293), designed by Domènech i Montaner, and visit **b.d.** the shop in its basement, which is like an exhibition of 21st-century furniture design. Reach the **Mercat de la Concepció** on València by taking either Roger de Llúria (notice J. Murria on the corner, an exceptional delicatessen frozen in time, and the inner patio of the **Casa Elizalde**, a civic centre on València)

RIGHT:
the Casa Macaya.

or more directly by Bruc. This is a fine example of a 19th-century market, remodelled in true Barcelona late 20th-century style with striking results. Its flower market never closes. A couple of good restaurants on the cobbled street to one side, an ironmonger's, health food and earthenware shops all contribute to the local atmosphere, which is typical of residential Eixample and an essential part of its charm.

Make your way to **Casa Macaya** ❾, formerly the cultural centre of the Fundació La Caixa (now in Montjuïc *see page 196*) and temporarily housing the Foundation's Science Museum while its buildings in Tibidabo are being extended on a large scale. The hallway and staircase are beautiful.

Gaudí's celebrated temple

And so to the **Sagrada Família** ❿ (open 9am–8pm in summer, 9am–6pm in winter; entrance charge), the symbol of Barcelona for many, and the reason the name Gaudí spread around the world. Here, in the centre of this bustling, ordinary neighbourhood, it is a staggering sight. It is visited by more than one million people every year, not counting those who simply gasp on the pavement. This extraordinary building should probably be tackled in the morning rather than at the end of a long walk, as there is much to see (*see page 93*). It is well connected by metro and bus. Whether you love or hate this building, you will never forget the first time you set eyes on it.

Along Avinguda de Gaudí is the much less known *modernista* complex, the **Hospital Sant Pau** (1902–12). Made up of over 20 buildings, it is the work of the prolific Domènech i Montaner. As it is a public hospital, you can wander through into the garden and pavilions behind.

Parc Joan Miró

Venturing beyond the central part of the Eixample is a good way to complete the picture of Barcelona from the mid-19th century to the millennium. On the extreme left of the Eixample you will find one of the first parks to be created in the 1980s as part of the new Barcelona. Covering four Eixample blocks above Plaça d'Espanya where Diputació and Aragó meet Tarragona (metro Espanya or Tarragona), the **Parc Joan Miró** is also known as the **Parc de l'Escorxador** because it was the location of the municipal slaughterhouse until 1979. It is a great area for kids to run wild in. The 22-metre (70-ft) Miró statue, *Dona i Ocell* ("Woman and Bird"), is striking in its simple setting on a small island in the middle of a pool in the park. One of Miró's last works, it was unveiled in 1983, just a few months before he died.

You could link a visit to the park with a trip to Montjuïc (*see page 193*). Alternatively, combine it with a walk along Gran Via (noisy, but some interesting buildings) or one of the streets parallel to it to get a sense of the day-to-day real life of the city. The apartment blocks along this route follow the Cerdà plan religiously even though, on the whole, they grew up later and are smaller and more modest than earlier buildings in the Eixample. ❑

Map on page 208

BELOW: the neo-classical Teatre Nacional.

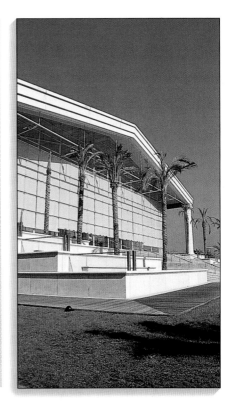

PLAÇA DE LES GLÒRIES

At the extreme right of the Eixample, just beyond the Monumental Bull Ring on the Gran Via, is Plaça de les Glòries Catalanes. What seems a no-man's land occupied by a roundabout and flyovers, actually hides a nucleus of activities: a new civic centre in an impressive old flourmill, **La Farinera**, and the much frequented Els Encants, a sprawling flea market, which opened in 1928.

Newcomer to the area is the high profile, high cost, cultural complex that was long awaited, much discussed and finally opened in the late 1990s: the **Teatre Nacional de Catalunya** (TNC) and **L'Auditori**, the National Theatre and the Concert Hall. The theatre is in the unmistakable neoclassical style of its architect Ricardo Bofill. Its three stages cope with a varied programme, mainly in Catalan, of classic and experimental theatre and dance. This is the Generalitat's protégé, unlike the Ciutat de Teatre at the other end of town near Montjuïc, which is the domain of the municipal cultural department.

L'Auditori, designed by Rafael Moneo, is the new home of the Barcelona Orchestra (OBC). It comprises a large hall (2,500 seats), a smaller room for chamber music and will eventually house the Music Museum and a music conservatory.

THE FANTASTIC VISION OF ANTONI GAUDÍ

Antoni Gaudí's astounding buildings established him as the most original European architect in the early years of the 20th century

Antoni Gaudí (1852–1926) was born at Reus, Catalonia, the son of a coppersmith, and spent almost all his career in Barcelona. He was a patriotic Catalan and is said to have insisted on using the Catalan language even when talking to the King of Spain. The other major forces that shaped his life were a devotion to his work and a devout Christian faith. In 1878 he graduated from the Escuela Superior de Arquitectura, Barcelona, and soon afterwards met Eusebio Güell (1847–1918), a wealthy industrialist and Catalan nationalist who became his main patron, commissioning the Parc Güell (*above*) and other works.

A BIZARRE STYLE

Gaudí's work was influenced by various sources, including Gothic and Moorish architecture, and it has features in common with the Art Nouveau style fashionable at the time. However, his buildings have a sense of bizarre fantasy that sets them apart from anything else in the history of architecture. Walls undulate as if they were alive, towers grow like giant anthills, columns slant out of the vertical, and surfaces are encrusted with unconventional decoration, including broken bottles.

Gaudí died after being hit by a trolley bus. Mistaken for a tramp, he was taken to a paupers' ward in the hospital. He died there, leaving several of his works, including the Sagrada Família, unfinished.

▷ **RAISING THE ROOF**
The undulating roof of the Casa Batlló, with its overlapping scale-like tiles, has been compared to the writhing of a dragon.

◁ **VIBRANT DECORATION**
Richly coloured ceramic decoration in playful, abstract designs typifies Gaudí's work at Parc Güell.

△ PARC GUELL
The Parc Güell is part of a garden suburb that Gaudí worked on for his patron Eusebio Güell from about 1900 to 1914 but never completed.

▽ COLOURED FACADE
Gaudí used blue-green ceramic material on the facade of the Casa Batlló; the artist Salvador Dalí compared it to "the tranquil waters of a lake".

◁ SLOW EVOLUTION
Gaudí began work on his masterpiece, the church of the Sagrada Família (Holy Family), in 1883, but the huge building is still unfinished.

▽ DRAGON GUARDIAN
The dragon gate linking two entrance lodges (1884–88) for Eusebio Güell's estate on the outskirts of Barcelona is one of Gaudí's finest pieces of ironwork.

RESIDENTIAL BUILDINGS

In 1904–06 Gaudí remodelled a house for José Batlló y Casanovas, a Barcelona textiles manufacturer. The house had been built in the 1870s and was elegant but unremarkable. Gaudí completely transformed the exterior, adding an extra storey, topping it with a spectacular roof, and adorning the windows with flowing frames and balconies. Inside the house, the subtle interplay of forms continues (*above*).

Immediately after the Batlló house, Gaudí designed an apartment block (1906–10) for Don Pedro Milá, Batlló's partner. The Casa Milá has been aptly nicknamed "La Pedrera" (The Quarry) because the curving facade looks like a strange cliff-face. The sense of movement and fantasy continues on the roof, where the chimneys and ventilation stacks are a riot of exuberant shapes – see the example below.

ABOVE THE DIAGONAL

Avinguda Diagonal effectively cuts the city in two. In the little-explored area north of this divide are some of the city's most distinctive districts and worthwhile excursions

Map on page 222

Two well-worn clichés about urban Barcelona are that it has traditionally turned its back to the sea, and that people who live above the Diagonal (the arterial road that slices through the city at an angle, from west to east) never come down below it. The development of the waterfront in the 1990s has gone some way to dispelling the former and, along with the whole urban renewal programme, has succeeded in attracting uptown people downtown. Nightlife in the Old Town also boomed in the 1990s – young *pijos* and *pijas* (a snooty set who favour polo shirts and navy blue, and insist on speaking Castilian despite their Catalan roots), whose natural habitat is around **Plaça Francesc Macià**, do now venture down on a Friday night.

The converse seems to be the case for tourists. Many visitors never make it above the Diagonal, and are at best unaware and at worst dismissive of this large part of the city. It is well worth taking a closer look, in order to gain a broader picture of Barcelona.

PRECEDING PAGES:
fast-moving
fairground ride.
LEFT: Parc Güell.
BELOW: colonnade
in Parc Güell.

Gaudí's colourful creation

There are, of course, isolated pockets above the Diagonal which are star attractions. One is the **Parc Güell ❶** (open daily 10am–8pm; admission free), the second most visited park in Barcelona after the Ciutadella. It owes its magnetic attraction to the fact it was designed by Gaudí. It was originally planned as a garden city on the estate of Eusebi Güell, encompassing 60 building plots, but only five buildings were completed: the two pavilions flanking the entrance, both designed by Gaudí, and three others inside the park, one of which is today the **Casa-Museu Gaudí** (open 10am–8pm in summer, 10am–6pm in winter; entrance charge) where the architect lived from 1906 until his death in 1926. Some of his furniture, drawings and projects are housed here.

In creating Parc Güell, Gaudí used shapes which harmonised with the landscape. Always aware of the struggle between man and nature, he built a complex garden of staircases, zoomorphic sculptures, sinuous ramps and viaducts. The most important single element of the park is a two-tiered plaza 86 by 40 metres (280 by 130 ft). The lower part, made up of a series of columns in the form of a *sala hipóstila*, was designed to be the housing estate's market-place. The upper portion is an open area with grand views over the city, surrounded by an undulating bench of mosaics, whose detailing is largely the work of Josep Maria Jujol. Recently restored, this serpentine seat is quite spectacular and, like the park, should not be missed. Built between 1900 and 1914, it has been declared a monument of world interest by UNESCO.

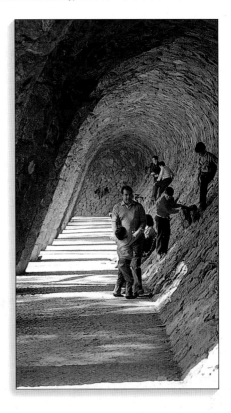

A classic example of residential life "above the Diagonal" is the area around **Parc Turó ❷**, pinpointed by the roundabout **Plaça Francesc Macià** (on many bus routes, including the luxurious Tombbus from Plaça de Catalunya) where one begins to leave the 19th century Eixample and enter the upper reaches of the Diagonal. Modern office blocks, hotels, smart shops and expensive properties are the trademark, and the streets are peopled by yuppies on mobile phones, well-dressed girls on mopeds, lawyers with slicked-backed hair, tanned, well-kept elderly men in dark suits, and women whose faces have seen a thousand lifts. In the park, just at the end of **Pau Casals** (a monument to the famous Catalan cellist is at the entrance), it is common to see well-behaved children in crisp pale blue under the watchful eye of a fully uniformed nanny.

Also known as **Jardins Poeta Eduard Marquina**, the park was a project of landscape architect Rubió i Tudurí, and has two distinct areas. One is made up of lawn, hedges and flowerbeds laid out in a classic geometric pattern, the other contains children's playgrounds, a small lake and an open-air theatre. Sculptures by Clarà and Viladomat, among others, dot the interior of the park.

Royal palace

From Plaça Francesc Macià the Diagonal is wider and the traffic faster, revving up for one of the main routes out of town. Walk, or catch a bus, along its tree-lined way as far as the **Palau Reial de Pedralbes ❸**, absorbing the atmos-phere of this other side of Barcelona, and passing the large shopping centre **La Illa** on the left. The Royal Palace is the result of a 1919 conversion of the antique Can Feliu into a residence for King Alfonso XIII during his visits to Barcelona. It is elegant and the classical garden peaceful, but has little sense of

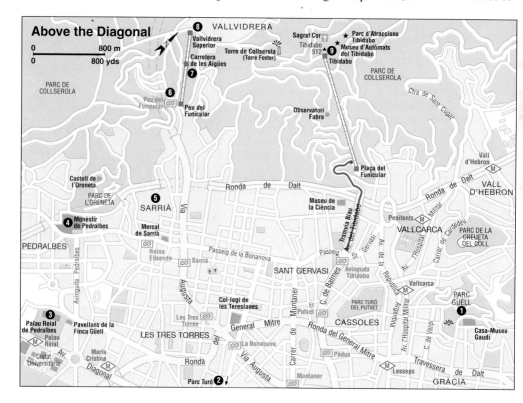

history. The main building cannot be visited, apart from the two museums it houses. The **Museu de Ceràmica** (open Tues–Sat 10am–6pm, Sun 10am–3pm; entrance charge) shows the history of Spanish pottery from the 12th century, and has some interesting 20th-century pieces from Artigas, Miró and Picasso. The **Museu de les Arts Decoratives** (same opening times) shows the development of craft techniques from medieval times to the present day, ending with Spain's only industrial design collection.

Map on page 222

Exclusive Pedralbes

The garden, built to a "geometric decorative outline" in the 1920s, also by Rubió i Tudurí, integrated the existing palace garden with land ceded by Count Güell. What remains of his neighbouring estate are the lodge and gates, the **Pavellons de la Finca Güell**, designed by Gaudí, which can be seen by going back down the Diagonal and turning left into **Avinguda Pedralbes**. This avenue sweeps up through ever-more exclusive blocks of apartments, with verdant gardens, manicured lawns and the inevitable swimming pools. This is the district of Pedralbes. No corner *colmados* or neighbourhood spirit here, each flat is its own exclusive island. A few beautiful modernista *torres* (large, detached houses) remain, though most have become homes for the elderly, institutions, colleges, or even a consulate (USA). Some have been left to deteriorate to make way for a more profitable building plot.

At the top, by the Creu de Pedralbes, are the welcomingly old stones of the monastery complex: the **Monestir de Pedralbes ❹** (open Tues–Sun 10am–2pm; entrance charge). This is, without doubt, one of the most peaceful corners of the city, the perfect antidote to the crowds of the Old Town and the frenetic

A vase in the Museu de Ceràmica, where there's a fascinating display of Spanish pottery.

BELOW: the Palau Reial de Pedralbes.

Treasure in the monastery, where you can also see the nuns' cells and refectory

BELOW:
a day out in the
Parc de Collserola.

Eixample with its roaring traffic. The monastery was founded in 1326 by Queen Elisenda de Montcada, widow (and fourth wife) of King Jaume II. She herself took the vows of the Order of St Clare, and today some 20 nuns are still in residence. The fine Gothic architecture, most notably the unusual three-tiered cloister, evokes the spiritual side of monastic life, while the rooms that are open to the public provide an insight into the day-to-day life of the monastery's inhabitants. There are some remarkable 14th-century murals by Catalan Ferrer Bassa.

Part of the complex houses the **Col.lecció Thyssen-Bornemisza** (open Tues–Sun 10am–2pm; combined entrance ticket to monastery and collection available). Some 72 canvasses and eight sculptures from the medieval, Renaissance and Venetian baroque periods were selected for Barcelona from the main collection in Madrid, and include works by Canaletto, Velázquez and Tintoretto. The monastery is easily reached by bus or FGC train to **Reina Elisenda** station.

Genteel Sarrià

While up here at the foot of the **Collserola** hills, take the opportunity to visit **Sarrià ❺** by walking a little further along Passeig Reina Elisenda de Montcada, which leads straight into the **Plaça Sarrià** (also reached in under 10 minutes from Plaça de Catalunya and other central stations on the FGC line). Recognisable as a former village, albeit a sought-after city residence today, it is infinitely more charming than Pedralbes, and the wealth more discreet.

This is a real neighbourhood with a soul: it has a market, old ladies in cardigans queuing for lottery tickets, smoky bars and the attractive church of Sant Vicenç at the centre of things. The main street leading down from the church, **Major de Sarrià**, has now been paved, encouraging strolling. The famed pas-

try shop **Foix de Sarrià,** founded in 1886, makes an elegant corner. **Casa Joana,** another old established business and little changed, still serves good home cooking at a reasonable price. However, the predominance of beauty salons, hairdressers and bijou gift shops means that this old village is now the domain of those who can afford to live in it. Nevertheless, it has genteel charm, reminiscent of a provincial Catalan town: passageways lead off through the backs of pretty houses with small gardens bursting with bougainvillea; and in a side street with *modernista* villas you can still find a haberdasher's with a bentwood chair at the counter and walls lined with underwear in boxes.

Map on page 222

Escape from the city

From Sarrià you can get a taste of the **Parc de Collserola** by taking a walk on the city side of the hill, overlooking the whole of Barcelona. The trip is equally manageable from the centre with the efficient and frequent FGC train service from Plaça de Catalunya. Another overlooked part of Barcelona, the Parc de Collserola is a green belt measuring 17 by 6 km (11 by 4 miles), which is literally on the city's doorstep. Its 8,000 hectares (20,000 acres) of vegetation border on the Ronda de Dalt ring road, and spread over the Collserola range of hills to Sant Cugat and beyond.

This easily accessible area is a bonus to city living. It is best known for its highest peak, Tibidabo (512 metres/1,664 ft) and its distinctive skyline, with the Sagrat Cor church and the Torre de Collserola communications tower, which forms a backdrop to Barcelona. But it is a lot more besides. There are endless activities on offer from horse riding to nature trails, picnic spots, restaurants and *merenderos*, open-air restaurants where you can barbecue your own food.

BELOW:
El Sagrat Cor
church on Tibidabo.

TIP

An added bonus: the standard metro ticket is valid on the FGC line that goes through the hill as far as Les Planes in the Collserola park, and for the funicular up to Vallvidrera.

If you prefer to walk with one eye on the city, the next stop after Sarrià on the FGC train is **Peu del Funicular ❻** (which translates as "foot of the funicular") to **Vallvidrera**, a suburban village on the crest of the hill where there are desirable homes with a view. Recently modernised, there are frequent services from this station and, by particular request (at the press of a button), the funicular will stop halfway to Vallvidrera at **Carretera de les Aigües ❼**.

This is an ideal spot for a quick burst of fresh air and exercise, or relative cooling-off in the heat of the summer: the *carretera* is a track cut into the side of the hill, that winds on to way beyond Tibidabo. Popular with joggers, cyclists, ramblers, dog-walkers and model aeroplane clubs, it is perfect for stretching city legs, particularly on bright blue, pollution-free days (worth waiting for) when the view is breathtaking. The whole layout of Barcelona and its geographical context becomes clear. For a good round trip, walk as far as the point where the track crosses the Tibidabo funicular, where a badly indicated footpath leads down to the Plaça del Funicular. Here catch the tram, or walk to Avinguda Tibidabo FGC station which will return you to the city centre.

Panoramic view

Alternatively, return to the Vallvidrera funicular, taking it as far as **Vallvidrera Superior ❽**, an attractive *modernista* station in this pleasant village, evocative of the days when city dwellers would spend the summer up here for the cooler air. The air still feels a few degrees cooler, even in the height of summer, and definitely cleaner.

The No. 211 bus will take you to the striking communications tower, the **Torre de Collserola**, designed by Norman Foster for the 1992 Olympics and

BELOW:
it's a steep ride up on the funicular.

sometimes known as the **Torre Foster** (open Wed–Fri 11am–2.30pm, 3.30–8pm, Sat & Sun 11am–8pm, until 6pm in winter; entrance charge). Up close it is even more awesome, with giant stays anchoring it to the hill. A transparent lift will take you up for a panoramic view 560 metres (1,837 ft) above sea level.

The Collserola park on the other side of the hill is another world, a mere train ride through the tunnel to **Baixador de Vallvidrera** station (just 13 minutes from Plaça de Catalunya). The contrast of the pine-scented cooler air that hits you as soon as the train doors open is quite extraordinary. Walk up a well-land-scaped path to the **Centre d'Informació del Parc de Collserola**, the information centre (open 9.30am–3pm daily): a helpful base with an exhibition about the wildlife in the natural park, maps, advice and a bar/restaurant.

Close to it is **Villa Joana**, an atmospheric 18th-century rural house with sleepy dogs lying in the shade of a tree. This is where the much-loved Catalan poet Jacint Verdaguer lived until his death, in 1902. It is now a museum dedicated to him with some rooms preserved from the year he died (open weekends 11am–3pm). Various footpaths lead off into the woods of pine and cork oak to *fonts* (natural springs) and picnic spots. After several days in the steamy city, especially with children in tow, this area is the heaven-sent answer.

Tibidabo heights

The best known and visible summit of the Collserola range is **Tibidabo ❾**. Its popularity implies moving in large crowds and queuing, but it still has its charms. You can reach the summit from Sarrià, by going along Bonanova, which leads to Avinguda del Tibidabo, becoming Passeig Sant Gervasi at the end. It is a tiring street to walk along since, as an important route along this top

Map on page 222

TIP

If you want to stop for a bite to eat in Vallvidrera Superior, Antiga Casa Trampa is a good restaurant offering traditional Catalan fare in the centre of the village.

BELOW: a plane ride in the amusement park.

Map on page 222

An old-fashioned sign at the museum of automatons.

BELOW: colourful exhibit in the Museu de la Ciència.

part of town, it is always congested with traffic, The daily traffic swells even further in the mornings and mid-afternoons when parents deliver and collect their children from the abundance of expensive schools in the area, and by ladies of leisure driving to the gym. On a bus the journey is pleasanter and shows an interesting slice of life.

However, a trip to Tibidabo is more likely to be a day or half-day's excursion directly from the centre of town. The FGC train goes to Avinguda Tibidabo station. Coming out in **Plaça John Kennedy**, pause a moment to take in the colours of La Rotonda, a *modernista* house opposite that has been converted into a hospital. At the base of Avinguda Tibidabo is Barcelona's last remaining tram service, the **Tramvia Blau**. This open-sided blue wooden tram has been plying the route to the base of the Tibidabo funicular since 1901.

Nearby is the excellent **Museu de la Ciència** in Teodor Roviralta (open Tues–Sun 10am–8pm; entrance charge), if it has reopened. Ambitious plans to extend it are underway which will involve its closure for a year. A reduced version will be in the Casa Macaya as a temporary measure (*see page 214*). The current museum is state of the art, with plenty of hands-on exhibits and fascinating temporary exhibitions. There is plenty to do for all ages, even 3–6-year-olds in the "Clik dels Nens", a space to play and learn created by high-profile designer Javier Mariscal. Funded by the affluent cultural foundation of La Caixa savings bank, and driven by a dynamic director, the reborn science museum will be more enlightening and more entertaining than Tibidabo.

The Tramvia Blau rattles up Avinguda Tibidabo, an avenue of beautiful *modernista* houses that winds up the hill. Its former elegance is now diminished, many of the large houses having been converted into institutions, advertising agencies or flats. Furthermore, it was dissected in the early 1990s by the Ronda de Dalt. The tram stops at the **Plaça del Funicular**, where there are some attractive bars and a good restaurant, **La Venta**, with a very pretty terrace.

Old-fashioned fairground

From Plaça del Funicular you can catch the funicular to the summit. This lofty playground has been a popular tradition since the turn of the century. It tends to look more interesting from a distance, but the air is sweet, the views spectacular – and children love it. The church, the **Sagrat Cor**, has little charm but this doesn't prevent the crowds flocking to it. Floodlit at night, it forms a dramatic part of the Barcelona skyline, particularly when wrapped in swirling mists.

The **Parc d'Attracions** funfair has a wonderful retro air and is not exhaustingly large or terrifying. Some of its attractions date back to 1901 when the funicular first reached the top, and some are from renovations that took place in 1986. There is also a museum of automatons, the **Museu d'Autòmats**, with some fascinating pieces built between 1901 and 1954.

The whole complex is open from Easter to December, but the times change according to daylight hours and peak season – check with tourist information offices locally. The tram and funicular run in conjunction with the opening times. ❑

Gràcia

The district of Gràcia lies "above the Diagonal", but has none of the connotations usually associated with the phrase. On the contrary, it is a neighbourhood with its own history and distinctive personality. Its character is preserved in the narrow streets and squares contained within an invisible boundary, which in turn has managed to keep out large-scale projects and expensive residential developments.

Traditionally a *barri* of artisans, it is now becoming a centre for New Age movements. Generations of families remain loyal to the district, and since the 19th century a strong gypsy community has been well integrated here. There are few newcomers, apart from a few young people, students and a sprinkling of foreigners charmed by the district's down-to-earth character.

The *vila* (a cut above "village") of Gràcia was once reached from Barcelona by a track through open fields (today's **Passeig de Gràcia**). Its established buildings imposed the upper limit on the Eixample, Cerdà's 19th-century expansion plan for Barcelona; the streets of **Còrsega** and **Bailèn** were built right up to its sides. The upper boundary is loosely **Travessera de Dalt**, and on the western side **Príncep d'Astúries**, although the official municipal district goes a little further.

The main route into Gràcia is along **Gran de Gràcia**, the continuation of Passeig de Gràcia, but it is also well served by the metro (Fontana and Lesseps L3; Joanic L4; Gràcia FGC line). Gran de Gràcia is a busy but elegant street full of shops and *modernista* apartment blocks. It also has one of the best and most expensive fish restaurants in the city, the Galician **Botafumeiro**.

Walking up the hill, take any of the turnings to the right and zig-zag up through streets bustling with a selection of small businesses, workshops, wonderfully dated grocers' and trendy fashion shops. At night, shuttered doors open to reveal an infinity of bars and restaurants, ranging from typical Catalan to the best Lebanese in town. You need to visit Gràcia both during the day and in the evening to fully appreciate its charms.

The whole area is dotted with *plaças*, one of which is named after John Lennon; watch out for the attractive **Plaça del Sol**, which acts as an unofficial centre for the district. Nearby is the **Verdi** multi-screen cinema in a long street of the same name; this is an essential stop on any filmgoer's itinerary, as it always shows *v.o.* (original version, i.e. undubbed) films.

There is an early Gaudí house, **Casa Vicens** in **Carolines**, a street on the other side of Gran de Gràcia, just above metro Fontana. It is worth a detour to see the facade of this striking house, which Gaudí built for a tile manufacturer.

If you visit Barcelona in steamy August you may coincide with the Festa Major de Gràcia, the main festival of the district. For at least a week around 15 August, the patron saint's day and a national holiday, the narrow streets are extravagantly decorated, music fills the squares both day and night, and everyone has a wild time. Not to be missed. ❑

RIGHT: celebrating the Festa Major in the streets of Gràcia.

THE PARC DE COLLSEROLA

Collserola is a natural park which forms part of the metropolitan area of Barcelona, yet it is surprisingly underused

Most visitors to Barcelona have been to Tibidabo, with its amusement park and temple, or at least spotted it from the city centre, looking like some floodlit Disneyworld, but it is only the tip of the Collserola iceberg. The Collserola massif, part of Catalonia's coastal range, is 17 km (10 miles) long, and 6 km (4 miles) wide, forming a protective backdrop to the city, and providing a wonderful playground for city dwellers. Tibidabo is its highest summit (512 metres/1,680 ft), but a huge park area stretches out behind the seaward side, towards Sant Cugat and the industrial plain of the Vallès.

ESCAPE FROM THE CITY

Some 8,000 hectares (19,700 acres) of classical Mediterranean terrain – woodlands of pine, oak and holm oak, flora and fauna – can easily be reached from Plaça de Catalunya (FGC train service) or by car through the Túnels de Vallvidrera or the more tortuous routes over the hills. The area abounds with tracks for walking, cycling and horse riding, picnic spots, restaurants, natural springs and some interesting old country houses open to the public. A good starting point is the park's Centre d'Informació, a pleasant walk from Baixador de Vallvidrera station: leaflets, maps and advice can be obtained here and there are various walks in the vicinity.

▷ SAGRAT COR
The Temple del Sagrat Cor, a looming neo-Gothic pile dominates the park and the surrounding countryside.

▷ FAIR WITH A VIEW
Even if the "Hurakan" or "Krüeger Hotel" don't appeal, the breathtaking views of Barcelona from Tibidabo are quite spectacular on a clear day.

△ GETTING THERE
A trip to the top of Tibidabo on the *tramvia blau* (blue tram) can be followed by the funicular and a mini train ride.

△ FAMILY FUN
The amusement park has an old world charm combined with enough modern thrills to keep everyone happy.

DESIGNER COMMUNICATIONS

Of the many changes to Barcelona's appearance in the 1990s, one of the most distinctive was the construction of the Torre de Collserola which dramatically changed the familiar skyline. Designed by British architect Norman Foster, this striking communications tower was completed in June 1992, in time to play an important role in the Olympic Games.

Also known locally as the Torre Foster it stands 288 metres (945 ft) high on the Vilana peak. A lift goes up to a glassed-in observation deck on the tenth floor, from where you can see the sacred mountain of Montserrat and the Pyrenees on a clear day.

The tower is open to the public from Wednesday to Friday (11am–2.30pm and 3.30pm–8pm) and all day at weekends and fiestas.

▷ **ACTIVE TRACK**
Cut into the hillside, the Carretera de les Aigües is a weekend favourite for cyclists, joggers, dog-walkers, and model aeroplane enthusiasts.

▽ **SERIOUS PICNICKERS**
Lunch in the open air is still a serious affair, enjoyed to the full in the dappled shade of woodland near Baixador de Vallvidrera.

▽ **MOUNTAIN PAELLA**
Paella cooked on an outdoor wood fire and eaten under a rambling vine takes some beating. Some restaurants let you grill your own food.

AROUND BARCELONA

The Catalonian hinterland and long stretches of coastline on either side of Barcelona provide some exceptional opportunities for excursions from the city

Map on page 236

Barcelona

Barcelona is a great city to be in, but it is also desirable to take a break from the hectic pace now and again. Luckily, there are beaches, mountains, wine country, religious retreats and historic provincial cities all within easy reach. Travelling to and from the city can be a nightmare if you work in Barcelona during office hours, with congested roads and trains at peak times, particularly on Sunday evening, all weekend in summer, and around annual holidays at Christmas, Easter and in August. But visitors who travel outside these times will enjoy straightforward, stress-free journeys.

Each of the suggested excursions is manageable in a day. Taking extra time over them will allow you to relax more, perhaps climbing higher into the Pyrenees or going a little further south. There are two options for journeys to the south of Barcelona (Sitges and Tarragona), two to the west (Sant Sadurní and Montserrat), two going inland to the north (Montseny and Vic), two going up into the province of Girona (Figueres and Girona), one to the Maresme coast just north of Barcelona (Caldetes), and one to the Costa Brava (Santa Cristina).

Sitges, Santa Cristina and Caldetes all have fine beaches; Montserrat and Montseny, two mountain-top retreats virtually overlooking Barcelona, are also superb natural attractions; Vic, Tarragona, Figueres and Girona are historic provincial centres; Sant Sadurní d'Anoia is at the heart of the Penedès wine-growing region.

Best beaches

A smooth 40-minute train ride or a quick drive through the Garraf tunnels on the C 32 motorway will whisk you south to **Sitges ❶**, the closest clean and uncrowded bit of the Mediterranean coast. While sand and sun can be enjoyed in Castelldefels, 20 minutes from Barcelona, or even on Barcelona's city beaches, the gleaming, whitewashed houses and flower-festooned balconies of Sitges are well worth the extra journey time, making you feel a world away in terms of atmosphere. A day on the beach, with a *paella* for lunch at one of the many restaurants overlooking the sea, is a good idea at any time of the year. What's more, the weather is reputed always to be better in Sitges, so you could leave Barcelona in cloud and arrive to find glorious sunshine.

Fringed by palms and populated by an intriguingly cosmopolitan range of bathers, including a large gay community, the gently curving **Platja d'Or** (golden beach) runs from the rocky point, La Punta, at the northeast end of Sitges Bay; it starts from the 17th-century Església Sant Bartomeu i Santa Tecla, perched on the headland, and extends 5 km (3 miles) south and west past the Hotel Terramar. The beaches on the other side of the church are also worth exploring.

The **Museu Cau Ferrat** (open Tues–Sat 9.30am–2pm, 4–6pm, Sun 9.30am–2pm) is an interesting museum. Once the studio of Picasso's contemporary Santiago Rusiñol, it was a meeting place for artists in the early 20th century. In this 16th-century house built over the rocks are two El Greco paintings, several Picasso drawings, and a unique collection of Catalan wrought iron. The work inside and Mediterranean close by outside are a powerful combination of art and nature. **Museu Maricel** (*mar i cel* means "sea and sky" in Catalan), two buildings connected by a bridge over the street, is most notable for the mural paintings by Josep Maria Sert. The **Museu Romàntic** at Sant Gaudenci, gives a good insight into 19th-century living conditions and houses the **Lola Anglada** antique doll collection (opening times for both museums as for Cau Ferrat).

Roman remains

Ninety minutes from Barcelona by train or car, **Tarragona ❷** still has the feel of a provincial capital of the Roman Empire. Captured by Rome in 218 BC and

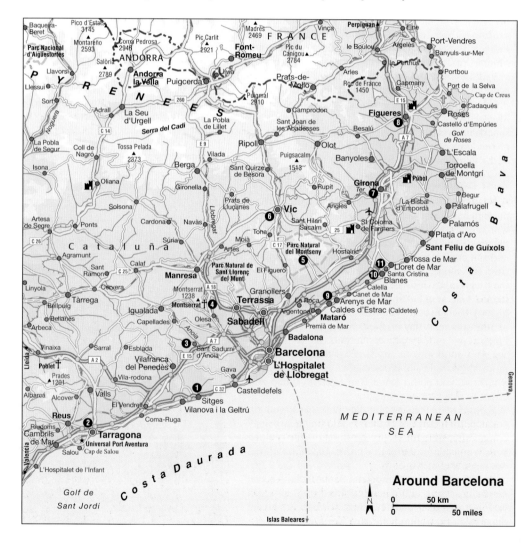

Around Barcelona

MEDITERRANEAN SEA

Costa Daurada

Golf de Sant Jordi

Islas Baleares

0   50 km
0   50 miles

Map on page 236

later the capital of the Spanish province of Tarraconensis under Augustus, the town was the major commercial centre on this part of the Mediterranean coast until Barcelona and Valencia overshadowed it after the Christian Reconquest of Spain in the early 12th century.

Rich in Roman ruins and stunningly beautiful ancient buildings, Tarragona may be approached from top to bottom, beginning within the walled upper part of the city surrounding the cathedral, continuing on for a tour of the wall itself, the **Passeig Arqueòlogic** or Archaeological Promenade. You can then descend to the next level of the city, featuring the **Rambla**, and conclude with a stroll through the fishing port and lunch on the quay.

Tarragona's **cathedral**, the centrepiece of the top part of the city, has been described by Catalonia's own travel writer Josep Pla, who had something to say about every town, as "easily and serenely mighty, solid as granite, maternal – a cathedral redolent of Roman virtues projected on to carved stone – a lion in repose, drowsy, unabashedly powerful". The mass of the wall itself and the tiny perforations in and out of this ancient cloister are hauntingly archaic, as if leading to some secret older than time itself.

The Passeig Arqueòlogic offers views south over the city, west out to the mountains, north to the hills and trees surrounding the city, and finally east to the coastline and the sea. Below the walls is the middle section of Tarragona, with the wide and stately Rambla ending in the Balcó del Mediterrani (Mediterranean Balcony) suspended over the ocean below. The city's luminosity at this point has been much commented on and is indeed remarkable: a crisp elegance and clean air shimmer over the golden sandstone of Roman structures, which are more than 1,000 years old.

The Serrallo section of the port is the main attraction in the lower part of the city, the multicoloured fishing fleet unloading the Mediterranean's varied marine life every afternoon, the fish auctioned off within minutes. A late lunch at a dockside restaurant – featuring Tarragona wines, fundamental to the Roman Empire, and seafood just out of the nets – makes a delicious ending to a visit.

Just 8 km (5 miles) south of Tarragona is the seaside resort of **Salou**, popular for packages, and its neighbouring theme park **Universal Mediterrania** including **Port Aventura**, the second largest in Europe after Disneyland Resort Paris (open Mar–Jan: daily 10am–8pm, until midnight in high season; Fri–Sun only in Nov and Dec; entrance charge). People travel for miles to experience the thrills and spills it offers. In 2002 two hotels opened here.

Spanish *cava*

If you feel safer with the more indigenous pleasures of Catalonia, a trip to **Sant Sadurní d'Anoia ❸**, a small town responsible for 80 per cent of *cava* production, is recommended. Sparkling wine made in Catalonia is not champagne; it is *cava*.

A 45-minute train ride from Sants or Plaça de Catalunya stations in Barcelona will drop you in Sant Sadurní next to Freixenet, the world's leading producer of *cava*, with vineyards in California and oper-

BELOW: wine is big business in the Penedès region.

A tile in the Museu del Vi in Vilafranca shows a medieval reveller.

ations in the People's Republic of China. Freixenet offers a spectacular tour, including a screening of its famous series of Christmas advertisements, featuring such stars as Liza Minelli, Gene Kelly, Raquel Welch, Plácido Domingo, Penelope Cruz and Paul Newman. A glass of *cava* is presented to guests as a finale. *Cava* has been produced in Sant Sadurní since 1872 by Josep Raventós, founder of the Codorníu empire who carefully studied the wine-making techniques, the *méthode champenoise*, of Dom Perignon and made Catalonia's first bottle of *cava*. It is an important part of life in Catalonia: baptisms, weddings, even routine Sunday lunches are occasions for popping corks. On 20 November 1975, the day Franco died, *cava* was given away free in Barcelona.

Gastronomy and wine

In addition to tours of the Freixenet and beautiful *modernista* Codorníu wine cellars, or any other of the 80 producers in this area, Sant Sadurní offers excellent gastronomical opportunities at local restaurants well-known for fine *cava* and seafood. Between late January and mid March, the *calçotada* is a traditional feast starring long-stemmed *calçots* (somewhere between a spring onion and a leek), dipped in a kind of *romesco* sauce made of oil, peppers, garlic and groundnuts. *Cava*, of course, flows freely at these earthy banquets, accompanied by lamb or rabbit grilled, as are the *calçots,* over coals.

About 14 km (8 miles) from Sant Sadurní is **Vilafranca del Penedès**, a centre of still wine production which is dominated by the world-famous Torres, whose winery and extensive vineyards can be visited. Wine making in this region can be traced back to the 5th century BC. The town has one of Europe's best wine museums, the **Museu del Vi** (open Tues–Sat 10am–2pm, 4–7pm, all day in

BELOW: Tarragona's Roman remains.

summer, Sun 10am–2pm; entrance charge). The Penedès region, one of the world's leading wine producers, has over 300 wine- and *cava*-producing companies, most of which can be visited. Information is centralised through the tourist office in Vilafranca (tel: 93 892 0358).

The region itself is attractive for walking or cycling. The Montserrat massif to the north rises above row after row of vines stretching down to the Mediterranean in the south, with moist sea breezes and 2,500 hours of sunshine a year. Around Sant Sadurní even children have opinions on *bruts, secs* and *brut natures*; in the Penedès, Bacchus reigns.

Mountain retreat

Catalonia's most important religious retreat is **Montserrat ❹**. Here athletes pledge barefoot pilgrimages if prayers are answered and vital competitions won. Groups of young people from Barcelona and all over Catalonia make overnight hikes at least once in their lives to watch the sunrise from the heights of Montserrat. "La Moreneta" (the black virgin), Catalonia's favourite saint, resides in the famous sanctuary of the Mare de Deu de Montserrat, next to the Benedictine monastery nestled among the towers and crags of the mountain.

Montserrat (*mont*, mountain; *serrat,* serrated), 48 km (30 miles) west of Barcelona, can be reached easily and spectacularly by train (and cable car) from Plaça d'Espanya station. The advantage of going by car, however, is the opportunity of seeing this landmark from different angles, especially from the northern or southern sides. In the words of Catalan poet Maragall, from varying perspectives Montserrat can look like "a bluish cloud with fantastic carvings, a giant's castle with a hundred towers, thrown towards the sky, its needles veiled

Map on page 236

Taking a break along the Way of the Cross at Montserrat.

BELOW: the monastery at Montserrat.

During the 40-year Franco regime, when the Catalan language was officially forbidden, baptisms and weddings were still held in Catalan at Montserrat.

by the fog hanging among them like incense… above all an altar, a temple." Looming 1,236 metres (4,055 ft) over the valley floor, Montserrat, the highest point of the Catalan lowlands, stands central to the most populated part of Catalonia. Visible from Barcelona, Sabadell, Terrassa, Manresa, Igualada, and Vilafranca, the massive conglomerate stone monolith is ideally located to play an important role in the cultural and spiritual life of Catalonia. The basilica is packed with works of art by a long list of prominent painters and sculptors, including works by El Greco in the sanctuary's museum. Catalan poets have dedicated some of their most inspired verse to Montserrat while maestros such as Nicolau and Millet have composed some of their finest pieces in honour of this mystical Catalonian retreat. Goethe is said to have dreamed of Montserrat and Parsifal sought the Holy Grail here in Wagner's musical drama. The monastery's famous *escolans*, the oldest boys' choir in Europe, sings twice a day.

Montserrat's highest point, **Sant Jeroni**, can be reached by funicular from the Romanesque monastery of Santa Cecilia. From Sant Jeroni almost all of Catalonia can be seen; the Pyrenees, Mount Canigó in France and even, on a clear day, as far away as Mallorca in the Balearic Islands.

Rugged forest

Montserrat and the Montseny range of mountains in the **Parc Natural de Montseny** ❺ occupy, in some way, polar extremes in Catalonian spiritual life. Whereas Montserrat is dramatically vertical, acute and passionate, Montseny is smooth, horizontal, massive and placid. *Seny* in Catalan means sense, restraint, patience, serenity and is a byword for a description of the national characteristics; the Montseny, well-named, seems to be a rich lode of this resource.

BELOW: sunbathers at Vilassar de Mar.

Best explored by car, this monumental mountain forest, considered one of Europe's most important sources of oxygen, is presided over by four peaks: Turó de l'Home, Agudes, Matagalls (all around 1,500 metres/5,000 ft) and Calma i Puigdrau, a lower peak at 1,215 metres (4,050 ft). Lesser terrain features and water courses connect and define these four pieces of high ground, tracing out an autonomous geographical entity which always appears hulking and mist-shrouded on the horizon, often confused with cloud formations.

The village of **Montseny** itself, an irresistible nucleus of stone and vegetation attesting to sounder, saner times and places, can be reached via Palautordera and Sant Esteve de Palautordera. This road continues on to Brull, through the pass at Collformic and over to Tona, near Vic on route C 17, thus traversing the entire Montseny massif. The road up from Sant Celoni, just off the *autovia* towards France, via Campins and Fogars de Montclus, arrives at the **Santa Fe hermitage**, a vantage point which seems little more than a stone's throw from Montseny's highest points. Santa Fe, surrounded by oaks and poplars, becomes bright with colour as the leaves turn in autumn, an unusual sight in Catalonia where forests and deciduous trees are uncommon.

Montseny, no more than 40 minutes from Barcelona, is a botanical anthology, including some of the southernmost fir trees in Europe, other specimens from all over the continent, and evergreen oak.

Country towns

An easy hour north by train or car, **Vic ❻** is an elegant market town with interesting buildings, sophisticated shops and good food. It is the meeting place of industry, commerce and agriculture, a mixture of rural and urban life with a

Map on page 236

BELOW: a view over Caldes d'Estrac, also known as Caldetes.

strong ecclesiastical and cultural tradition. Especially known for its Romanesque bell tower, Sert's epic murals, and the magnificent Plaça Major with its Saturday market, Vic is an entity distinct from Barcelona. The Vic accent in Catalan is unmistakable and becomes, if anything, more acute in the Catalonian capital as natives of this small city emphasise their separate identity.

Vic's **Cathedral**, a neoclassical structure completed in 1803 and with a graceful 11th-century bell tower, is best known for the series of murals covering the interior walls. Josep Maria Sert left his personal vision in the voluptuous, neobaroque figures performing colossal deeds. His triptych on the back of the cathedral's western door depicts the injustices in the life of Christ and, by association, in the history of Catalonia.

With the cathedral in ruins as his background, Jesus expels the moneylenders from the Temple and is, in turn, condemned to be crucified while Pilate washes his hands and Barabbas, the thief, is cheered by the crowd. Certain faces (Pilate, Barabbas) are said to be those of Franco's lieutenants, but El Generalísimo himself, during a visit to Sert's work while it was in progress, did not seem to see the resemblance.

Philosopher Jaume Balmes (1810–48), a native of Vic, is buried in the 14th-century cloister, as is Sert. The **Museu Episcopal** has an impressive collection of Romanesque and Gothic pieces, including altarpieces and sculpted figures collected from local chapels and churches. It is well worth visiting, especially now its treasures are re-housed in a new building designed by leading Barcelona architects Correa and Milà. Note especially the Romanesque textiles and *El Davallament de la Creu* (*The Descent from the Cross*), an especially fine 12th-century sculptural work in carved, polychrome wood.

BELOW: a wedding at the Cathedral.

The **Plaça Major**, or central square, surrounded by low arcades, is a metaphor for the sense and feel of this agro-industrial town. Open, unrelieved by the equestrian statue some critics feel it should have, the square stands on its own, as the city itself does, flat and firm on the plain, the Plana de Vic.

Map
on page
236

Girona province

The cities of Girona and Figueres can be combined for a memorable excursion from Barcelona. **Girona ❼**, the capital of the province, is an attractive small city bursting with history and pride, and only an hour's drive from Barcelona. It is known for its **Ciutat Antiga** (Old Town) and especially for its 13th-century **Jewish quarter**, which is considered (along with Toledo's) one of the two most important and best preserved in Spain. The Onyar river separates Girona's old section from the modern part of the city, which lies west of the river.

The footbridges over the Onyar provide some of Girona's most unforgettable views into the old city, including reflections of the buildings on the banks of the river as well as taller structures such as the **Sant Feliu** bell tower and the cathedral. The 12th-century **Església de Sant Pere de Galligants** is one of the city's oldest monuments, with a delightful Romanesque cloister built before 1154. From here you can walk around the city walls as far as Plaça Catalunya.

Girona's old city, built on a hill, is known for its lovely stairways, such as the baroque *escalinata* of 96 steps leading up to the Cathedral, or the stairs up to **Església de Sant Martí**. **Santa Maria Cathedral**, described by the ever-present Josep Pla as "literally sensational" in its force and magnitude, was built by architect Guillem Bofill, who succeeded in covering the structure with Europe's largest Gothic vault.

BELOW: Blanes port is always busy in summer.

Vintage toy car and motorcycle collection at the Museu de Joguets in Figueres.

The Cathedral's **museum** (open Tues–Sat 10am–2pm, 4–7pm, Sun 10am–2pm entrance charge) is most notable for its *Tapis de la Creació*, a stunning 12th-century tapestry depicting God surrounded by all the flora and fauna, fish and fowl of Creation. Equally impressive is Beatus's *Llibre de l'Apocalipsi* (Book of the Apocalypse), dated 975. The **Església de Sant Feliu**, the **Arab baths** and the lofty plane trees of **Devesa Park** are other important landmarks of this ancient city of sunless alleys, graceful stairways, and the Onyar, flowing through as imperceptibly as time.

Dalí's birthplace

Figueres ❽, only another half hour north on the A 7 motorway, is the major city of the **Alt Empordà** (Upper Ampurdàn), a fresh, busy country town which, in many ways, could be on either side of the border with France. Like many provincial cities in Spain, Figueres seems to have some time on its hands. The **Rambla** is the scene of the traditional *passeig,* the constitutional midday or evening stroll. This is the perfect opportunity for the locals to run into friends or share an aperitif with an old chum they haven't seen in years (or days) – an encounter tailor-made for a 20-minute chat. Also on the Rambla, on the top floor of the Hotel de Paris, is Spain's only toy museum, the **Museu de Joguets** (open Wed–Mon; entrance charge). The huge collection of beautifully made, old-fashioned toys will enthrall adults as well as children.

However, Figueres is best known as the birthplace of the surrealist artist Salvador Dalí, whose museum is aptly located in the former municipal theatre. The **Teatre-Museu Dalí** (open July–Sept daily 9am–7.15pm; Oct–June: 10.30am–5.15pm; closed Mon; entrance charge) is one of the most visited

BELOW:
mellow buildings in Girona, beside the River Onyar.

museums in Spain and has a wide range of the internationally famous artist's work including a new area of jewellery. Whether you regard him as a genius or not, there is no denying that this museum, with all its tricks and illusions, provides an entertaining show. The day can be happily completed with a meal in one of Figueres' many good restaurants, or made utterly perfect by dinner in the **Hotel Ampurdán**, on the outskirts of town and one of Catalonia's most famous restaurants. The hotel is also a good base for Dalí-tourism in the region: both Dalí's house in **Port Lligat**, near Cadaqués, and the castle he bought for his wife, Gala, in **Púbol**, are now open to the public.

Costa del Maresme

The beaches just north of Barcelona have a much lower profile than Sitges, and are much maligned for the railway line that runs alongside them. As a result, they are often less crowded. In recent years most have been overhauled, with some beaches being widened, promenades landscaped and marinas built. It is worth travelling beyond Badalona, which is more of an industrial suburb of Barcelona. However, if you only have half a day both Masnou and Vilassar de Mar are acceptable. Inland from Mataró, an industrial town and capital of the region, the quiet village of Argentona makes a pleasant detour.

One of the most attractive resorts along this coast is **Caldes d'Estrac ❾**, also known as **Caldetes**. The slightly longer journey is well rewarded – about 40 minutes by car on the speedy new C 32 and about an hour on the train which runs from Plaça Catalunya, a useful service for reaching any of these coastal spots. Caldetes is a spa town – several hotels have thermal baths – and the small town has many charms and pretty *modernista* houses. The long, sandy beaches

Dalí memorabilia is on sale everywhere, from prints to melting watches, but the most memorable souvenir of the painter is his beloved landscape, ever-present in his work and all around you.

BELOW: lush decoration in the Teatre-Museu Dalí.

DALÍ TOURISM

Dalí would have loved it: Margaret Thatcher went for the day; rock stars dash up between gigs in Barcelona. The hordes are flooding into the province of Girona to visit the surreal world of Salvador Dalí, which through the endeavours of the Gala-Salvador Dalí Foundation now includes his very surreal private world. Visiting Dalí's home in Port Lligat, Gala's castle in Púbol or the museum itself, it is clear the two worlds were inseparable.

The best introduction to this triumvirate is the museum in his home town Figueres, the Teatre-Museu Dalí, to get a broad view of the art and a vivid idea of the man. Thirty km (20 miles) away on the coast, near Cadaqués, is the Casa-Museu Salvador Dalí, a fascinating glimpse of Dalí's life with Gala, where he ate, slept, entertained and painted. These old fishermen's cottages have limited space, so small groups are admitted every 10 minutes. Book in advance (open daily 10.30am–9pm in summer; 10.30am–6pm in winter, closed Mon and Jan to mid-Mar; tel: 972 25 10 15).

Bought by Dalí for his wife in 1970, the Castell Gala Dalí is very atmospheric, set in a landscaped garden in Púbol, in the stunning Baix Empordà (open daily 10.30am–8pm in summer; 10.30am–6pm in winter, closed Mon and Nov to mid-Mar). Gala is buried in the crypt.

Map on page 236

Outside the botanical gardens in Blanes.

BELOW: green folds where the mountains swoop down to the sea.
RIGHT: the old ways of life still go on, not far from the tourist resorts.

never seem to get too crowded, and the sea is usually clear. Large family villas along the waterfront are redolent of a time when wealthier families would move out of Barcelona for the hot summer months.

The early evening is a pleasant time, when freshly showered families dress up in casual-smart clothes – a Catalan skill – to promenade. A strangely old-fashioned esplanade with a fish pond, a retro merry-go-round and a bustling bar (with good snacks and meals) is the central meeting point. You can enjoy all this, have dinner and get back to Barcelona for the night without too much effort.

The beaches of Caldetes merge with those of **Arenys de Mar**, known for its fishing port and internationally famous restaurant, the Hispania, favoured by King Juan Carlos. The next town north, **Canet de Mar**, also has a refurbished waterfront and some interesting 19th-century architecture, notably the home of leading *modernista* architect Domènech i Montaner. His studio can be visited at weekends (open 11am–2pm; entrance charge). Just beyond Canet de Mar is **Sant Pol**, a pretty, whitewashed village.

The Costa Brava

To feel completely cut off from Barcelona it is worth going as far as the southernmost beaches of the famed **Costa Brava**. Officially beginning at **Blanes ⑩**, this stretch of coast is distinguished by its bold, rocky shoreline punctuated by small sandy inlets. The clear, bright water and this rugged coast mark the difference between the beaches of the Maresme and those of the Costa Brava. The further north you go, the more rugged and magical the coast becomes.

During the summer, passenger boats work in and out of the *calas* or coves. You can board a boat at Blanes for **Santa Cristina ⑪** or be dropped at some remote *cala* which may be at the bottom of a sheer cliff and inaccessible from land.

Santa Cristina, between Blanes and **Lloret de Mar**, is one of the first inlets of the Costa Brava, and is only about an hour from Barcelona. Access to Santa Cristina is easy – you can go by train to Blanes and bus, or by car along the coast, but the proximity of this sandy enclave to the city has made it extremely popular with Barcelonans. Other visitors might do well to stay in town at the weekend and save this trip for during the week.

With its twin beaches bordered and divided by rocky promontories, Santa Cristina's lovely hermitage stands at the top of the steep paths down to the water. The chapel and house were left to the town of Lloret de Mar by a wealthy 18th-century landowner who moved to Cuba. At that time the shorefront was worth nothing; the valuable property in those days was inland, where there were arable fields.

At Santa Cristina there are several simple restaurants on the beach where *paella* can be prepared anytime during the afternoon. These places are relaxed, outdoor spots where dining in bathing suits is quite normal, and they might not mind adding a few crabs or mussels to the *paella* if you find any among the rocks. They also serve excellent seafood *tapas* or small specialities of squid, sardines, wild mushrooms, shrimp or prawns. ❑

INSIGHT GUIDES
TRAVEL TIPS

Insight FlexiMaps

Maps in Insight Guides are tailored to complement the text. But when you're on the road you sometimes need the big picture that only a large-scale map can provide. This new range of durable Insight Fleximaps has been designed to meet just that need.

Detailed, clear cartography
makes the comprehensive route and city maps easy to follow, highlights all the major tourist sites and provides valuable motoring information plus a full index.

Informative and easy to use
with additional text and photographs covering a destination's top 10 essential sites, plus useful addresses, facts about the destination and handy tips on getting around.

Laminated finish
allows you to mark your route on the map using a non-permanent marker pen, and wipe it off. It makes the maps more durable and easier to fold than traditional maps.

The world's most popular destinations
are covered by the 125 titles in the series – and new destinations are being added all the time. They include Alaska, Amsterdam, Bangkok, Barbados, Beijing, Brussels, Dallas/Fort Worth, Florence, Hong Kong, Ireland, Madrid, New York, Orlando, Peru, Prague, Rio, Rome, San Francisco, Sydney, Thailand, Turkey, Venice, and Vienna.

INSIGHT GUIDES

The world's largest collection of visual travel guides

CONTENTS

Getting Acquainted

The Place

Barcelona is the capital of the Autonomous Region of Catalonia in northeast Spain.

Area: 99 sq km (38 sq miles).
Situation: Approximately 42°N, 2°E on the same latitude as New York City and Beijing. Barcelona is situated on the Mediterranean roughly 150 km (95 miles) south of the Pyrenees.
Population: 1.6 million; 2.9 million in the greater metropolitan area. Forty percent of the population comes from other parts of Spain.
Currency: the Euro.
Electricity: 220 volts, two-pin plug.
Weights and measures: metric.
Languages: Catalan and Spanish (Castilian).
Religion: Predominantly Roman Catholic, though there is a strong anti-clerical tradition.
Highest point: Mt Tibidabo, 516m (1,700 ft).
Time zone: One hour ahead of GMT in winter, two hours in summer. Six hours ahead of Eastern Seaboard Time.
International Dialling Code: 34.

Climate

Average temperature: 54° F (10° C) in winter, 75° F (25° C) in summer.

December and January have the lowest temperatures, though the cold is often accompanied by bright sunshine.

Rains tend to be in November and February/March. Spring and autumn are pleasant with mild, sunny days. July and August are aggravated by humidity. There are 2,500 hours of sunlight a year.

Government

Spain is a constitutional monarchy headed by King Juan Carlos I, who came to the throne in 1975. He appoints the prime minister from the party which has a majority in the Cortes (parliament). This has a Chamber of Deputies (Lower House) with 350 members elected by proportional representation every four years. The 17 Autonomous Regions (of which Catalonia is one) elect 49 members to the Senate (upper house).

The Autonomous Region of Catalonia is governed by the Generalitat in Barcelona, opposite which is the Ajuntament (Town Hall), where the mayor and the city council preside. For more than two decades (after free elections), the Generalitat has been governed by the conservative Convergencia i Unió under Jordi Pujol, and the Town Hall has been socialist, now under Mayor Joan Clos.

Economy

Catalonia, and in particular Barcelona, is of outstanding economic importance to the Spanish state. It has 25 percent of the nation's industry, and supplies nearly 20 percent of the Gross Domestic Product. In European terms, the economy of Catalonia has a greater turnover than Portugal or Ireland. Foreign investment has increased in recent years, a reflection of confidence in Catalonia as a progressive and dynamic region.

Planning the Trip

Entry Regulations

Passports are required for all nationalities entering Spain. Carry a photocopy for everyday use so that the original document can be left in a secure place (such as a hotel safe). If your passport is lost or stolen, report the fact immediately to the National Police.

Visas are needed by non-EU nationals, unless their country has a reciprocal arrangement with Spain.

Animal quarantine There are no regulations in Spain but you will need health certificates before you bring your own animal into the country: the regulations vary according to country of origin; the airline with which you are travelling should be able to provide the information required.

Consulates in Spain

Australia
Gran Via Carles III, 98, 9°
Tel: 93 490 90 13
Fax: 93 411 09 04.
Canada
Passeig de Gràcia 77, 3°
Tel: 93 204 27 00.
Ireland
Gran Via Carles III, 94
Tel: 93 491 5021
Fax: 93 411 29 21.
United Kingdom,
Avinguda Diagonal, 477, 13°
Tel: 93 366 62 00
Fax: 93 366 62 21.
United States
Passeig Reina Elisenda, 23
Tel: 93 280 2227
Fax: 93 280 61 75.

Useful Addresses

If you would like information about Barcelona before leaving home, contact your nearest Spanish Tourist Office:

Canada
2 Bloor Street West, 34th Floor
Toronto, Ontario M4W 3E2
Tel: 416-961 31 31
Fax: 416-961 19 92.

United Kingdom
22–23 Manchester Square
London W1U 3PX
Tel: 020-7486 8077 or 09063-640630 (for brochures)
Fax: 020-7486 8034.
www.tourspain.es

United States
666 Fifth Avenue, New York
NY 10103
Tel: 212-265 8822
Fax: 212-265 8864.

Barcelona on the web:
www.barcelonaturisme.com
www.bcn.es

Catalonia on the web:
www.gencat.es

Spain on the web:
www.spaintour.com/indexe.html

What to Bring

Catalan men and women dress elegantly, though men rarely wear ties. In July and August cotton and loose-fitting garments are necessary. Respect local traditions: bathing costumes and bikinis are strictly for the beach. Fashionable shorts are fine, especially for men, but avoid really short shorts. A light jacket is useful any time of the year. In winter, bring a warm jacket which can accommodate various layers, especially in January and February, when the wind blows. Be sure to bring comfortable shoes – Barcelona is a very walkable city.

Health Matters

Barcelona is a modern European city and there are no special health risks to be aware of. Take the usual travel precautions and break yourself into the climate and the food gently. The sun is getting stronger and between June and September you should wear a hat and suncream when out during the day.

Food and Drink

In most areas of Barcelona tap water can be drunk without fear, but it is often dosed with purifying salts which make the taste unpleasant. Mineral water is easily available, and Vichy Catalan is soothing for queasy stomachs. Cheap wine can be rough, so take it easy.

Catalan cooking is healthy and nutritious, but a change of diet can affect some digestive systems. Avoid bars and restaurants where oil is obviously used to excess.

Another danger area can be in *tapas* (snacks), which in hot weather can be a source of infection. Most notorious is any-thing mayonnaise-based, such as *ensaladilla rusa* (Russian salad), a potential source of salmonella; in some parts of Spain home-made mayonnaise has been banned.

With common sense it is easy to spot the "tired" *tapas* which should be avoided.

Insurance

Residents of EU countries, Iceland and Norway are entitled to receive state medical treatment in Spain if they present a form known as an "E111", which must be obtained in their own country. In the UK this can be done through the Post Office.

For greater peace of mind, take out private insurance which can be organised before setting off or on arrival through any travel agency. If you are insured privately or prepared to pay for private healthcare, Barcelona Centro Medico (Avinguda Diagonal, 612, tel: 93 414 0643 or 24 hrs, tel: 639 30 34 64) operates an information service for consultations and appointment bookings. Patients are referred to one of the clinics or hospitals associated with this scheme and informed in advance of the cost of treatment.

Buying Medicines

Pharmacies *(farmacias)* are easily spotted as they normally have a red or green flashing neon cross outside. When closed, there will always be a list posted outside of nearby pharmacies which are open. Pharmacies stock prescription and non-prescription medications, toiletries, baby food and supplies.

The **Allergyshop** (París, 156, tel: 93 322 2668) specialises in treatments for allergies and offers advice.

Dentists

Dentists in Spain are not covered by any of the reciprocal agreements between countries.

The following clinics offer an emergency service:

Amesa
Gran Vía, 680
Tel: 93 302 6682.
Open: 9.30am–1pm and 3–6pm.

Clínica Janos
Muntaner 375, 6° 2ª
Tel: 93 200 2333.
Open: 9am–1pm and 4–8pm daily (including Saturday). Sunday 10am–2pm.

Institut Dexeus
Passeig de Bonanova, 67
Tel: 93 418 4433.
Famous for its gynaecological work and for producing the first test-tube

Emergency Medical Treament

In an emergency go to the "Urgencias" department at one of the main hospitals:

Hospital Clínic
Carrer de Casanova, 143
Tel: 93 227 5400.

Hospital de la Creu Roja
Carrer de Dos de Maig, 301
Tel: 93 433 1551.

Hospital Sant Pau
Carrer de Sant Antoni Maria Claret, 167
Tel: 93 291 9191.

Or visit an **Ambulatorio** (medical centre). They can be found in every district – ask in any pharmacy for the nearest one.

Public Holidays

Many bars, restaurants and museums close in the afternoons and evenings on public holidays and Sundays. If a holiday falls on a Tuesday or a Thursday it is common to take a *puente* (bridge) to link the interim day with the weekend. August is the annual holiday month and many businesses, including restaurants, close down for three or four weeks.

These are the public holidays:
1 January – New Year's Day
6 January – Reis Mags: Epiphany
Good Friday – variable
Easter Monday – variable
1 May – Festa del Treball: Labour Day
Whitsun – (Pentecost) variable
24 June – Sant Joan: Midsummer's Night
15 August – Assumpció: Assumption
11 September – Diada: Catalan national holiday
24 September – La Mercè: the patron saint of Barcelona and the city's main fiesta
12 October – Hispanitat/Pilar: Spanish national day
1 November – Tots Sants: All Saints' Day
6 December – Día de la Constitució: Constitution Day
8 December – Immaculada Concepció: Immaculate Conception
25–26 December – Christmas

baby in Spain, this clinic also provides an emergency dental service Tues–Fri 8–9am.

Money

The monetary unit is the euro (€). Banknotes are issued in €5, 10, 20, 50, 100, 200 and 500; coins in demoninations of 1, 2, 5, 10, 20, 50 centimos, and €1 and 2. Pesetas can be changed at any branch of the Banco de España.

Most banks have automatic tills or cashpoints, operating 24 hours a day, where money can be withdrawn using most credit and debit cards.

Keep a record of the individual numbers of your travellers' cheques. If they are lost or stolen they can be replaced quickly if you have this information.

Tax

Tax (IVA) on services and goods is 16 percent, and for restaurants and hotels, 7 percent. Visitors from non-European Union countries are entitled to tax reclaims on their return home at a Global Refund Office. Look out for Tax Free signs in shop windows. When you leave the EU, Barcelona Customs must confirm the purchase and stamp the Tax-Free cheque; you can then take it to the airport branch of Banco Exterior de España and cash the cheque into the currency required. For further information *see Shopping, page 277.*

Banks

Bank opening hours vary, but as a general rule are Mon–Fri 8.30am–2pm, and Sat 8.30am–1pm between 1 October and 31 May. The *Cajas* or *Caixes* (savings banks) offer the same service, but are open on Thursday afternoons instead of Saturday mornings between 1 October and 31 May. They also have 24-hour cashpoints.

There are many currency exchange offices in the centre, including the Ramblas and in the Plaça Catalunya Information Centre.

Foreign banks in the city:
American Express
Passeig de Gràcia, 101
Tel: 93 255 0000.
Offers the usual services to clients, including poste restante, and replacing stolen credit cards.
Lloyds Bank
Rambla de Catalunya, 123
Tel: 93 236 3300.
Barclays Bank
Passeig de Gràcia, 45
Tel 93 481 2000.

Credit Cards

Major international credit cards, such as Visa, Eurocard and MasterCard can be used. The larger hotels also exchange money, though often at a less favourable rate.
American Express
Tel: 91 572 0303.
Diner's
Tel: 901 101011.
Eurocard, MasterCard, Mastercharge, Serrived and **Visa**
Tel: 91 519 2100/900 971 231.
Visa International
Tel: 900 99 1124.

Getting There

BY AIR

Iberia, the national carrier, and other major airlines connect with most parts of the world, sometimes via Madrid. Various companies compete over cheap deals to Barcelona, especially off-season, and there are charter flights in summer. Increasingly popular are the companies who sell via the Internet, such as:
EasyJet: www.easyjet.com
Go: www.go-fly.com
The airport is 12 km (7 miles) south of the city. The distribution of airlines in the three terminals sometimes changes, so confirm on arrival from which terminal your flight will depart. Airport tel: 93 298 3838.

Airlines flying out of Barcelona to other parts of Spain include:
Iberia, Diputació, 258.
Information and bookings:
Tel: 902 400 500.
Air Europa
Tel: 93 298 3328. For bookings call 902 401 501.
Spanair
Tel: 902 131 415.
Air Nostrum (part of Iberia)
Tel: 902 400 500.

BY TRAIN

An international service, the Talgo, runs daily from Paris, Milan, Zurich and Geneva. It is a high-speed, comfortable train. All other international connections involve a change at the French border, in Port Bou on entering Spain and Cerbère when leaving. These trains have few facilities, so travel prepared.

The direct trains (Talgo) terminate in the Estació de França (Avinguda Marquès de l'Argentera, near Parc de la Ciutadella) and the rest go to Estació de Sants, Barcelona's central station, Plaça Països Catalans. Some stop in Plaça Catalunya. For international train information and reservations, tel: 902 243 402.

National long-distance trains terminate in Estació de Sants and some in Estació de França.

For national train information, tel: 902 240 202.

BY BUS

The international bus companies Julià, Via (Eurolines) and Linebús run a regular service all over Europe, linking up with the national bus companies in each country. Buses arrive and depart either from Estació d'Autobusos Sants (tel: 93 490 4000), or Barcelona Nord (tel: 93 265 6508). In the UK, contact Eurolines, tel: 01582 404511.

BY CAR

Barcelona is 160 km (100 miles) or 1½ hours' drive from La Jonquera on the French border and can be easily reached along the A7 motorway (autopista, toll payable) and then, nearer Barcelona, the C33. The cost from France into town is approximately €10. Alternatively, the national route N11 is toll-free but tedious.

Be careful when you stop in service stations or lay-bys: professional gangs work this route, engaging travellers in conversation, or seeking help, while their companions skilfully rob them. If you stop for a drink or a meal try not to leave the car unattended.

The worst times to travel, particularly between June and September, are Friday night, (6–10pm), Sunday evening, (7–12pm) or the end of a bank holiday, when tailbacks of 16 km (10 miles) are common. Normal weekday rush hours are 7–9am and 6–9pm.

The ringroads (cinturones) surrounding the city can be very confusing for first arrivals, and you may find yourself driving swiftly to somewhere other than your desired destination; you are strongly advised to study a road map carefully beforehand. The Ronda de Dalt curves around the top part of the city, and the Ronda Litoral follows the sea.

Distances

Distances to other cities in Spain by road from Barcelona:

Tarragona: 98 km (60 miles)
Girona: 100 km (62 miles)
La Jonquera (French border): 149 km (93 miles)
Valencia: 349 km (217 miles)
San Sebastián: 529 km (329 miles)
Bilbao: 620 km (385 miles)
Madrid: 621 km (386 miles)
Salamanca: 778 km (483 miles)
Málaga: 997 km (620 miles)
Seville: 1,046 km (650 miles)

Practical Tips

Business Hours

In general, offices are open 9am–2pm and 4–8pm though some open earlier, close later and have shorter lunch breaks. Most official authorities are open 8am–2pm and close to the public in the afternoon. Companies in the outer industrial zones tend to close at 6pm. From mid-June to mid-September many businesses practise horas intensivas, from 8am–3pm in order to avoid the hottest part of the day and to get away early on a Friday.

Media

PRINT

Newspapers
The main daily newspapers are:
El País
Based in Madrid but with a Barcelona edition, El País is the most internationally respected Spanish paper. An English version is published by the International Herald Tribune.
La Vanguardia
The traditional newspaper of Barcelona has good coverage of local news and activities. Conservative.
El Periódico
The more popular Barcelona newspaper, but limited on international news, published in Castilian and Catalan.
Avui
The original Catalan paper.

International newspapers can be found on the newsstands on the Ramblas and Passeig de Gràcia, and also in several international bookshops, such as Libreria

Useful Numbers

Operator Services
Information: **1004**.
Directory Enquiries: **1003**.
International Directory Enquiries:
025.
International Operator (Europe)
1008; (Rest of the world) **1005**.

Country Codes:
International code: **00**
Australia: **61**
Canada: **1**
Eire: **353**
United Kingdom: **44**
United States: **1**

Francesa (Passeig de Gràcia, 91) or
FNAC (Plaça Catalunya).

Magazines

A wealth of magazines cover every
interest and indulgence. The main
fashion magazines, such as *Vogue*,
Marie Claire and *Elle* publish a
Spanish edition. Most notable of
the national magazines are:
Hola: The most famous Spanish
magazine, with illustrated scandal
and gossip on the rich and royal.
Guia del Ocio: A useful weekly
listings magazine for Barcelona.
Visit their website on:
www.guiadelociobcn.es
Metropolitan: Barcelona's first
monthly magazine in English is now
well established. Targeted at
residents, it makes interesting
reading and carries useful listings.
Distributed free at key points in the
city (and around e.g. Sitges) –
bookshops, bars and cinemas.
Check out their website on:
www.showcom/metropolitan.
Barcelona Business: A pink monthly
newspaper with incisive comments
on business affairs, unveiling some
of the mysteries of local law and
politics. It is distributed free at over
100 points across the city.

TELEVISION

The principal channels are TVE1 and
TVE2 (state-owned), TV3 and Canal
33, the autonomous Catalan

channels. The local channel is BTV.
Commercial channels include
Antena 3 (general programming),
Tele 5 (directed towards
housewives) and Canal Plus (mainly
films, for subscribers only). Satellite
programmes are obtainable in many
of the larger hotels.
   News bulletins in various
languages are on TVE and TV3 from
July to September. Check the daily
press for details.

Postal Services

Stamps for letters, post cards and
small packets can be bought very
conveniently in the many *estancos* to
be found in every district. These are
state-owned establishments licensed
to sell stamps, cigarettes and
tobacco, and easily recognisable by
their orange and brown logo, Tabacs
S.A. Opening hours are loosely
9am–1.30pm and 4.30–8pm. Post
boxes are yellow. Express letters can
be posted in special red boxes,
marked *Urgente*, but it is easier to
find the post office than one of
these, and possibly more direct.
   The main post office is at the
bottom of Via Laietana near the
port, in Plaça Antoni López. It has
collections every hour and is open
Mon–Fri 9am–9pm, Sat 9am–1pm.
Other post offices close at 2pm,
apart from the one in Carrer

d'Aragó, 282 (near Passeig de
Gràcia) which is open until 7pm but
with limited services.
   Poste Restante letters can be
sent to the main post office
addressed to the Lista de Correos,
08080 Barcelona. Be sure to take
personal identification with you
when claiming letters.

Telecommunications

Telephones

Telephone booths are well
distributed throughout the city. As
long as you find one that works,
they are easy to use and efficient,
especially for international calls.
Most bars have either a pay-phone
or a metered telephone, but be
tactful and at least have a coffee
while you are there.
   Public telephones take all euro
coins and most accept credit cards.
The minimum charge for a local call
is 7 centimos. Telephone cards are
available in *estancos* and post
offices. International reverse charge
calls cannot be made from a
phonebox.
   There are also privately run
exchanges *(locutorios)* mainly in the
Old Town, where you talk first and
pay after; useful for calls outside
Europe and North America.
Telephone calls reduced in price
after privatisation of the Spanish

Tourist Information Offices

Plaça de Catalunya
The main city tourist information
centre. Well-equipped and good for
hotel and theatre bookings,
currency exchange. tel: 906 301
282, from abroad 93 368 9730.
Open: 9am–9pm.
El Prat Airport
Tel: 93 478 4704.
Open daily: 9am–9pm in Terminals
A and B.
City Hall
Plaça Sant Jaume. Open: Mon–Fri
9am–8pm, Sat 10am–8pm; Sun
10am–2pm.
Sants Station
open daily: 8am–8pm (summer).
Rest of year: Mon–Fri 8am–8pm,

weekends/holidays 8am–2pm.
**Tourist Information Centre for
Catalonia**
Information on Barcelona and the
rest of Catalonia in the grandiose
Palau Robert, which has
comfortable reading rooms with
sofas and worktables and Internet
connections as well as a garden.
Passeig de Gràcia 107, tel: 93
238 4000; www.gencat.es/
probert. Mon–Fri 10am–7pm Sat
10am–2pm.
   In addition to the above,
information booths are situated in
Plaça Catalunya, the **Port** and the
Sagrada Família in summer. They
are open daily: 9am–9pm.

telecommunications industry, but they are still higher than many other countries, particularly the US.

Principal walk-in telephone exchanges are situated in Sants railway station (fax service), Barcelona Nord bus station and La Rambla, 88 (fax service).

US access codes: AT&T: 900 99 0011; MCI: 900 99 0014 Sprint: 900 99 0013.

Telegrams, Telex and Fax

These can be sent from the main post office Mon–Sat 8.30am–9.30pm or from a small office at Ronda Universitat, 23, 9am–7pm. They can also be sent by telephone, tel: 93 322 2000.

Both these offices have a telex and fax service, but will not receive a fax unless the recipient is present. A more convenient and cheaper service is offered by **Prisma-fax** (Jaume I, 18, fax: 93 310 5865), which will accept incoming faxes.

Internet

There are several internet cafés and lounges in the city, including:
Café Internet
Gran Via de les Corts Catalans, 656
Tel: 93 302 1154
Mon–Sat 9am to midnight.
Easy Internet Café
La Rambla, 31 and Ronda Universitat, 35.
These two branches of the easy Empire are open 24 hours daily all year for cheap Internet access.
Net Movil Consulting
Rambles, 140
Tel: 656 83 8101/2/3
Daily 10am–10 pm.

Tourist Information

For general information about the city, call 010. This is the Barcelona City Council's service that will provide a wealth of information, or at least tell you where to telephone. English spoken.

You can also take advantage of the **"Red Jackets" service**. This consists of a team of young people, recognisable by their red and white uniforms, who offer help and

The Police

There are three main types of police:
Policia Municipal.
Tel: 092
The City Police, known as Guardia Urbana, responsible for traffic, civilian care and security; recognisable by the blue-and-white checked band around their caps and on their vehicles.
Policia Nacional.
Tel: 091
The State Police, who wear navy-blue uniforms. They are responsible for law and order and civilian security.
Mossos d'Esquadra
The autonomous police of Catalonia, in Toni Miró-designed navy-blue and red. They are mainly responsible for the Generalitat buildings.

information in the summer. You will usually find them in the Barri Gòtic, the Ramblas and in Passeig de Gràcia.

Security and Crime

Take care, as in any large city. Loosely swinging handbags, ostentatious cameras and even rucksacks are regularly snatched in broad daylight. Do not be alarmed: Barcelona is not a den of iniquity, and with due care and attention, and common sense, you can avoid dangerous situations.

The old town has a bad reputation for petty crime so be aware when wandering through it or watching street artists. Wear your handbag across your chest, keep your camera hidden and do not flash your wallet around. Carry enough money for the day, leaving the rest in the safe deposit box at your hotel.

At airport, railway and bus stations, keep your luggage together and don't leave it unattended. Never leave anything valuable in a car, especially radios, even in a crowded street.

Don't get caught by a few small gangs who perpetrate various tricks

to waylay you, like commenting on the dirt on your back and, while "helping" you to remove it, slip the purse from your pocket. Another is a game known as *trila*, a variation of the three-card trick, played by crooks, regulars on La Rambla, in the guise of innocent bystanders. When travelling by car, be careful at traffic lights: a familiar scam is where one person causes a diversion while the other pinches your bag from the back seat, or slashes your tyres.

Lost Property

There is a Lost Property Office in Carrer Ciutat, 9 just off Plaça Sant Jaume, 9.30am–1pm
Tel: 93 402 3161.

Reporting a Theft

In the case of a theft, assault or loss, you should first contact the Policia Nacional to make a state-ment *(denuncia)*. This is vital if you want to claim on an insurance policy or seek further help from the City Police or your consulate. The main police station is at Nou de la Rambla, 76, or call **112**.

Assistance for Tourists

The City Police have a special scheme for tourists, at their headquarters (Ramblas, 43, tel: 93 301 9060, 7am–noon; 7am–2am in summer), offering legal advice, medical assistance, provision of temporary documents in the event of loss or robbery and an inter-national telephone line for the speedy cancellation of credit cards,

Emergency Numbers

Fire Brigade
Tel: 080
Ambulance services
Tel: 061
Road accidents
Tel: 088
Policia Nacional
Tel: 091
Policia Municipal
Tel: 092
General emergencies
Tel: 112

Tipping

If you feel the need to tip, make it a token rather than an extravagant one. As a yardstick, in restaurants it should be around 5–10 percent and about the same in a taxi. In a bar or café 80 centimos–€1.50 is enough, depending on the size of the bill.

etc. There is usually someone there who can speak one of the following languages: French, English, German, Italian and Russian.
Police assistance for tourists
Tel: 93 317 7020.
Police station with interpreter service available
Via Laietana, 49
Tel: 93 302 6325.

Religious Services

Mass is usually said between 7am and 2pm on Sunday and feast days. Evening mass between 7pm and 9pm on Saturday, Sunday and feast days.
Catholic Mass: Parroquia Maria Reina, Ctra. d'Esplugues, 103
Tel: 93 203 4115.
Sundays 10am (in English).
Anglican: services in English are held at Saint George's Church
Sant Joan de la Salle, 41
Tel: 93 417 8867.
Sunday 11am.
Judaism
The Synagogue, Avenir, 24
Tel: 93 200 6148.
Islam
Centro Islàmico
Avinguda Merid-iana, 326
Tel: 93 351 4901.
Toarek Ben Ziad
Hospital, 91
Tel: 93 441 9149.

Travelling with Kids

Barcelona, like everywhere else in Spain, or Southern Europe for that matter, is very child-friendly and there will be few places where kids will be excluded. Spanish children are allowed to stay up much later

than elsewhere, particularly in the summer months. Eating out is quite easy with children; the variety of local food means that there will always be something to appeal to a child's palate.

However, take care with children when out in Barcelona. Busy roads and inconsiderate drivers call for extra care. You can escape from the traffic in the old town, where there are many pedestrian streets. The city's beaches are obviously wonderful options for kids, as for anyone else. When you really need to let them run wild take the 10-minute train ride to the Parc de Collserola *(see pages 230–31).*

Attractions for Children

Special attractions for the entertainment of your children in Barcelona could include:
L'Aquàrium de Barcelona
Moll d'Espanya, Port Vell
Tel: 93 221 7474.
Zoo de Barcelona
Enter via the Ciutadella park or Carrer Wellington if you're coming from the seafront.
Tel: 93 221 2506.
Tibidabo funfair
Parc d'Atraccions de Tibidabo
Plaça del Tibidabo
Tel: 93 211 79 42.
Parc de la Ciutadella
Apart from open greenery, boats can be hired on the pond, and rocks studied in the Museu de la Geologia, tel: 93 319 6895.
The museums listed below should appeal to a young audience:
Museu de Cera
The Wax Museum
Passatge de la Banca, 7
Tel: 93 317 2649.
Museu Marítim
Avda de les Drassanes
Tel: 93 318 3245.
Museu de la Ciència
Teodor Roviralta, 55
Tel: 93 212 6050.
Places further afield:
Illa de Fantasia
Finca Mas Brassó, Vilassar de Dalt
Tel: 93 751 4553.
An aquatic park 24km (15 miles) from Barcelona in Premià de Mar.

Port Aventura
near Tarragona
108km (67 miles) from Barcelona
Tel: 977 77 9090.
A theme park based on five world locations: the Mediterranean, Mexico, the Wild West, China and Polynesia.

Women Travellers

Women should have no occasion to feel ill at ease in Barcelona; Spain is different in this respect from, for example, Italy, and women won't encounter harassment just walking around or eating alone. Everyone should be careful, however, when out late in narrow, dark streets.

A good source of information on women-related issues is: Librería Pròleg, Dagueria, 13. This is the city's specialist bookshop for feminist subjects and women writers. It is also an exhibition space and holds talks occasionally.

Gay & Lesbian Travellers

The gay scene is thriving in Barcelona and generally very well accepted. Nearby Sitges (half an hour south of the city on the coast) is a real mecca for gays, particularly in summer, and well worth a visit. The drag parade during Carnival in February is renowned.

For advice and information on the latest venues, the lesbian and gay hotline is **Telèfon Rosa**: tel: 900 601 601.

Other useful addresses are:
Casal Lambda
Ample 5,
Tel: 93 319 5550.
From 5pm onwards. A cultural centre.
Coordinadora Gai-Lesbiana
Buenaventura Muñoz, 4
Tel. 93 309 7997.
Col.lectiu Gai de BCN
Paloma, 12
Tel: 93 318 1666.
Sextienda
Rauric, 11
Tel: 93 318 8676.

Getting Around

On Arrival

Whether you arrive in the airport, rail or bus station, or in your own car, you probably will stand out as the vulnerable tourist, so be alert and keep your bags or car attended until you are in a hotel or *pension*.

FROM THE AIRPORT

Barcelona is only 12 km (7 miles) from El Prat airport and is easily reached by train, bus or taxi.

Trains to Sants, the central station, depart every 30 minutes from 6.14am–10.44pm and take about 18 minutes. The same service from Sants to the airport operates from 5.44am–10.14pm. Approximate cost is €2.60. Although advertised as the train to Sants, it continues to Plaça de Catalunya and Arc de Triomf, which can be more convenient for central parts of the city.

Aerobús, an efficient bus service, is perhaps the best way to and from the airport. It runs to Plaça Catalunya from each terminal every 15 minutes, stopping at strategic points en route. It operates 6am–11pm (6.30am–10.50pm at weekends) and the fare is €3.50 single and €5.65 return.

There is also a bus service (line EA) to and from Plaça d'Espanya but it is rather irregular. The night service (EN) is useful, however. It leaves from Plaça d'Espanya 9.40pm–3.15am.

To reach most central parts of Barcelona by taxi will cost about €12–18, plus an airport supplement and a token amount for each suitcase. To avoid misunderstandings, ask how much it will cost before getting in to the taxi. "*Cuánto vale el recorrido desde el aeropuerto hasta... (e.g.) Plaça de Catalunya?*". Get the taxi driver to write down the answer if necessary. To be really thorough, you can check with the taxi authorities in the airport.

Iberia information: tel: 902 400 500.

Airport: tel: 93 298 3838.

renfe (train services): tel: 902 24 02 02 (national routes), 902 24 34 02 (international routes).

Using Public Transport

Barcelona is a manageable city to get around, whether on foot or by public transport. The latter is efficient and good value. The only means of transport to avoid is your own: the parking problems, the threat of a police clamp or removal lorry, local driving habits and the traffic system all conspire to make travelling by car in this city a nightmare. Leave your car in a car park. For travelling around Catalonia, however, a car is useful.

METRO

The Metro is Barcelona's underground network. It has five colour-coded lines – I, II, III, IV and V. Line V is equipped for wheelchairs and prams, with lifts at every station. Trains are frequent and cheap, with a set price per journey, no matter how far you travel. It is more economical to buy a card that allows you 10 journeys (*tarjeta multi-viaje* T-10) available at any station, at banks or *estancs* (tobacconists). It can be shared and is valid for FGC trains *(see below)* and town buses. Trains run 5am–11pm Monday to Thursday, 5–2am on Friday and Saturday, and 6am–midnight on Sunday.

The train service, Ferrocarrils de la Generalitat de Catalunya (FGC), interconnects with the Metro, looks like the Metro and functions in the same way but extends beyond the inner city area to towns on the other side of Tibidabo, like San Cugat, Terrassa and Sabadell (all from Plaça de Catalunya) and to Manresa and Igualada (from Plaça d'Espanya). It is a useful service for reaching the upper parts of Barcelona and for parts of Tibidabo and the Parc de Collserola.

The Metro ticket is valid on this line within a limited area, but to travel beyond is more expensive. The FGC lines are shown in a darker blue on the Metro map. Within town the timetable is the same as the Metro, but beyond it varies according to the line. Check in a station or call 010, a useful number for transport information.

Taking Taxis

All Barcelona taxis are black and yellow, and show a green light when they are available for hire. There are taxi ranks at the airport, Sants station, Plaça de Catalunya and other strategic points but taxis constantly move around town and can be hailed at any street corner. Rates are standard and calculated by meter, starting at a set rate and clocking up at a rate governed by the time of day: nighttimes, weekends and fiestas are more expensive. Travelling by taxi is still extremely affordable here compared to other major cities.

If you go beyond the metropolitan area, the rate will increase slightly. The final charge is what shows on the meter, except when supplements are due for luggage, dogs or a journey to or from the airport. Drivers do not expect a tip though a small one is always appreciated. A sticker inside the rear window outlines (in English) rates and conditions. Taxis equipped for wheelchairs or a group (7 seats) are available. Contact:

Radiotaxi Verd, tel: 93 266 3939, or **Taxigroc**, tel: 93 490 2222.

Tourist Buses

A convenient way of getting an overall idea of the city is to catch the Tourist Bus (Barcelona Bus Turistic) which follows a circuit that takes in the most interesting parts of the city. You can select a northern route or southern, and get on and off freely. It also offers discounts on entrance charges.

These buses operate from March to early January and there are frequent services, the first leaving Plaça Catalunya at 9am. The fleet includes buses equipped for wheelchairs and open-air double deckers.

For information and tickets ask at the tourist information office in Plaça Catalunya or the one in Estació de Sants.

Other companies offering bus tours around the city inlcude:

Julia Tours
Ronda Universitat, 5.
Tel: 93 317 6454/6209.
Pullmantur
Gran Via C.C., 635.
Tel: 93 317 1297.

BUS

The bus service is good for reaching the areas the Metro doesn't, and for seeing more of Barcelona – at speed. Thanks to bus and taxi lanes, journeys can be fast, so hold on tight. Single tickets are the same price as Metro tickets and can be bought from the driver, or a multiple card (*tarjeta multi-viaje* T-10) of 10 journeys can be punched inside the bus. Most buses run 5 or 6am–10pm. There are some night services (the Nit bus), but lines vary so check on the map or at bus stops.

A more exclusive bus, the Tomb Bus, is convenient for covering the shopping area between Plaça de Catalunya and the top end of Avinguda Diagonal (Plaça Pius XII), which is not well connected by Metro. The Tibibus runs from Plaça Catalunya to Plaça del Tibidabo (on the top of the hill).

Cycling

Barcelona is now a cyclist-friendly city, with bike lanes, parking facilities and many great traffic-free places to cycle, such as the port, marinas, and along the beach front from Barceloneta to the Olympic village. Bikes can be taken on trains free of charge.

Barcelona on Foot

Walking is one of the best ways of getting around Barcelona, though sometimes the traffic fumes in the busy Eixample suggest it may not be the healthiest. However, it is ideal for seeing the many details of Barcelona that cannot possibly all be charted by maps or guide books – *modernista* entrances and doorways, ancient corner shops, hidden roof gardens, balconies, local characters, daily life.

Several companies offer guided walking tours of the city:

Barcelona Walking Tours,
Saturdays in English at 10am and Spanish at noon. Information and booking: Turisme de Barcelona, Plaça Catalunya, tel: 906 301 282.
The Route of Modernism,
tickets and information: Centre del Modernisme, Paseig de Gràcia, 41, pral, tel: 93 488 0139.
Gaudí Tour, Barcelona, lasts 4 hours; information and sales: Centre Cultural Caixa Catalunya, tel: 93 484 8909.
La Ruta del Gòtic: If you are in a group (min. 10 people) you have the opportunity to do a 3-hour guided tour of the Gothic quarter. Information and tickets: Museu d'Història de la Ciutat, Plaça del Rei, tel: 93 315 1111.
Guided Tours of Palau de la Música Catalana, Sant Francesc de Paula, 2, tel: 93 268 1000.
There is also a guided tour by bicycle: **Un Cotxe Menys**, Espartaría, 3, tel: 93 268 2105.

Barcelona Addresses

Addresses in this section are indicated by street name, number, storey, door. So Muntaner, 375, 6° 2ª means Muntaner street No. 375,

Tour Guides

If you want to recruit a professional tourist guide or interpreter, contact:
Barcelona Guide Bureau
Tel: 93 268 2422
City Guides Tel: 93 412 0674
Professional Association of Barcelona Tour Guides
Tel: 93 319 8416

6th floor, 2nd door. The first floor of a building is *Principal*, often abbreviated to Pral.

Maps

The Tourist Board issues a good general map of the city *(plano de la ciudad)*. A transport map is also available from Metro stations. The *Guia Urbana*, the taxi drivers' bible, is the most comprehensive map of the city on sale at newstands.

Travelling outside Barcelona

BY TRAIN

The following stations currently function as described, but before planning any journey it is advisable to call RENFE (the national train network) for the latest information and ticket deals, tel: 902 240 202. It is wise to purchase tickets in advance (on this number) especially at holiday times.

Estació de Sants, in Plaça Països Catalans, is for long-distance national and international trains. Some of these will also stop

Left Luggage

Left luggage lockers *(consigna)* are available in Sants railway station 4.30am–midnight. There is an equivalent service at Estació de França and Passeig. de Gràcia stations and at Barcelona Nord bus station. At the sea terminal on Moll Barcelona there is a left luggage office which is open 8am–1am.

in **Passeig de Gràcia** station, which is very convenient for central parts of town. Confirm beforehand that your train really does stop there.

Regional trains leave Sants for the coast south and north of Barcelona including a direct train to Port Aventura theme park and the high-speed Euromed to Alicante, which makes a few stops in between. In Sants station, queues can be long and ticket clerks impatient and not very helpful.
Estació de França, Avinguda Marqués de l'Argentera: long distance national and international trains.
Plaça de Catalunya: apart from the Metro and Generalitat railways (FGC), RENFE has a station in Plaça de Catalunya. Trains to Manresa, Lleida, Vic, Puigcerdà, La Tour de Carol, Mataró (Maresme Coast) and Blanes.
Plaça d'Espanya: FGC trains to Montserrat, Igualada and Manresa.

BY COACH

There are regular long-distance coach lines running all over Spain which leave from the Estació d'Autobusos Barcelona Nord, Ali-bei, 80 or Sants bus station. For information, tel: 93 265 6508. Bus services to other parts of Catalonia are operated by:
Costa Brava: Sarfa
Tel: 902 302 025.
Costa Maresme: Casas
Tel: 93 798 1100.
Delta del Ebro: Hife
Tel: 93 322 7814.
Montserrat: Julià
Tel: 93 490 4000.
Pyrenees: Alsina Graells
Tel: 93 265 6866.

BY SEA

There is a regular passenger and car service between Barcelona and Mallorca, Menorca and Ibiza with the Trasmediterránea company, based at the Estación Marítima, Moll de Barcelona, tel: 902 454 645; www.trasmediterranea.es for information, or book through a travel

agent. There is also a Fast Ferry service, which takes four hours as opposed to the usual eight. Another company, Buquebus, has catamaran-type boats which can get you to to Palma in three hours. For information and bookings contact: Fast Ferries, tel: 902 414 242.

Driving in Catalonia

Driving is definitely the most flexible way to see the rest of Catalonia, but cars are better left in a parking place while you travel around town. Avoid parking anywhere that is not legal, particularly entrances and private garage doors: the police tow offenders away with remarkable alacrity, and charge for retrieval is heavy. You will know if this has happened if you find a document with a triangular symbol stuck on the ground where your car was. This paper will give details of where you can retrieve your vehicle. Street parking, indicated by blue lines on the road and a nearby machine to buy a ticket, is limited. Convenient (but fairly expensive) car parks are in Passeig de Gràcia, Plaça de Catalunya, Plaça de la Catedral and many side streets.

Drivers are supposed to stop for pedestrians at zebra crossings and when the green man is illuminated on traffic lights but often drive through while people are still crossing. This is an abuse of the road system and not to be copied.

Car Rental

Hiring a car is a good way to explore the area around Barcelona. It may be cheaper to make arrangements from home before you leave. A few of the car hire companies are:
Avis, Casanovas, 209
Tel: 93 209 9533; 93 298 3601 or 93 298 3602 (airport).
Budget, Josep Tarradellas, 35
Tel: 93 410 2508 or 93 298 3500 (airport)
Europcar, Estacio de Sants
Tel: 93 491 4822 or 93 298 3300 (airport).
Hertz, Tuset, 10.
Tel: 93 217 3248 or 93 298 3639 (airport).

National-Atesa, Muntaner, 45
Tel: 93 323 0701 or 93 298 3433 (airport).
Vanguard, Londres, 31.
Tel: 93 439 3880.
Motorbikes also for hire.
www.easycar.com is a good option if you are not planning excessive mileage.

Breakdowns

In case of a breakdown on the road it is best to call the general emergency number **112**, which has a foreign language service, and can connect you with the relevant service. Another useful organisation is the RACC (Royal Automobile Club of Catalonia), tel: 900 365 505.

On motorways and main roads there are SOS phone boxes with specials buttons to call for help.

Licences and Insurance

Members of the EU can use the driving licence from their own country of residence. Those outside the EU must have an international driving licence. You should have a Green Card (international motor insurance) from your insurance company.

Useful Addresses

Royal Automobile Club of Catalonia (racc), Avinguda Diagonal 687, tel: 93 495 5000 or 900 365 505 (24 hours). Towing service.
24-hour repairs, workshop/towing service: Vicmavel, Sagrera, 107, tel: 93 351 1203.

Speed Limits

- Urban areas: 50 kph (30 mph)
- Roads outside urban areas: 90–110 kph (55–70 mph)
- Dual carriageways outside urban areas: 120 kph (75 mph)
- Motorways: 120 kph (75 mph)

Where to Stay

Choosing a Hotel

Barcelona has more than 400 hotels, offering a wide range of accommodation from the humble *pensión* to 5-star luxury. Take care when choosing a *pensión*: it could have all the charms and comforts of staying with a local family or it could equally well be the local brothel.

Under new regulations for the classification of establishments in Catalonia, *hostales*, *hostal-residencias*, *casas de huespedes* (CH – Guest Houses) and *fondas* should all be re-categorised either as hotels or as *pensiones*. It will probably take some time to enforce the new categories so be prepared to find the old names above the door – and in this listing.

The official categorisation is: *Hotels* (one star to five star) – a bathroom for every room is obligatory.

Pensiones: One star – 15 percent of rooms with bath. Two star – 25 percent of rooms with bath.

All the establishments in the following list are hotels unless otherwise stated. Remember that a flight and hotel package often works out cheaper than reserving direct.

Barcelona is an extremely popular tourist and business destination and conference centre. Hotels are therefore busy and relatively expensive, and it's advisable to book accommodation well in advance of a visit. You may find more availability and better prices in July and August than in September and October, which is considered high season. Many hotels have been renovated or refurbished in recent years and there is now an almost standardised Barcelona style –

either a modern version of "classic" or a contemporary design using bright colours.

Hotel Chains

Aside from the hotels listed below you could also contact the central offices of the following hotel chains to see what they have available:

Derby Hotels
Tel: 93 414 2970.
www.derbyhotels.es/
Guitart Hotels
Tel: 972 347 000.
www.guitarthotels.com
Hoteles Catalonia
Tel: 93 418 4818.
www.hoteles-catalonia.es/
NH Hotels
Tel: 93 412 2323.
www.nh-hoteles.es

Hotel Listings

The following hotels are categorised by price, with the most expensive first; within each price category, they are listed in alphabetical order.

VERY EXPENSIVE (€€€€)

Arts
Passeig de la Marina, 19
Tel: 93 221 1000
Fax: 93 221 1070
www.harts.es
The hotel with the highest profile in town, it is one of the two towers that mark the entrance to the Olympic Village, on the sea front. It has a light and airy feel; the piano bar overlooks the hotel gardens which in turn overlook the sea. Rooms with panoramic views.
Avenida Palace
Gran Vía, 605–607
Tel: 93 301 9600
Fax: 93 318 1234
www.avenidapalace.com
Classic old-world gilt and chandeliers at new world prices. Comfortable, good service. Request one of the rooms that still has original fittings, or the fourth floor upwards, for good city views.
Colón
Avinguda Catedral, 7
Tel: 93 301 1404

Fax: 93 317 2915
www.hotelcolon.es
A classic, in the centre of the Barri Gòtic, directly facing the cathedral. Bedrooms seem more English in their floral style than Spanish. Request a room with a view of the Cathedral Square.
Claris
Pau Claris, 150
Tel: 93 487 6262
Fax: 93 215 7970
Well positioned in the middle of the Eixample, its strikingly well designed interior was built behind the original façade of the Palace of Vedruna and is crammed with valuable art work.
Comtes de Barcelona
Passeig de Gràcia, 75
Tel: 93 488 2200
Fax: 93 467 4785
Contemporary elegance in two Modernist buildings facing each other in the Quadrat d'Or of the Eixample. Rooms available with private balcony; there is a roof terrace with mini-pool.
Gallery
Rossello, 249
Tel: 93 415 9911
Fax: 93 415 9184
Well situated between Passeig de Gràcia and Rambla de Catalunya. Very pleasant bar on the first floor overlooking the street, and a restaurant which has tables outside in the attractive garden behind.
Le Meridien Barcelona
Rambla, 111
Tel: 93 318 6200
Fax: 93 301 7776
www.lemeridien-barcelona.com
A large plush hotel, well renovated in keeping with the refurbishment of Barcelona.
Majestic
Passeig de Gràcia, 70
Tel: 93 488 1717
Fax: 93 488 1880
www.hotelmajestic.es
Takes up 3 buildings on Paseig de Gràcia. Renovation was completed in 1999 to transform what was 70s style into polished sophistication. The oldest daughter of the family that owns it has chosen all the art on display with great skill. Two restaurants, including the famed

INSIGHT GUIDES

The classic series that puts you in the picture

Alaska	Dublin	**M**adeira	Rome
Amazon Wildlife	**E**ast African Wildlife	Madrid	Russia
American Southwest	Eastern Europe	Malaysia	**S**t Petersburg
Amsterdam	Ecuador	Mallorca & Ibiza	San Francisco
Argentina	Edinburgh	Malta	Sardinia
Arizona & Grand Canyon	Egypt	Mauritius, Réunion	Scandinavia
Asia, East	England	& Seychelles	Scotland
Asia, Southeast	**F**inland	Melbourne	Seattle
Australia	Florence	Mexico	Sicily
Austria	Florida	Miami	Singapore
Bahamas	France	Montreal	South Africa
Bali	France, Southwest	Morocco	South America
Baltic States	French Riviera	Moscow	Spain
Bangkok	**G**ambia & Senegal	**N**amibia	Spain, Northern
Barbados	Germany	Nepal	Spain, Southern
Barcelona	Glasgow	Netherlands	Sri Lanka
Beijing	Gran Canaria	New England	Sweden
Belgium	Great Britain	New Orleans	Switzerland
Belize	Great Railway Journeys	New York City	Sydney
Berlin	of Europe	New York State	Syria & Lebanon
Bermuda	Greece	New Zealand	**T**aiwan
Boston	Greek Islands	Nile	Tenerife
Brazil	Guatemala, Belize	Normandy	Texas
Brittany	& Yucatán	Norway	Thailand
Brussels	**H**awaii	**O**man & The UAE	Tokyo
Buenos Aires	Hong Kong	Oxford	Trinidad & Tobago
Burgundy	Hungary	**P**acific Northwest	Tunisia
Burma (Myanmar)	**I**celand	Pakistan	Turkey
Cairo	India	Paris	Tuscany
California	India, South	Peru	**U**mbria
California, Southern	Indonesia	Philadelphia	USA: On The Road
Canada	Ireland	Philippines	USA: Western States
Caribbean	Israel	Poland	US National Parks: West
Channel Islands	Istanbul	Portugal	**V**enezuela
Chicago	Italy	Prague	Venice
Chile	Italy, Northern	Provence	Vienna
China	Italy, Southern	Puerto Rico	Vietnam
Continental Europe	**J**amaica	**R**ajasthan	**W**ales
Corsica	Japan	Rio de Janeiro	
Costa Rica	Jerusalem		
Crete	Jordan		
Cuba	**K**enya		
Cyprus	Korea		
Czech & Slovak Republics	**L**aos & Cambodia		
Delhi, Jaipur & Agra	Lisbon		
Denmark	London		
Dominican Rep. & Haiti	Los Angeles		

☉ INSIGHT GUIDES

The world's largest collection of visual travel guides & maps

Price Guide

Prices vary dramatically in each establishment depending on the season and demand because of Trade Fairs etc. Approximate price per night for a double room with bath:

€€€€ = €200 and over
€€€ = €150–200
€€ = €75–150
€ = €75 and below

Drolma, which has only 10 tables for gourmets to sample the exquisite menu by well-known chef.

Melia Barcelona
Avinguda Sarria, 48–50
Tel: 93 410 6090
Fax: 93 410 6173
You could forget you're in Barcelona in this hotel and be anywhere in the world, but if comfort is what you're after then this is an obvious option.

Rey Juan Carlos I
Avinguda Diagonal, 661–671
Tel: 93 364 4040
Fax: 93 364 4264
www.hrjuancarlos.com
Vast modern construction using plenty of glass and steel. At the end of Diagonal and therefore a taxi ride away from everything. Maximum comfort and security, favoured by Royalty and politicians.

Ritz
Gran Vía, 668
Tel: 93 318 5200
Fax: 93 318 0148
www.ritzcarlton.com
Luxury maybe, but exorbitant even for business accounts. Splendid entrance hall and lobby where tea can be taken. Dalí had a permanent suite here.

Rivoli Ramblas
Rambla, 128
Tel: 93 302 6643
Fax: 93 317 5053
E-mail: reservas@rivolihotels.com
Behind the elegantly cool façade is a modern hotel with tasteful rooms. The barman of the Blue Moon cocktail bar downstairs plays great music, which makes a refreshing change from typical hotel musack.

EXPENSIVE (€€€)

Ambassador
Pintor Fortuny, 13
Tel: 93 412 0530
Fax: 93 302 7977
Just off the Ramblas. Rooms are comfortable. Its little rooftop garden makes a pleasant retreat from the bustle.

Barcelona Plaza
Plaça d'Espanya, 6–8
Tel: 93 426 2600
Fax: 93 426 0400
Popular with business clientele due to its proximity to the Fira de Barcelona trade fair site. Situated at the foot of Montjuïc, it's also well located for exploring the city.

Catalunya Plaza
Plaça Catalunya, 7
Tel: 93 317 7171
Fax: 93 317 7855
On the square itself. Standard hotel comfort behind attractive façade.

Diplomatic
Pau Claris, 122
Tel: 93 272 3810
Fax: 93 272 3811
Superbly sleek and crisp in its stylish, faintly 60s design, and a refreshing change from classical cosiness. The downstairs lounge is spacious, simple and streamlined. Amazing views from the roof terrace, which also has a gym and saunas. Excellent value.

Duques de Bergara
Bergara, 11
Tel: 93 301 5151
Fax. 93 317 3442
You may be delighted by the beautiful, late 19th/early 20th century entrance hall but don't get too excited: the rooms are disappointing in comparison since everything has been modernised. The hotel has every comfort but is somewhat impersonal and dull. The nicest feature is the small, peaceful terrace with pool.

Gran Hotel Barcino
Jaume I, 6
Tel: 93 302 2012
Fax: 93 301 4242
www.hotelbarcino.com
The location is the chief factor. A bit expensive for what is on offer.

Gran Hotel Havana
Gran Via Cortes Catalanes, 647
Tel: 93 412 1115
Fax: 93 412 2611
www.hoteles-silken.com
The rooms here are on the smaller side but well thought out and pleasant. Attractive luminous interior.

Regente
Rambla de Catalunya, 76
Tel: 93 487 5989
Fax: 93 487 3227
Pleasant hotel in excellent position. Some attractive original features have survived amid the standard hotel furnishings. Rooftop pool.

Regina
Bergara, 2–3
Tel: 93 301 3232
Fax: 93 318 3236
www.reginahotel.com
High quality and central location just off Plaça Catalunya.

Royal
La Rambla, 117
Tel: 93 301 9400
Fax: 93 317 3179
Despite the rather mediocre 1970s exterior, the interiors are fully refurbished.

Sant Moritz
Diputación, 262
Tel: 93 412 1500
Fax: 93 412 1236
More of interest for its location than its style, but the **San Galen** restaurant is recommended in the Michelin Guide. On the ground floor there is a set of rooms for guests with disabilities.

Turó de Vilana
Vilana, 7
Tel: 93 434 0363
Fax. 93 418 8903
www.turodevilana.com
For anyone who prefers to be out of the noise and touristy areas, this small hotel with only 20 rooms is at the top of the town, not far from the Norman Foster Communications tower and the Parc de Collserola. Modern, compact and pretty.

MODERATE (€€)

España
Sant Pau, 9
Tel: 93 318 1758

Fax: 93 317 1134
E-mail: hotelespanya@tresnet.com
Magnificent Modernist décor on the ground floor by Domènech i Montaner is refreshingly set off by kitsch touches and the 50s style of the bar. Rooms modernised, but fairly basic. Popular among American intellectuals. At least eat here: the set lunch is good value and the wonderful surroundings are worth every euro.

Gran Vía
Gran Vía, 642
Tel: 93 318 1900
Fax: 93 318 9997
E-mail: hgranvia@nnhoteles.es
Faded old Spain splendour which can be a welcome change from the pervading designer modernity of the city. Well situated near Passeig de Gràcia. Interior rooms are preferable to avoid Gran Vía traffic. Downstairs there is a large, restful parquet-floored lounge leading to a spacious terrace.

Mercure Barcelona Rambla
La Rambla, 124
Tel: 93 412 0404
Fax: 93 318 7323
A mix of old and new. Bedrooms are modernised but down to earth, whilst there is an upstairs lounge revealing how the hotel looked in former times.

Mesón de Castilla
Valldonzella, 5
Tel: 93 318 2182
Fax: 93 412 4020
Furniture is old-fashioned; cupboards and chairs in a sort of rustic style. A bit quirky, but at least gives the feeling of being somewhere "different" (as opposed to anywhere). Very good location. The owners are friendly and helpful.

Nouvel
Santa Anna, 20
Tel: 93 301 8274
Fax: 93 301 8370
www.hotelnouvel.com
Located in a pedestrian street off the Ramblas, an attractive old building, with modernised interior and comfortable, spacious rooms.

Oriente
Rambla, 45
Tel: 93 302 2558
Fax: 93 412 3819

One of Barcelona's best known hotels. Not what it was despite the price increases but still full of character.

Park Hotel
Avinguda Marquès de l'Argentera, 11
Tel: 93 319 6000
Fax: 93 319 4519
This is a natty little piece of pure 50s architecture, opposite the Estació de França, and near the Parc de la Cuitadella. It is on the edge of the Born district, which is awash with cafés, restaurants and bars. Rooms are pleasantly designed.

Reding
Gravina, 5–7
Tel: 93 412 1097
Fax. 93 268 3482
In a quiet side-street just off Pelai. Well equipped, fairly standard, comfortable hotel accommodation but well located.

Rialto
Ferrán, 42
Tel: 93 318 5212
Fax: 93 318 5312
Modernised and straightforward, nothing fancy. In an interesting street just off Plaça Sant Jaume.

Price Guide

Approximate price per night for a double room with bath:

€€€€ = €200 and over
€€€ = €150–€200
€€ = €75–€150
€ = €75 and below

Sant Agustí
Plaça Sant Agustí, 3
Tel: 93 318 1658
Fax: 93 317 2928
www.hotelsa.com
Comfortable and clean, overlooking a quiet square. It is well worth paying more for one of their luxury rooms on the fourth floor.

Suizo
Plaça de l'Angel, 12
Tel: 93 310 6108
Fax: 93 310 4081
Pleasant, homely, comfortable in a

good position in the Barri Gòtic. Request a room on Baixada Llibreteria for an attractive outlook and more peace.

INEXPENSIVE (€)

This category includes hotels, *hostales* and *pensiones*. The Barri Gòtic (Gothic Quarter) is full of *pensiones* but choose them with care: the streets between Carrer de Ferrán and Plaça de Catalunya are better than those nearer the port. Several reasonable places are in Carrer de Carme, Portaferrissa and Santa Anna.

Ginebra
Rambla de Catalunya, 1
Tel: 93 317 1063
Fax: 93 317 5565
This is on the simple, basic side; not all rooms have *en suite* bathrooms. However, it is very clean, staff are friendly and the location is central, with views of Plaça de Catalunya from some rooms. All windows are double-glazed. A good deal.

Hostal Ciudad Condal
Mallorca, 255
Tel: 93 215 1040
Very clean, respectable little *pensión* in the heart of the best part of the Eixample.

Hostal Lesseps
Gran de Gràcia, 239
Tel: 93 218 4434
Owned by the same family as the *pensión* above and similar in style, though a little further up the city.

Hostal Palacios
Gran Vía, 629 bis
Tel: 93 301 3792
Fulfils the basic requirements and cheap considering the location. For unfussy customers.

Jardí
Plaça Sant Josep Oriol 1/
Plaça del Pi
Tel: 93 301 5900
After months of refurbishment this extremely popular hotel is still quite basic, but worth trying to get in if you can, overlooking two of the most attractive squares in the Barri Gòtic.

Marina Folch
Mar, 16, pral
Tel: 93 310 3709
Fax: 93 310 5327
Just behind Passeig Joan de Borbó is another world, that of the real Barceloneta, resembling bits of Naples. Looking at the façade you may get the wrong impression. The interior is completely renovated and the rooms surprisingly tasteful. There are only 10 rooms, and even company directors like staying here, so booking is essential.

Paseo de Gràcia
Passeig de Gràcia, 102
Tel: 93 215 5824
Fax: 93 215 3724
Another vestige from the past, with some original fittings. Ask for a room on the 8th floor. Prime location and good value for money in this area.

Peninsular
Sant Pau, 34
Tel: 93 302 3138
Fax: 93 412 3699
There used to be many more *pensiones* like this one but they are now so rare that this one is almost a jewel; the staff are proud of the promotion to hotel and say that its one star shines brilliantly. The inner patio is filled with hanging plants, and paintwork is in the traditional Mediterranean green of years gone by, but all maintained in tip-top condition.

Residencia Windsor
Rambla de Catalunya, 84
Tel: 93 215 1198
A gem: intact and impeccably clean, light and airy in contrast to the usual drab, sad *hostales*. Essential to book in advance and to request a room looking on to Rambla de Catalunya. Excellent position near Diagonal.

Roma Reial
Plaça Reial, 11
Tel: 93 302 0366
Fax: 93 301 1839
In a corner of a stunning square; rooms are basic but acceptable, though for the price something better can probably be found in a less ostentatious location, such as nearby Carrer Boquerìa, which has many cheaper hotels.

Triunfo
Paseig de Picasso, 22
Tel: 93 315 0860
Fax: 93 315 0860
A simple, clean *pensión* between the Born and the Parc de la Ciutadella which makes this a good spot to stay. The buildings on this wide avenue are elegant.

Self-catering Hotels

Aparthotel Bonanova $$$
Bisbe Sevilla, 7
Tel: 93 418 1661
Fax: 93 418 4497
In a quiet residential area in the upper part of Barcelona. Ask for a room with a terrace.

Citadines Barcelona-Ramblas $$
La Rambla, 122
Tel: 93 270 1111
Fax: 93 412 7421
Excellent value for money. Food shopping can be done at the Boquería market or local super-market. Very pleasant breakfast buffet bar and good views from the rooftop.

Youth Hostels

Hostal de Joves
Passeig De Pujades, 29
Tel/Fax: 93 300 3104

Kabul
Plaça Reial, 17
Tel: 93 318 5190
Fax. 93 419 301 4034

Mare de Déu de Montserrat
Mare de Déu de Coll, 41–51
Tel: 93 210 5151
Fax: 93 210 0798

Pere Tarrès
Numància, 149–151
Tel: 93 410 2309
Fax: 93 419 6268

Studio
Duquessa d'Orleans, 56
Tel: 93 205 9601

Camp Sites

There are 300 camp sites in Catalonia, 70 percent of the total number in Spain. Twelve of these are within easy reach of Barcelona. Most are south of the city, near the stretch of beach which begins at

the end of the airport tarmac and runs through Viladecans, Gavá and Castelldefels. The road into Barcelona is notoriously busy and dangerous, the beaches and sea are crowded and of dubious cleanliness, but the air provides a refreshing change from the city. The following campsites all have a swimming pool, supermarket, laundry and facilities for the disabled Further details are available on www.barcelonaturisme.com.

South from Barcelona
El Toro Bravo
(1,200 sites)
Autovía de Castelldefels km 11, Viladecans
Tel: 93 637 3462
Fax: 93 637 2115

Filipinas
(1,063 sites)
Km 12 on the same road
Tel: 93 658 2895
Fax: 93 658 2115
E-mail: filipinas@retemail.es

La Ballena Alegre
(1,500 sites)
Km 12.5 on the same road
Tel: 93 658 0504
Fax: 93 658 0575
E-mail: ballenal@ballena-alegre.es

Tres Estrellas
(407 sites)
On the same road, but in Gavá, at Km 13.2
Tel: 93 633 0637
Fax: 93 633 1525

Estrella de Mar
(525 sites)
Castelldefells
Tel/fax: 93 633 0784

North of Barcelona
Masnou (120 sites)
Camilo Fabra, 33
Tel/fax: 93 555 1503
11 km (7 miles) north of the city (no laundry).

Where to Eat

Restaurants

Barcelona has a huge number of restaurants and bars covering everything from exorbitant deluxe to simple suppers for less than €8; the important thing is that eating out is accessible to everyone in this city and is generally excellent value for money.

The following have been selected for their good food combined with atmosphere or pleasant location. Nearly all serve Catalan food and many other regional dishes. At lunch time try any corner bar for a 3-course *menu del día*. The standard price is between €6 and €12.

Be aware that many places close on a Sunday evening and/or Monday, and in August.

VERY EXPENSIVE (€€€€)

Botafumeiro
Gran de Gràcia, 81
Tel: 93 218 4230
This is a Galician restaurant and one of the best places to eat seafood in Barcelona. Oysters served at the bar.

Ca l'Isidre
Les Flors, 12
Tel: 93 441 1139
A family-run restaurant, within the Ciutat Vella, with regular, well groomed clientele who come to appreciate the meticulous attention to detail in food, decoration and service.

El Passadís d'en Pep
Pla de Palau, 2
Tel: 93 310 1021
This is a place for people "in the know", the kind of place you will walk past if you are not. Be prepared to spend a lot, but otherwise relax; you don't even have to choose from a menu; food is simply brought to you.

Hofmann
Argentería, 74–78
Tel: 93 319 5889
Food by cordon bleu chefs for serious gourmets, served in a set of cosy rooms on the first floor, next to the adjoining cooking school. Essential to book in advance.

Jean Luc Figueras
Santa Teresa, 10
Tel: 93 415 2877
Small restaurant with a big reputation for artful Mediterranean cuisine. Located in a restored building in Gràcia.

Neichel
Avinguda Pedralbes, 16 bis
Tel: 93 203 8408
A prize-winner for its modern, stylish design and 2 stars in the Michelin guide, this restaurant looks onto a garden of lemon trees. The owner describes the food as "avant-garde Mediterranean". There is a special "tastes and aromas" menu.

Talaia
Marina, 16
Tel: 93 221 9090
One of the best restaurants at the Olympic Port, with a guaranteed high standard of creative cooking. Specialises in fish.

EXPENSIVE (€€€)

Cal Pep
Plaça de les Olles, 8
Tel: 93 310 7962
A restaurant which has got it all right. The chefs perform a kind of ballet preparing fish dishes with the very best of fresh ingredients. You can observe the action (and eat much more cheaply) if you sit and order a few *raciones* at the long bar counter – don't dream of sitting anywhere else, even if you have to queue.

Can Majó
Almirall Aixada, 23
Tel: 93 221 5818
One of the best and most established of the Barceloneta fish restaurants, and one of the few places you can be sure of a good paella.

Carballeira
Reina Cristina, 3
Tel: 93 310 1006
Excellent Galician fish. At lunchtime try a simple *tapa* of *arroz a banda* (delicious rice cooked in fish stock) at the bar. Accompany it with a glass of Ribeira (Galician white wine); in particular try the cloudy variety, *turbio*.

Casa Leopoldo
Sant Rafael, 24
Tel: 93 441 3014
Worth hunting down in the narrow streets of the Barri Xines, a family-run Barcelona classic. Favourite of artists and intellectuals, serving excellent fish.

Els Pescadors
Plaça Prim, 1, Poble Nou
Tel: 93 225 2018
A lesser-known corner of Barcelona, Poble Nou is past the Olympic village, following the coast. This simple but very elegantly designed restaurant specialises in seafood. Pretty terrace with tables on square.

Jaume de Provença
Provença, 88
Tel: 93 430 0029
Classic Catalan and international cooking.

La Balsa
Infanta Isabel, 4
Tel: 93 211 5048
Prize-winning restaurant of classy wood and glass design with views of surrounding greenery in up-town Barcelona. Terraces for dining al fresco. International cuisine.

La Venta
Plaça Doctor Andreu
Tel: 93 212 6455
Attractively decorated building and leafy terrace at the foot of the funicular to Tibidabo. Perfect for springtime lunches or summer nights.

O'Nabo de Lugo
Pau Claris, 169
Tel: 93 215 3047
Excellent Galician seafood.

Real Club Nàutico de Barcelona
Moll d'Espanya
Tel: 93 221 6508
A large restaurant at the port.

Since it's almost all-round glass there are extremely good views. This is a high-class place: the King of Spain is a fairly regular customer, along with others from the boating world.

Roig Robí
Seneca, 20
Tel: 93 218 9222
At the upper end of the expensive category, a beautifully subtle, elegant space with a terrace, and food and service to match.

Price Guide

Price for a 3-course meal for one person, including service charge and house wine:

€€€€ = €55 and over
€€€ = €30–55
€€ = €18–30
€ = under €18

Set Portes
Passeig Isabel II, 14
Tel: 93 319 3033
Over 150 years old and sympathetically restored, recapturing the original atmosphere. A classic, popular for family Sunday lunches. Specialises in rice dishes, one for each day of the week. Also has the advantage of remaining open through the afternoon and evening until 1am.

MODERATE (€€)

A Contraluz
Milanesat, 19
Tel: 93 203 0658
In a quiet street in the residential Tres Torres area (en route to the Museu-Monestir de Pedralbes), this house and garden is a relaxing place to dine. Makes a refreshing change from the downtown heat, dust and noise. Try their reasonably-priced *menú del día* at lunch time.

Agua
Passeig Marítim, 30
Tel: 93 225 1272
About as near as you'll get to eating

on the beach in Barcelona, this is a fun place to eat fish, especially at lunchtime. Book early for the terrace, especially at weekends.

Agut
Gignás, 16
Tel: 93 315 1709
Bright, noisy, always busy restaurant with comfortable yet jovial atmosphere. Good for getting the "Barcelona feel" and for succulent Catalan specialities.

Antigua Casa Solé
Sant Carles, 4
Tel: 93 221 5012.
In the heart of Barceloneta, literally and metaphorically, and a favourite with locals. Great seafood and fish at traditional marble tables.

Bilbao
Perill, 33
Tel: 93 458 9624
Very animated atmosphere in this traditional eatery in Gràcia, frequented mainly by journalists, artists and writers. Especially busy at lunchtime.

Café de l'Academia
Lladó, 1
Tel: 93 315 0026
Nouvelle Catalan cooking, well presented. Warm interior with pleasant art on the stonework walls. Part of a medieval building in pretty square in the Barri Gòtic, with outdoor tables in the summer. Good value.

Carpanta
Sombrerers, 13
Tel: 93 319 9999
Located in a narrow street to one side of the Santa María del Mar church. Catalan food in a completely modernist interior.

El Caballito Blanco
Mallorca, 196
Tel: 93 453 1033
Another old-fashioned, popular place which always has a large number of international and Catalan dishes to choose from. Ingredients are selected from what is in season.

El Salón
Hostal del Sol, 6
Tel: 93 315 2159
Inspiring and delicious food which draws from a variety of sources, resulting in imaginative

combinations. Warm and pretty candle-lit space, decked out with old-style Spanish furniture.

El Suquet de L'Almirall
Pg Juan de Borbón, 65
Tel: 93 221 62 33
Comfortable and tatefully decorated restaurant, where the Mediterranean food is not so much about elaborate concoctions as how well the basic ingredients are prepared.

Flash-Flash
Granada del Penedès, 25
Tel: 93 237 0990
Wonderful 1960s white leatherette seating and black and white Warhol-type prints on the walls. A great place for tortillas (the speciality, of which they have a wide range), sandwiches and snacks if you are hanging around "mid-town".

Ponsa
Enric Granados, 89
Tel: 93 453 7674
Also a classic. Old-fashioned good taste and great food, in a quieter street of the Eixample.

Santa Maria
Comerç, 17
Tel: 93 315 1227
A popular place offering an unusual way of eating in this city. On the menu are extremely dainty but delectable little plates of oriental and Mediterranean extraction. The idea is to treat the tastebuds rather than to gorge.

Senyor Parellada
Argentería, 37
Tel: 93 310 5094
A mixture of unusual and classic Catalan dishes in a sophisticated, very pleasant environment.

Silenus
Angeles, 8
Tel: 93 302 2680
A good-looking, comfortable and artsy café/restaurant with a selection of Mediterranean and international dishes. In warm weather there are tables outside in the pretty tree-lined street near MACBA.

Taktika Berri
Valencia, 169
Tel: 93 453 4759
Basque delights in a modernist building, once a textile workshop.

Tragaluz
Pge. Concepció, 5
Tel: 93 487 0196
In a charming passageway off
Passeig de Gràcia, and a wonderful
example of Barcelona design. The
enormous skylight, which lends its
name to the restaurant, gives the
impression of eating on a light, airy
terrace.

INEXPENSIVE (€)

The following are especially good
(and economical) at lunchtime:
Can Culleretes
Quintana, 5
Tel: 93 317 3022
The second-oldest restaurant in
Spain, founded in 1785 and full of
character, with paintings and photos
of famous visitors throughout.
Can Tripas
Sagués, 16
Tel: 93 200 7642
Cheap, cheerful and crowded: a
paradox amid the elegant shops of
the Diagonal/Plaça Francesc Macià
area.
Casa Joana
Major de Sarriá, 59
Tel: 93 203 1036
Very good value for this generally
expensive part of town. A cosy,
family-run restaurant serving
traditional recipes.
Egipte
La Rambla, 79
Tel: 93 317 7480
Once behind the Boqueria market, a
popular, lively place that has grown
from being a small market
restaurant into several well
decorated floors.
El Gran Café
Avignon, 9
Tel: 93 318 7986
A splendid, classic old restaurant,
expensive unless you order the set
lunch menu.
Kasparo
Plaça Vicenç Martorell
Tel: 93 302 2072
Charming terrace bar in secluded
square just off the Ramblas.
Delicious and cosmopolitan light
snacks. Play area in the square for
children.

La Cassola
Sant Sever, 3
Tel: 93 318 1580
Family run restaurant, with good
home-made Catalan food.
La Llotja de les Drassanes Reials
Avinguda Drassanes
Tel: 93 302 6402
Part of the medieval building in
which the Maritime Museum is
housed. A choice setting for dining
on Catalan specialities.
La Singular
Francisco Giner, 50
Tel: 93 237 5098
A wonderful little restaurant in
Gràcia, with a warm environment,
friendly atmosphere and great
cooking using seasonal local
produce.

Price Guide

Price for a 3-course meal for one
person, including service charge
and house wine:

€€€€ = €55 and over
€€€ = €30–55
€€ = €18–30
€ = under €18

Madrid-Barcelona
Aragó, 282
Tel: 93 215 7026
A fun, bustling place to lunch on
Catalan-Spanish food, just off
Passeig de Gràcia.
Rodrigo
Argenteria
Tel: 93 310 3020
Another endearing, busy, family-run
restaurant. Delicious food.
Romesco
Arc de Sant Agustí
No phone
The dazzling fluorescent lighting
deters no-one. Popular prices for
good food. Famous for its *frijoles* –
an entire meal on a single plate,
consisting of black beans, rice,
minced meat in a sauce, fried egg
and fried banana!
Turia
Petxina, 7
Tel: 93 317 9509
Traditional food and fresh, seasonal
produce. Traditional style and décor

also. Inexpensive at lunch time if
you have the *menu del día*. The kind
of place where anyone can be
found: high-flying professionals,
actors and civil servants.

World Cuisine

If you don't want to eat
Spanish/Catalan, there's an
increasing range of food from other
parts of the world served in the many
restaurants in the maze of streets of
the Gràcia area and in the Old Town.

American

From **Hard Rock Café** in Plaça de
Catalunya to **Planet Hollywood** in
the Olympic Village, American
chains and fast food outlets are
invading Barcelona.

Greek

Dionisus €
Torrent de l'Olla, 144
Tel: 93 237 3417
If you feel like a supper (or lunch) of
Greek roast lamb with all the
trimmings, here's where you'll find
the genuine article. You can visit
this branch in Gràcia, or the
tastefully designed new one with
the same name in Avinguda de
L'Argentera, 27, opposite the
Estació de França.

Italian

La Verónica €
Avinyó 30
Tel: 93 412 1122
Colourful, modern space designed
for a colourful, modern crowd in the
heart of the old city. The terrace is
a popular meeting place for lunch
(there's a *menú del día*) or supper.
Delicious creations with local fresh
produce used to make pizzas and
excellent salads.

Japanese

Koyuki €
Córcega, 242
Tel: 93 237 8490
This is one of the simplest but best
among the growing number of
Japanese restaurants in the city,
less expensive than most and
frequented by comic-reading
Japanese.

Lebanese
Amir de Nit €
Plaça del Sol, 2
Tel: 93 218 5121
There are quite a few Lebanese places in Barcelona. This one is excellent, has a large choice of well-prepared dishes and the advantage of a great location. You can eat outside at the tables in one corner of this popular square in Gràcia.

Mexican
Mex & Cal €
Aribau, 50
Tel: 93 323 4316
The best place to eat à la Baja California. Authentic and tasty nachos, burritos, plus cocktails. Attractive and animated atmosphere.

Moroccan
La Rosa del Desierto €
Plaça Narcís Oller, 7
Tel: 93 237 4590
Pioneers of Moroccan cooking in Barcelona serving extremely good couscous.

Pakistani
Shalimar €
Carme, 71
Tel: 93 329 3496
Above average (for Barcelona) Pakistani and Indian cooking, at a reasonable price.

Paraguayan
El Paraguayo €
Parc, 1
Tel: 93 302 1441
A magnet for passionate carnivores but this restaurant has a lot more besides delicious grilled meat. Not least, it always has a lively atmosphere.

Peruvian
Peimong €
Templaris, 6
Tel: 93 318 28 73
A small, very simple restaurant just behind Plaça Sant Jaume serving authentic *ceviche* and other Peruvian specialities, including Peruvian beers and Inca Kola.

Syrian
Xix Kebab €
Córcega, 193
Tel: 93 321 8210
Soothing atmosphere and delicate, very tasty food.

Regional Clubs

Barcelona has 85 clubs run by and for people from other regions of Spain. They usually have restaurants open to the public at midday. As well as being very good value places to eat these clubs give a glimpse of life in the rest of the country. Among them are the **Hogar Extremeño** (Extremadura) at the bottom of Avinguda Portal de l'Angel, the **Centro Murciano** (Murcia) in Carrer de Portaferrissa, and the **Casa de Madrid** at Carrer de Ausias Marc, 37.

Vegetarian Food

Biocenter €
Pintor Fortuny, 25
You can choose between an enormous, nutritious *menú del día* (4 courses) or a substantial *plato combinado*. Either way you will enjoy a hearty meal, in surroundings where everyone always seems to be in a good mood.

Comme Bio €
Via Layetana, 28
Tel: 93 319 8968
Upstairs are two restaurants (day-time and evening); downstairs an eat-as-much-as-you-want buffet. There are also two shops: one for organic groceries, and one open 'til late. Comme-Bio II is in Gran Via, 603.

Fresc Co €
Carme, 16
Tel: 93 301 6837
Latest in this chain of attractive salad and pasta bars with the irresistible offer of eat till you burst.

Juicy Jones €
Cardenal Casañas, 7
Tel: 93 302 4330
Right by the Ramblas is this small vegetarian/vegan restaurant and juice bar, a reflection of how Barcelona is absorbing outside influences. Great juices. Open 1–11pm.

Mama Café €
Doctor Dou, 10
Tel: 93 301 2940
Neither strictly vegetarian nor strictly organic but a wide selection of both options available. An aesthetically pleasing place, in line with what's in fashion in other major cities. Open for lunch – when you can get a *menú del diá* – and evenings for supper or just a drink.

Snacks, Light Meals

Café de l'Estiu
Plaça Sant Iu, 5–6
Refreshments and light snacks in a lovely courtyard next to the entrance to the Museu Frederic Marès. Open March–September.

Café Textil
Montcada, 12
Accessory to the Museu Textil and shop. The café has tables indoors but also occupies the beautiful patio of this Gothic palace. An international type of light meal is available: salads, quiches and so on. Refreshments at any time of day.

Can Conesa
Llibreteria, 1
Occupies a tiny corner of the Plaça de Sant Jaume. Toasted *bocatas* are their speciality. Cheap, simple and very good.

La Cerería
Baixada de Sant Miquel, 3
If you want something more substantial for breakfast than *cafè amb llet* and a sugary pastry as fuel for stomping around the city, this is a wise choice. In this "wholemeal" environment (it's a co-op) you can select from a large range of home-made milk-shakes, cakes, sandwiches – the list is endless and is all delicious. It's open from 9am through to 10pm, so you can have lunch or supper.

Mora
Avinguda Diagonal, 409
If you're on a "shop until you drop" spree in the Eixample, Mora is a good place to drop (into) for coffee, cakes, tapas, a lunch or just a drink.

It's versatile, civilised and unique in personality. Their window displays are always beautiful pieces of design.

Mordisco

Rosselló, 265

Just off Passeig de Gràcia, this very pleasant day-time café has an adjoining restaurant. The café turns into a place to have supper in the evenings. The design has definitely got the Barcelona stamp – friendly, with a sense of humour.

Cafés

You don't have to look for a place to drink coffee in Barcelona – there are bars everywhere. The most popular ways to drink coffee are: *cafè sol* (black expresso coffee), *cafè amb llet* (white coffee) and *cafè tallat* (a small glass of strong coffee with just a dash of milk).

If you don't fancy a traditional Catalan bar, there are now a lot of café chains – such as Caffe di Roma and Café Jamaica – to choose from; but their branches don't have much individual character. If you want charm, try the following:

Cafè de l'Opera

La Rambla, 74

Opposite the Liceu opera house, an all-time favourite shared by locals and visitors. Traditional and old-fashioned. Has a summertime terrace on the Ramblas.

Cafè del Pí

Plaça del Pí

Tables outside most of the year in the leafy square. As well as coffee and other drinks, the tapas are

Horchata

In the summer, ask in bars for *horchata*, a cold drink made from pulverised *chufas* (tiger nuts) mixed with water and sugar.

Planellas Donat (Avinguda Portal d'Angel, 27) and other *horchaterías* in the same street make their own *horchata*, *granizados* (iced, fruit-flavoured drinks) and ice-creams. In the winter they sell their own *turrón* (see Shopping, page 276).

good. If you can't find a free table here there are plenty more cafés with outdoor tables in the neighbouring squares.

Cafè Zürich

Pelai, 39

A city institution, the Cafè Zürich in the El Triangle shopping mall on Plaça de Catalunya has retained its original flavour after restoration.

Escribá

La Rambla, 83

This most famous of Barcelona's famous *modernista* patisseries has a litle café at the back and outdoor tables so that you can enjoy its excellent cakes *in situ*.

Foix

Plaça de Sarriá, 12

Another very select establishment which makes art in the form of chocolates and patisserie to swoon over. There are two outlets in upper Barcelona. In this one you can also sit down for coffee.

Tapas Bars

Tapas are not a Catalan tradition but most foreign visitors don't know this or care. Due to the demand, there is a large number of tapas bars in the city. Passeig de Gràcia, no longer quite as elegant as it was, caters to this fast consumerism. It is lined with "mega" tapas bars, some better than others, but all looking pretty much alike.

Elsewhere, among the longer-standing and better quality tapas bars are:

Can Tomàs

Major de Sarriá, 49

Down-to-earth and very popular bar famous for Catalan *patates bravas* and other tapas.

Estrella de Plata

Plaça del Palau

Supreme tapas. Not cheap but money extremely well spent.

Euskal Etxea

Montcada, 1–3

Tel: 93 310 2185

Basque tapas bars are springing up rapidly, but this one is firmly established. At specific serving times a vast spread of goodies is laid out before you. You can feast

Granjas

In the olden days *granjas* were milk suppliers which kept cows on the premises. The cattle have gone but these cafés still sell dairy produce. In the winter you might order *xocolata*, a chocolate drink as thick as custard into which sponge cake is dipped. You may see some of the *granjas'* older customers order a plate of whipped cream. Some *granjas* in the old quarter are:

Viader

Xuclá, 4

Xocoa

Petrixol, 11

La Granja

Banys Nous, 4

merrily for as long as they last. Own up afterwards to how many you have scoffed and you will be charged accordingly.

José Luis

Avinguda Diagonal, 520

Elevated prices worth paying for sophisticated, well prepared tapas amidst an up-town crowd.

Montesquieu

Mandri, 56

Very mixed clientele in this well known, lively, exuberant place up-town with very good tapas of all kinds.

Mundial

Plaça Sant Agustí Vell, 1

Especially good for shellfish. Another old treasure of a place worth visiting, but try not to get lost in the maze of little streets in which it stands. If you do get lost, look as though you know where you're going and watch your bag.

Roble

Lluis Antúnez, 7

Tel: 93 218 7387

Also well known for its paella, which is served at Thursday lunchtime and for which you must book. Bustling atmosphere of a local bar.

Sol Soler

Plaça del Sol, 13

Good alternative tapas in attractive environment of ceramic tiles and marble tables. Relaxed atmosphere in the evening.

Wine, Cava & Apéritifs

Can Paixano
Reina Cristina, 7
Wild and wonderful bar in a neon-lit import-export niche crammed with shoppers looking for the best electrical goods bargains. As you enter this cavernous bar full of hanging hams, don't think of standing comfortably because you will be packed together with everyone else trying to order the extraordinarily good (and cheap) *chistorras, chorizos* and other meat or cheese *bocatas*, to go with a glass of cava.

El Xampanyet
Montcada, 22
Near Passeig del Born and Picasso Museum. Pretty ceramic-tiled bar that serves a fizzy white wine of the same name. Perfect for an apéritif with anchovies.

La Bodeguita
Rambla de Catalunya, 100
Almost an antique. Spain was once full of such *bodegas*, with massive old fridges, where you could buy wine or sit at marble tables and nibble olives, *tacos de manchego* and *jamon serrano* while you sip a full-bodied *vino tinto*. Here you still can.

La Viña del Senyor
Plaça Santa María, 5
A civilized way to begin the evening, you may select from a wide range of choice cavas and interesting wines served in this very pleasant bar.

Pla de la Garsa
Assaonadors, 13
A serene and intimate candle-lit wine and cava bar where cheeses and patés with *pan tomàquet* are served.

Culture

Cultural Events

The combination of Catalonia's rich cultural heritage and the dynamism of contemporary movements has made Barcelona one of Europe's cultural capitals. In 2004, a Universal Forum of Cultures will be held in and around the city, and across the world by Internet. Apart from its architecture and 46 museums, there is a busy calendar of music and arts festivals, opera, visiting exhibitions and constant activity in design, theatre and the arts in general, to say nothing of daily performances from street artists in the Ramblas and small squares of the Barri Gòtic.

Posters, banners, the daily and weekly press all herald what's on. The City Council has a Cultural Information Centre in the Palau de la Virreina, Rambla, 99 *(see below)*, which is very helpful and has leaflets and information on nearly all cultural activities. It also sells tickets. The Generalitat also has a cultural information centre (closed at lunchtime) at base of Centre d'Art Santa Mònica *(see below)*. The tourist information office in Plaça Catalunya sells tickets at half-price on the day of a performance. Also two of the savings banks have an efficient system for ticket sales:
Tel-Entrada of the Caixa de Catalunya, tel: 902 101 212
Servi-caixa of "la Caixa", in most branches of the bank.
Tel: 902 33 22 11
www.servicaixa.com

Exhibition Centres

The following centres regularly hold temporary exhibitions of the visual arts. Consult local press for details:

Centre d'Art Santa Mònica
Rambla Santa Mònica, 7
Tel: 93 316 2810
www.cultura.gencat.es
Caixa Forum cultural centre of "la Caixa" Foundation
Avinguda Marques de Comillas, 6–8
Tel: 93 476 8600/902 223 040.
Centre de Cultura Contemporània de Barcelona (CCCB)
Montalegre, 5
Tel: 93 306 4100
www.cccb.org
Seminars and a range of activities as well as installations, exhibitions of contemporary art, and film and music festivals.
Fundació Caixa de Catalunya,
Provença 261, La Pedrera
Tel: 93 484 5995
www.caixacat.es/cccc
Apart from all the Gaudí works, there are free temporary shows on first floor.
Fundació Antoni Tapies
Aragó, 255
Tel: 93 487 0315.
Permanent collection of work by the artist himself plus very good shows on other themes and by other internationally acclaimed artists. It has a beautiful art library upstairs.
Palau de la Virreina
Rambla, 99
Tel: 93 301 7775
www.ben.es/icub
Cultural information centre run by the city council: exhibition space, often photographic.

Art Galleries

Art galleries are usually open Tues–Sat 10.30am–1.30pm and 4.30–8.30pm. They tend to be congregated into three areas of the city. In rough order of importance these are as follows:

On the Passeig de Gràcia, the Rambla de Catalunya and on interconnecting streets (notably Consell de Cent):
Ambit, Consell de Cent, 282.
Carles Taché, Consell de Cent, 290.
Galería Alejandro Sales, Julian Romea, 16.
Galería Senda, Consell de Cent, 292.
Galería Estrany, Passatge Mercader, 18.

Music Hall and Cabaret

Barcelona has a long and colourful tradition of show business, centred on the Paral.lel area. The shows, the surrounding bars, the characters involved, all provide a sharp contrast to the high design and yuppiedom of the Eixample and upper parts of town. Sadly, with reducing demand, theatres are in decline. The most famous, El Molino, has been forced to shut, although campaigners are striving to re-open it. However, for a global view of Barcelona check in the listings what's on and try a show:

Café Concert Llantiol, Riereta, 7
Tel: 93 329 9009.
City Hall, Rambla de Catalunya, 2
Tel: 93 317 2177.
Teatre Arnau, Avinguda Paral.lel, 60
Tel: 93 441 4881.

Joan Prats, Rambla de Catalunya, 54.
Kreisler, Valencia, 262.
    In the old town around Plaça San Josep Oriol (classical), in the Born (contemporary) and in El Raval district, near the MACBA:
Antonio de Barnola, Palau, 4.
Ferran Cano, Plaça dels Angels, 4.
Metrònom, Fusina, 9.
Sala Artur Ramon, Palla, 23.
Trama, Petritxol, 8.
Urània, Doctor Dou, 19.
    In the streets behind Plaça Francesc Macià:
Fernando Alcolea, Plaça Sant Gregori Taumaturg, 7.
Lucia Homs, Avinguda Diagonal, 505.

Music and Dance

CLASSICAL MUSIC

A busy season of concerts by the Orquestra Sinfónica de Barcelona i Nacional de Catalunya (OBC) and visiting orchestras and soloists runs from September to early July. The Festival de Música Antigua (tel: 902 223 040) is held in April and May, and various international music festivals take place outside Barcelona in July and August, including the notable Festival de Peralada, Girona (tel: 93 280 5868).
    Barcelona's various arts festivals also include classical music. Among them is one for 20th-century music in October (tel: 93 301 7775) and the Festival de Guitarra de Barcelona in June (tel: 902 101 212/93 232 6167).

    The main places to hear classical music are:
Auditori Municipal
Plaça de les Arts.
A new, huge music auditorium in the Plaça de les Glories complex.
Caixa Forum (see page 72)
Palau de la Música Catalana
Sant Francesc de Paula, 2
Tel: 93 268 1000.
If you have an opportunity to go to a concert in this extravagant modernist concert hall by Domènech i Montaner, go – whatever the programme.

CONTEMPORARY MUSIC

CCCB
Montalegre, tel: 93 412 0781.
Fundació Miró
Montjuïc
Tel: 93 329 1908.
This gallery hosts a season of 20th-century music, with particular emphasis on Catalan composers.

JAZZ

The Terrassa Jazz Festival in the spring and the Barcelona International Jazz Festival in the autumn gather together some leading names. In addition there is a jazz festival in the Old Town, Ciutat Vella from mid-October to mid-December, and regular jazz and blues sessions in an ever-increasing number of venues. To name a few:

Harlem Jazz Club
Comtessa de Sobradiel, 8.
Jamboree Jazz and Dance Club
Plaça Reial, 17.
Jazzman, Roger de Flor, 238.
Jazz Sí Club, Requesens, 2.
La Cova del Drac, Vallmajor, 33.

ROCK/POP

Barcelona is on the itinerary of most major international tours. Booking for these is usually through banks and music shops, notably in Carrer de Tallers, just off the Ramblas. FNAC in the Triangle shopping centre at Plaça Catalunya sells tickets for most of the well known groups performing. On a smaller scale, some interesting off-beat musicians and eternal old timers often pass through. Check the listings. Some key venues:
Bikini, Deu i Mata, 105. People still talk of *the* Bikini (on another site) where anyone who was anyone went. It re-opened here a few years ago and now has a well selected, varied programme of live music – roots, soul and dance music.
Garatge Club, Pallars, 195. Fairly heavy-duty hardcore garage, rock and indie.
Luz de Gas, Muntaner, 246. Formerly a music hall. A pretty place for concerts of many descriptions: jazz, ethnic, rock, soul and so on. It turns into a dance place later on but by then you can consider going elsewhere – it's not their forté.
Palau Sant Jordi, Montjuïc.
Razzmatazz, Almogàvers, 122. Important venue. The former Zeleste repackaged and relaunched. Different spaces including a club.
Sala Apolo, Nou de la Rambla, 113. Once a music hall, now a trendy club with music from visiting DJs as well as live events.

SALSA

Antilla Barcelona, Aragó, 141–143.
Sabor Cubano, Francisco Giner, 32.
Samba Brasil, Lepant, 297.

CELTIC

The city's Irish pubs nearly all have live music sessions. Check the local listings.

OPERA & BALLET

Gran Teatre del Liceu, Rambla, 51–59, tel: 93 485 9913/902 332 211 (tickets). Barcelona's opera house re-opened in 1999 having been rebuilt after a devastating fire. Despite better technology and more productions, it is still difficult to get tickets.

CONTEMPORARY DANCE

Local companies and visiting groups perform sporadically throughout the year. An important part of the Mercat de les Flors programme, contemporary dance can also be seen at:
L'Espai
Travessera de Gràcia, 63
Tel: 93 414 3133.
Season's at the Liceu (above) and the Teatre Nacional (below) and outdoor locations during festivals.

Theatre

Naturally most theatre productions are in Catalan or Spanish, but for true enthusiasts the theatrical experience should compensate for language problems.
Among the main theatres are:
Artenbrut
Perill, 9–11.
Another small-scale cosy theatre with an interesting programme.
Circol Maldà
Pi, 5, Pral. 2ª
Intimate space in old palace for theatre, music and cabaret.
Lliure
Montseny, 47
Tel: 93 218 9251.
Good contemporary productions from the theatre's own company.
Malic
Fussina, 3
Tel: 93 310 7035.

Minute space for theatre and puppetry. Excellent.
Mercat de les Flors
Lleida, 59
Tel: 93 318 8599.
This is the former flower market converted into a theatre complex. It has a very active programme with many visiting international groups and unusual productions.
Poliorama
Rambla, 115
Tel: 93 318 8181.
Romea
Hospital, 51
Tel: 93 310 5504.
Teatre Nacional de Catalunya
Plaça de les Arts

Traditional Festivals

Every district (barri) of Barcelona has its own annual fiesta, known as the Festa Major, centred on its own patron saint. These usually last several days.
The sardana, the national dance of Catalonia, can also be seen every Sunday in Plaça Sant Jaume at 7pm (6.30pm in winter), and in the Plaça Catedral on Sundays at noon.
Gegants (giants) and cap grossos (comic characters with large heads) parade the streets and usually reunite in the evening at a Grand Ball in one of the public squares.
Castellers usually perform during fiestas. These acrobatic troupes erect human towers capped with the youngest and smallest.
All these things also feature in the traditional fiestas that are celebrated all over Barcelona:
Christmas. During early December the Santa Llùcia Fair of arts and crafts plus Christmas trees is held in the streets around the Cathedral.
Sant Esteve (St Stephen's Day), 26 Dec. Families meet for an even larger meal than on the 25th.
Reis Mags, Epiphany, 6 Jan. Children receive presents from the Three Kings, though modern commerce now indulges them in presents at Christmas as well. In

Tel: 93 246 0041.
Ricardo Bofill's ostentatious monument posing as a Greek temple is located next to the new auditorium near Plaça de les Glories. It has the space for large-scale productions and workshops.
Victoria
Avinguda Paral.lel, 67.
Often has musicals, ballet and flamenco spectacles.

Cinema

Barcelona has a great cinema-going tradition. Several cinemas show "version original" films (VO in listings) – foreign films that

Barcelona the Kings arrive from the orient by boat.
Carnival (Carnestoltes), Feb or Mar. Wild pre-Lent celebrations close with the "Burial of the Sardine" on Ash Wednesday, a riotous mock funeral. The most extravagant Carnival parades are at Sitges, on the coast.
Sant Jordi, 23 April. A traditional Catalan festival, St George's Day, is also now World Book Day, on which men give a rose to their lady, and receive a book in return.
Fira de Sant Ponç, 11 May. Aromatic and medicinal herbs, crystallised fruit and honey are sold in Carrer de l'Hospital.
Sant Joan, 23–24 June. Midsummer's Night, the eve of the Feast of St John, is a big event in Catalonia. It is celebrated with fireworks, cava and coca, a Catalan cake made with pine nuts and crystallised fruit.
Diada de Catalunya, 11 Sep. Catalonia's national day is less a traditional fiesta than an occasion for political demonstrations and national anthems.
The Feast of La Mercè, 24 Sep. Barcelona's main fiesta is held in honour of the city's patron saint. A week of merriment is crowned by the correfoc, a nocturnal procession of devils and fire breathing dragons.

have been subtitled rather than dubbed.

Most sessions begin around 4pm. The last and most popular screening will be around 10.30pm, although sometimes at weekends there will be a late-night show *(sesion de madrugada)*.

Alexis, Rambla de Catalunya, 90.
Boliche, Avinguda Diagonal, 508.
A cinema with 4 screens.
Casablanca, Passeig de Gràcia, 115
Filmoteca de la Generalitat de Catalunya
AvingudaSarrià, 33.
A film theatre showing less commercial films and retrospectives.
Icària-Yelmo
Salvador Espriu, 61. 15 screens.
Maldà, Pi, 5.
Méliès Cinemas
Villaroel, 102. Golden oldies.
Renoir-Les Corts
Eugeni d'Ors, 12. 6 screens.

Hot Artists

Catalonia has a long tradition of theatrical talent from Margarita Xirgu, actress and Lorca's collaborator, to Nuria Espert, internationally renowned both for her performances and her directing.

Outstanding among the contemporary performers are Josep Maria Flotats and the refreshingly satirical Albert Boadellas with his brilliant company Els Joglars. Els Comediants, based in Canet de Mar up the coast, make colourful shows to celebrate key events.

The avant-garde company, La Fura dels Baus, became internationally famous in the 80s with theatre to shock; not surprisingly they have lost some of their raw edge and are diversifying into film and opera.

On a lighter level, and sometimes to be found in the streets of Barcelona, are La Cubana group – offering satirical and fun entertainment. El Tricicle, meanwhile, is a team of three performing mime artists.

Verdi, Verdi, 32. And, around the corner, **Verdi Park**, Torrijos, 49. Together they have 9 screens. Interesting and reliable selection.

Arts Festivals

The Grec Festival, held from late June until early August, is Barcelona's biggest summer cultural event. It brings together a high standard of national and international talent in theatre, music and dance. Performances take place all over the city, but one of the most impressive and appealing venues on a summer night is the Grec Theatre itself, an outdoor amphitheatre on Montjuïc. For information and booking: Palau de la Virreina, Rambla, 99, tel: 93 301 7775 or call the city council information service, tel: 010.

The **Sitges Festival Internacional de Cinema de Catalunya** is a well established annual event every October (tel: 93 415 3938).

Nightlife

A Night on the Town

The first thing to understand about nightlife in Barcelona is that night means night, and, in terms of clubs, nothing really gets going until after 1am.

For an authentic Barcelona night out, start to think about cocktails around 9pm and dinner, at a leisurely pace, from 10-ish. This way you will be all set to begin the *juerga* (fun/wild time) by 1am, with enough energy to keep going until at least 4am. The insistent and persistent can continue to an"Afters" bar (open until past breakfast time).

This demanding schedule is usually practised from Thursday to Saturday – though the hardy are out playing any day of the week and still miraculously make it to their offices at 9am.

Bars

Of the trendy bars which are regularly featured in international design magazines, the "in" place changes every few months when yet another one opens and becomes the bar where anybody who thinks they are anybody goes. Some are just for drinking and socialising (and being seen) and some are for drinking and dancing (and being seen). This selection is loosely divided into pre-dinner and post-dinner bars, the former including some classics which never go out of fashion and those which are pleasant at any time of day; the latter includes a number of clubs and bars which only open from 8pm at the earliest.

PRE-DINNER BARS

Almirall, Joaquim Costa, 33.
Dark, enticing old *modernista* bar.
Berimbau, Passeig del Born, 17.
Brazilian bar with stunning
caipirinhas – the Brazilian cocktail
you will never forget.
Boadas, Tallers, 1.
A classic Barcelona cocktail bar.
The cartooned figure of the original
owner watches from highly polished
walls while his elegant daughter
mixes the snappiest Martinis and
her waiters attend to your every
need. Their *mojito*, Hemingway's
Cuban favourite, is highly
recommended.
Café del Sol, Plaça del Sol.
Terrace on the square. A good start
to an evening in the Gràcia district,
with its many alternative bars and
restaurants.
La Confiteria, Sant Pau, 128.
Relaxed atmosphere and good
sounds in this pretty bar housed in
a former pastry shop.
Dry Martini, Aribau, 162.
A large but cosy cocktail bar in
which to ensconce yourself; choose
between the green room or the red.
Serves excellent Martinis.
Els Quatre Gats, Montsió, 3.
Modernista landmark, famous due to
the artists, including Picasso, who
frequented it at the turn of the 20th
century. You can eat in the restaurant
or just have drinks at the front.
Gimlet, Rec, 24.
Very cool, small cocktail bar.
Margarita Blue, Josep Anselm
Clavé, 6.
You can eat Mexican food here both
day and night but also come for
evening drinks when the place will
be buzzing.
Mirablau, Plaça Dr.Andreu (at the
foot of the Tibidabo funicular).
Has a spectacular view over
Barcelona day and night.
Pastis, Santa Mònica, 4.
More than 40 years old, this small
corner of Marseilles at the bottom
of the Ramblas offering *pastis* to
the strains of Brel and Piaf, is a
welcome alternative to the high
design and high tech of bars
elsewhere. Tango and live music
some nights.

Casinos

The Spanish are avid gamblers,
playing the various lotteries being
a favourite pasttime. If you want
to do some more serious
gambling you have the following
waiting for you:

Casino Castell de Perelada
Perelada.
Tel: 972 53 8125.
In the province of Girona, 13
miles (20 km) from the French
border.
Casino de Lloret de Mar
Girona.
Tel: 972 366116.
Gran Casino de Barcelona
Marina, 19–21.
Tel: 93 225 7878.

Rita Blue, Plaça Sant Agustí.
Even buzzier than its older sister,
Margarita Blue, serving Tex-Med
food.
Snooker Club, Roger de Lluria, 42.
Elegant, modern snooker club for a
cool cocktail or an after-dinner
drink.
Velódrom, Muntaner, 213.
An old bar in the middle of the
Eixample with high, nicotine-stained
ceilings, peeling paint and
fluorescent lighting, but which never
loses its charm or popularity.

POST-DINNER BARS

Café Royale, Nou de Zambrano, 3.
Cool lounge bar just off Plaça
Reial.
El Salero, Rec, 60
Salero means salt cellar, and its
white interior is one of the most
beautiful spaces created in the city
in recent years. Open until late.
Gimlet, Santaló, 46.
Cocktails and slick, modern design.
London Bar, Nou de la Rambla, 34.
Popular with resident foreigners and
a local crowd, this old bar with
marble counter and chandeliers
gets more crowded and smokier the
deeper you go into it. Regular live
music on the tiny stage at the back
provides entertainment.

Los Tilos, Paseo dels Til.lers, 1.
Another up-town bar with terrace
and views where you dance and
drink until 4am.
Marsella, Sant Pau, 65.
This was probably the last old bar
with "No spitting and No singing"
signs on the walls. It was popular
with the locals until some years ago
when it underwent changes. As the
old locals expired it has became
popular with a young, international
crowd. Beware the absinthe.
Nick Havanna, Rosselló, 208.
Once famed for its design and for
the in-crowd it attracted, this is no
longer the most fashionable place
to go, but it's good value and gives
an idea of the Barcelona "design
bars" of the 80s.
Rosebud, Adrià Margarit, 27.
If you want a taste of the high life,
this sohisticated place has
magnificent views and a garden.
Torres de Avila, Poble Espanyol.
An extravaganza created by
designers Arribas and Mariscal (of
Olympic mascot fame), showing
Barcelona 90s design at its zenith.
No longer as trendy as it was.
Tres Torres, Via Augusta, 300.
What was once a huge private
house is now a flashy bar and
beautifully lit building. There's no
code in this smart drinking hole but
you'll find a certain type of wealthy
clientele here.
Universal, Marià Cubí, 184.
Striking decor on three floors. Dark
and loud for dancing downstairs.
More refined upstairs where you
can dine very well or drink in plush
surroundings.

EVEN LATER BARS & CLUBS

The "music boxes" of the Port Vell,
Maremagnum and the Olympic Port
don't need much explanation. If you
are after lots of coloured lights and
pumping disco, you can just turn up
and choose for yourself, since all
are open to the street.

Club venues are ever-changing.
Check in the local listings for
what's current, or better still, ask
around.

Discotek, Poble Espanyol.
A club with a lot of action.
La Boîte, Avinguda Diagonal, 477.
A medium-sized, intimate kind of club in the form of an underground box with glittery, 70s style interior. Live bands (jazz/soul/funk etc.) from midnight. DJs play very danceable music after they finish.
Dot, Nou de Sant Francesc, 7.
Although small, Dot is very popular. In-house and visiting DJs play the best of current styles every night of the week. You can drink, dance and watch movies all at the same time.
KGB Alegre de Dalt, 55.
An old favourite going through a revival, with live music on Fridays.
Moog, Arc del Teatre, 3.
Down an alleyway off the Ramblas. This is another small place but very good for techno/electronic. You can dance until 5.30am if you so desire, and even later at weekends.
Otto Zutz, Lincoln, 15.
One of the first designer-discos. Best after 2am. Live music occasionally.
Salsitas, Nou de la Rambla, 22.
One of the latest clubs where you can eat before you dance.
La Terraza, Avinguda Marquès de Comillas. This is up on Montjúic, around the back of Poble Espanyol and a great summer venue. Dance to electronic music on the hill until the early hours of the morning, with a fashionable crowd.

Pubs

Having great success amongst ex-pats and Catalans alike is the new wave of pubs, which are a far cry from the old clichéd "English pub" of the past.
Flann O'Brien's
Casanova, 264.
An Irish pub, of course.
The Clansman
Vigatans, 13.
Scottish pub with the malts to prove it.
The Quiet Man
Marquès de Barberà, 11
An Irish pub selling draught Guinness. Good atmosphere and live music.

Tablaos

A *tablao* is a bar/restaurant that has a flamenco show. *Tablaos* are not strictly Catalan, but this import from Andalusia has become popular among Catalans to the point of being trendy. It is advisable to confirm the times of the shows and whether or not dinner is obligatory.
El Patio Andaluz
Aribau, 242.
Tel: 93 209 3378.
El Tablao Cordobés
La Rambla, 35.
Tel: 93 318 6445.
El Tablao de Carmen
Arcs, 9, Poble Espanyol
Tel: 93 325 6895.
A good authentic show and reasonable dinner.
Los Tarantos
Plaça Reial, 17.
Tel: 93 318 3067.
Stylishly refurbished. One of the most genuine shows.
Sala Rocería Los Almonteños
Elkano, 67.
Tel: 93 443 2431.

Dance Halls

Cibeles, Córsega, 363.
La Paloma, Tigre, 27
Tel: 93 301 6897.
A Barcelona classic. Orchestra plays on Thursday–Sunday nights. Sessions 6–9.30pm and 11.30pm–3.30am. Both these traditional dance halls bring in the DJs after 2am at weekends for the young crowd.

The Gay Scene

If you start off with these places you'll soon get to know where all the rest are.
Bahia, Seneca, 12.
Warm and friendly lesbian bar with good music.
Metro, Sepúlveda 185.
A well-known gay club. Best after 1.30am.

Shopping

What to Buy

As Europe rapidly becomes one entity and most goods are available in most countries, the bargain that cannot be found back home is a rarity. However, for certain products the choice is much wider, and anything bought abroad is a nice souvenir once the holiday is over.

If you can't face trudging home with virgin olive oil, or fear your holiday budget will disappear if you venture into leather at Loewe, it is still worth seeing the spectacle of the food markets and doing some serious window shopping while in Barcelona.

Shopping Areas

The entire length of Passeig de Gràcia, the Rambla de Catalunya and the interconnecting streets provide enjoyable shopping ranging from chain store to top fashion and individual boutiques. The same goes for the Barri Gòtic, now studded with artisanal shops, galleries and trendy souvenirs, and bursting with hip clothes shops. The Avinguda Diagonal, from the top of Rambla de Catalunya up to the roundabout which forms Plaça Francesc Macià (still often referred to as Calvo Sotelo) and the streets behind this Plaça, Pau Casals, Mestre Nicolau and Bori i Fontesta are good for fashion, but expensive.

The upper parts of town have their own local district atmosphere and make a refreshing change from the Eixample and Barri Gòtic. Try Carrer de Muntaner, around the Metro station and upwards. Here you'll find interesting shops and bars. One of the best shoe shops in town, Las Maravillas, is at No. 356.

Shopping Hours

Most shops open between 9 and 10am and close religiously for lunch between 1 and 2pm, opening again between 4 and 5pm until 8pm. Many clothes and food shops close at 8.30 or 9pm. The large department stores and some of the shopping galleries remain open through lunchtime. In the summer many shops will close on Saturday afternoons.

If you need a break, good wines by the glass accompany delicate snacks in the Tivoli at No. 361.

Department Stores and Shopping Malls

The largest department store in Barcelona is **El Corte Inglés**, with two branches in Plaça de Catalunya, another in nearby Portal de l'Angel specialising in leisure, music, books sports, and others in Avinguda Diagonal. All branches are open Monday–Saturday 10am–10pm.

The main shopping centres and malls are:

La Avenida
Rambla de Catalunya, 121.
Barcelona Glòries
Plaça de les Glòries.
Bulevard Rosa (3 locations)
Passeig de Gràcia, 55; Diagonal, 474; Diagonal, 609–615. Smaller, more individual shops.
Diagonal Mar
Avinguda Diagonal, 3.
Another huge complex opened at the end of 2001 in new residential district by the sea with the usual shops. Large play area for kids.
Galeries Maldà
Portaferrissa, 22.
L'Illa
Avinguda Diagonal, 545.
Superior shopping centre for the uptown crowd.
Maremagnum
Moll d'Espanya.
Shops here are open until 11pm.

For out-of-hours shopping the best bets are:

7–11
Plaça Urquinaona.
Open 7am until 3am every day. Good for Sunday shopping.
El Triangle
A large development in Plaça de Catalunya including Habitat and FNAC (huge book and music store).
VIP's
Rambla de Catalunya, 7–9.
Open daily 8–2am, until 3am Thur–Sat.

Markets

There are covered markets in every district of the city selling fruit, vegetables, meat and fish. A trip to Barcelona would be incomplete without visiting at least one of them. Markets open every day except Sunday from early in the morning until around 3pm. Avoid Mondays; the selection is poor because the central wholesale market does not open on a Monday.

The largest and most colourful market is the Boqueria on the Ramblas, which stays open until 8pm Monday–Saturday. The most exotic and expensive fare is in the entrance; the bargains are to be found in the maze of stalls behind, especially from the local farmers in the adjoining Plaça Sant Galdric.

Book and antique fairs are held with great regularity in Barcelona: look out for posters or announcements in the press.

Other markets of interest are:
Coin and stamp market, Plaça Reial. Sunday 9am–2.30pm.
Coin, video games and book market, Mercat Sant Antoni. Sunday 9am–2pm. Attractive market building on the junction of Carrer de Tamarit/Comte d'Urgell.
Els Encants, Plaça de les Glòries.
A genuine flea market. Some expensive antiques, some old clothes, and a lot of trash, but amongst it all bargains can still be found. Very hot in the summer; early morning is better for bargains and comfort. Open: Monday, Wednesday, Friday and Saturday 8am–7pm (winter) and until 8pm (summer).

Mercat de Concepció, Valencia, between Carrer de Bruc and Carrer de Girona. In this district market you can see how Barcelona mixes new design with old.
Mercat Gòtic d'Antiguitats, Avinguda Catedral. Antique market every Thursday. Some interesting collections.
Moll de Drassanes. Weekend antiques market, by the sea.

Clothes

LEATHER

It is questionable whether leather garments are still worth buying in Spain, except perhaps at the top end of the market, where design and quality are outstanding. But shoes, handbags and suitcases are worth considering. The best in clothes, bags and accessories is **Loewe**, based in Madrid but with an important and sumptuous branch in Casa Lleó Morera (Passeig de Gràcia, 35).

There are many other shops specialising in leather. **Yanko**, Passeig de Gràcia, 95, is Spanish and specialises in shoes and jackets. Nowhere near as expensive as Loewe, but still pricey.

Cheaper, often good value leather shops can be found particularly in and around the Ramblas and Portal de l'Angel, some of them in strange first-floor surroundings selling at factory prices.

SHOES

These are good value. Look out for Catalan and Spanish designers such as **Yanko**, (address above) and **Farrutx** (Roselló, 218) which trade on sophisticated elegance. **Lotusse** (contemporary classical and very well made) and **Camper** (trendy, comfortable) can be found at Tascón, Avinguda Diagonal, 462. Camper has its own shops in Pelai and Valencia, just off Passeig de Gràcia. Another local designer, **Muxart** (Rambla Catalunya, 47 or Rosselló, 230), is wild and wonderful. The best areas for shoes and bags are Portal de l'Angel, Rambla de Catalunya, Passeig de Gràcia, Diagonal and the shopping malls.

TOP FASHION

Toni Miró is by far the most famous Catalan designer of men's and women's wear, and his clothes are somehow representative of how the middle-classes like to dress. They are characterised by their clean lines and subtlety (verging on the inconspicuous or sombre). His shops called **Groc** are at Rambla de Catalunya, 100 and Carrer de Muntaner, 385. An **Antonio Miro** is at Carrer Consell de Cent, 349.

Other designer names are:
Adolfo Dominguez, Passeig de Gràcia, 32.
David Valls, València, 235.
Jean Pierre Bua, Avinguda Diagonal 469. Good range of international labels for men and women.
José Tomas, Mallorca, 242.
Josep Font, Passeig de Gràcia, 10.
Lydia Delgado, Minerva, 21.
Noténom, Pau Clarís, 159.
On Land, València, 273.
Roser i Francesc, València, 285 and Roger de Llúria, 87.

CHEAPER FASHION

The two biggest fashion stores are **Zara** and **Mango**, with branches all over the city. On and around Carrer Avinyó there are a lot of trendy shops, such as **Loft Avignon**.

In **El Mercadillo** and **Gralla Hall**, both on Portaferrisa, you can spend some happy hours flitting from shop to shop. The former is cheaper and more alternative, the latter geared more towards smarter, or club clothing. Both places were old palaces and fun to visit whether you buy or not. When you've had enough, go for a drink or meal on the terrace upstairs at the back of El Mercadillo – such inner patios are scarce and a rare treat.

Food

A taste of Spain back home always extends the holiday. Olives marinated in garlic direct from the market, sausages (*chorizo* and *sobrasada*), ham (*jabugo* is the best), cheese (Manchego, Mahon, Idiazabal), nuts, dried fruit and handmade chocolates are all easy to carry. Virgin olive oil, wine, cava and moscatel are less portable, but still worth the effort. Buy from the markets or *colmados* (grocer's shops, on street corners in every district of the city). Some prime sites for purchasing are:
Casa Gispert, Sombrerers, 23.
A lovely old shop selling dried fruits, grains and coffees in sacks, as well as preserves and other delicacies.
Colmado Quilez, Rambla de Catalunya, 63.
Another excellent, well stocked and gorgeous old shop full of delicacies.
Escribà, La Rambla, 83.
The famous chocolate "sculptor", Antoni Escribà, whose family has been in the business since 1906, runs this beautiful shop. They certainly know what they're doing.
El Magnífico, Argenteria, 64.
Experts on coffee. They stock a vast range, including the best beans.
Fargas, Boters, 2 (corner of Pi and Cucurulla).
For chocolates, sweets and *turrones* (see under Planelles Donat below). Decorative old shop .
La Seu, Dagueria, 16.
Seasonal additive-free farmhouse cheeses from all regions of Spain. The Scots owners allow you access to the walk-in fridges; let you taste before you buy; and provide printed information on every variety. What you purchase will be packed specially for travel. They also sell the best, most natural olive oils.
Múrria, Roger de Llúria, 85.
The shop name should remind you of the street name; or vice-versa. This is where you will find the most seriously exquisite selection of foodstuffs in the prettiest of old *modernista* interiors. They have their own cava label as well.
Planelles Donat, Portal de l'Angel, 27 (and other branches).
Specialists in *turrón* (a sticky nougat-type delicacy traditionally eaten at Christmas). Good ice cream in summer.

The Best of Barcelona Design

Much of Barcelona's stylish image rests upon its reputation for design. To get an idea of how trendy Barcelonans decorate their homes, all you need to do is take a trip around the first floor of **Vinçon** at Passeig de Gràcia, 96.

Other design shops in the Eixample include:
Biosca & Botey, Rambla Catalunya, 129. Noteworthy among the hordes of lighting shops.

Dom, Passeig de Gràcia, 76. Inexpensive fun design.
Dos i Una, Rosselló, 275. Smaller lines include David Valls socks, Mariscal earrings and gimmicks to help solve gift problems.
En Línea Barcelona, Còrsega, 299. Beautiful Spanish and Italian furniture.
Pilma, just around the corner in Avinguda Diagonal, 403.

Among the design shops in the old town are:
Aspectos, Rec, 28. Owner Camilla

Hamm sells tasteful furniture and accessories by both international names and new, innovative designers. Very high prices though.
Ici et Là, Plaça Santa Maria del Mar, 2. More furniture and bits and bobs which are bright, humorous, and which reflect Barcelona's wacky alter-ego.
Matirile, Passeig del Borne, 24. One-off lamps made to order, using new and re-cycled materials.
Zeta, Avinyó, 22. In the same vein – contemporary, original designs.

Drink

Vila Viniteca, Agullers, 7–9.
A magnificent range of fine wines and spirits.

Xampany, Valencia, 200.
This is for serious purchasers of cava, with more than 100 types. There are also essential cava accessories and memorabilia.

Traditional Crafts

Barcelona has many small shops specialising in traditional crafts. Whether you are looking for lace, feathers, fans or religious artefacts, there is sure to be someone somewhere making it. Or you may want to commission a guitar, walking stick or lightning conductor. The best areas to try are the Barri Gòtic, around the Born or on Carrer de l'Hospital and Carrer del Carme. Many shops are over 100 years old.

The Generalitat runs the **Centre Català d'Artesania**, Passeig de Gràcia, 55, an exhibition centre with permanent displays, temporary shows, information and a shop.

Shoes

Calçats Solé, Ample, 7. For really original footwear, sturdy leather boots, Mallorcan sandals or rustic shoes from different parts of Spain. **La Manual Alpargatera**, Avinyó, 7. Sells an infinite variety of alpargatas or espadrilles – the classic rope-soled canvas shoes of old Spain. See them being made and choose your preferred design.

Antiques and Books

There are many elegant and expensive antique shops in the Eixample and the Barri Gòtic, notably the streets Banys Nous and Palla. Prints and antique books are also a feature of Barcelona, particularly in the labyrinth of pretty streets around the Cathedral. **Librería Violán**, just off the Plaça del Rei. Unusual books, prints and striking Art Deco posters.

Candles

From religious to decorative, candles are quite a speciality of Barcelona. There are several shops near the cathedral, especially: **Cereria Subirá**, Baixada Llibreteria, 7. Founded in 1762.

Ceramics

From earthenware cooking pots to elegant dishes or hand-painted tiles, the ceramics of Catalonia and other regions of Spain can be found all over the city, particularly in the Barri Gòtic, at **Molsa** in Plaça Sant Josep Oriol (who also have some antique pots), **La Caixa de Fang** in Carrer de Freneria and **La Roda** in Carrer de Call. Traditional ironmongers (ferreterías) usually have a good collection of the classic brown-earthenware pots at non-tourist prices, as well as wonderful cooking utensils.

Wickerwork

A rustic chair may not be very manageable on a charter flight, but a basket or a mat is easy to carry and will make a good present. Look on the corner of Carrer de Banys Nous and Carrer Ave Maria. Also: **Taller de Cistelleria**, Amargós, 16. Even more manageable for transport are these miniature versions of traditional baskets from Catalunya, made by a friendly elderly lady. She also has normal- sized baskets, but the miniatures are very popular.

Lace and Fabrics

A dying art but still popular. Many old shops, with beautiful exteriors, are still dotted around the Eixample. **Casa Oliveres**, Dagueria, 11. Full of antique treasures. Specialises in lace and will produce to order. **Coses de Casa**, Plaça Sant Josep Oriol, 5. Hand-woven Mallorquín fabrics.

Dona, Provença, 256. Embroidery and embroidery kits.
Rose Mary, Calaf, 4. White linen, bedclothes, tablecloths and towels with elaborate details.
Taller de Lencería, Rosselló, 271. Linen with hand-made lace borders.

Glass

Bells i Oficis, Palla, 15. Many choice pieces. They have their own resident designers.

Export Procedure

Under current laws anyone resident outside the EU is exempt from IVA (Value Added Tax) on individual purchases worth more that €0. The IVA rate is 7 or 16 percent, according to the goods. The relevant forms to fill in for Customs on leaving and on entering one's own country will be provided by the store. Ask for details at the time of purchase. Note that the goods may be subjected to an even higher tax on return home. You can also ring Global Refund Information on 900 43 54 82. Large stores such as El Corte Inglés have a packing/despatch service.

Espai Vidre, Angels, 8. International and Spanish modern glass design plus exhibitions.

Handmade Paper and Books

Papirum, Baixada Llibreteria, 2. Handmade paper and note-books of all sizes. They are not cheap but are beautiful and make great gifts.
Tarlatana, Comtessa de Sobradiel, 2. Marbled papers and book binding.

Gloves, Shawls, Fans and Hats

Almacenes del Pilar, Boqueria, 43. Traditional mantillas and shawls.
Alonso, Santa Anna, 27. Leather (and other) gloves in the winter; fans in the summer. A beautiful little treasure trove.
Guantes Ramblas, La Rambla, 132. Maybe you'll find those leather gloves here; or a wallet or a bag.
Mil, Fontenella, 20. Supplies of old and new types of headdress.
Paraguas, La Rambla, 104. Only umbrellas and fans. How exclusive can you get!
Sombreria Obach, Call, 2. Hats of many descriptions, mainly traditional (e.g. berets). The interior is old, but paradoxically it is so functional that it seems up-to-date.

Jewellery

For more conventional or very pricey pieces, look on Passeig de Gràcia (e.g. J. Roca, at No. 18), Rambla de Catalunya or many other Eixample streets. In the centre you can find many tiny jewellery shops; often they occupy only the entrance of a building, with most of their wares in the window display. For something a bit different, try:

Forum Ferlandina, Ferlandina, 31. Avant-garde gold and silver jewellery.

Hipòtesi, Rambla Catalunya, 105. A good, varied range of fine, modern, but not ultra-modern pieces.

Joaquín Berao, Rosselló, 277. Designer items with a very individual stamp: smooth and chunky. Only the best materials used.

Knives

Ganiveteria Roca, Plaça del Pí. Impressive window displays and inside, virtually every kind of cutting instrument for domestic use. Or you might like a Spanish-style pen knife for outdoor use.

Toys

A cluster of toy shops can be found leading off either side of Plaça del Pí. The most original of these is **El Ingenio**, at Carrer Rauric, 6–8.

Bookshops

Col.legi d'Arquitectes, Plaça Nova, 5. Well supplied bookshop specialising in architecture and some design.

Documenta, Cardenal Casañas, 4. Generally good bookshop.

Kowasa, Mallorca, 235. Photography books only displayed in a chic space. Wide selection.

Laie Llibreria Café, Pau Claris, 85. A good-looking bookshop selling mostly art and media books, and literature. Has a very good café/restaurant upstairs. Also has an excellent branch in the CCCB (Contemporary Culture Centre).

Quera, Petritxol, 2. Specialists in maps of Catalonia.

Tartessos, Canuda, 35. A bit of everything but a lot of photography. The collection is cosmopolitan, and they also stage small photo shows at the back.

Sport

Participant Sports

The city council has been very active in providing sports facilities to the community. Some are the legacy of the Olympic Games.

BOWLING

AMFF
Sabino de Arana, 6
Tel: 93 330 5048.
Open: Mon–Sat 11am–2am.

Pedralbes Bowling
Avinguda Doctor Marañón, 11
Tel: 93 333 0352.
Open: 10am–2am, and until 4am on Friday/Saturday.

CYCLING

Cycling is becoming more popular in Barcelona. The city council issues a guide/map which is available in tourist offices. It shows suggested routes and bike lanes, and gives advice on taking bicycles on public transport.

Bicycles can be hired at the following places:

Al punt de trobada
Badajoz, 24
Tel: 93 225 1585.

Barcelona by Bicycle
Tel: 93 268 2105.
Accompanied cycling tours of the old town, including a meal. Cycle and skates for hire.

Bici-clot
Passeig Marítim. On the beach near Olympic village, great for waterfront bike rides.

Broadway
Avinguda Icària, 129.

Filicletos
Passeig de Picasso 40

Tel: 93 319 7885.
Bicycles, tandems, and child seats for rent. Open: weekends and holidays 10am–dusk. Easy access to Parc de la Ciutadella, port and beach.

Icària Sports
Avinguda Icaria, 180
Tel: 93 221 1778.

Scenic
Marina, 22
Tel: 93 221 1666.

GOLF

There are many courses all over Catalonia. To play it is essential to prove membership of a recognised club. Weekend fees are usually double the weekday fee. Three courses close to Barcelona are:

El Prat
El Prat de Llobregat
Tel: 93 379 0278.
A premier course, often host to international competitions. Hire of clubs and trolleys.

Sant Cugat
Sant Cugat del Vallès
Tel: 93 674 3908.
Bar, restaurant, swimming pool. Hire of clubs and trolleys. Closed on Mondays.

Terramar
Sitges
Tel: 93 894 0580.
Hire of clubs and trolleys. Open all year.

Sports Centre

Can Caralleu sports centre (tel: 93 204 6905) is in an attractive location on the hill of Tibidabo. It has tennis courts, a *frontón* (a wall against which you play the Basque game *pelota*), volley ball courts and two swimming pools.

Indoor facilities are open to the public Mon–Fri 8–10am and 2–3.30pm, Sun 10am–1pm. Outdoor facilities are open from mid-June to mid-September, 10am–5pm. Tennis courts are available 8am–11pm.

To get there, take bus 94 from Tres Torres/Via Augusta.

Swimming Pools

When you just can't face another tourist sight and the summer crowds have got too much, a dip in a pool can be the perfect antidote to city fatigue. In and around Barcelona there are plenty to choose from; here are a selection:

Banys Sant Sebastià
Plaça del Mar.
Tel: 93 221 0010.
Large indoor pool overlooking sea, and outdoor pool. Well equipped.

Parc de la Creueta del Coll
Mare de Deu del Coll, 87.
Tel: 93 211 3599.
Large outdoor pool/lake, in one of Barcelona's new urban parks, complete with Eduardo Chillida sculpture. Boats can be hired in the winter. Swimming: June to end of August Monday–Friday

10am–4pm, Sunday and holidays 10am–7pm. Ideal for small children.

Piscinas Bernat Picornell
Avingudade l'Estadi, 30–40.
Tel: 93 423 4041.
Olympic pool in a beautiful location.

Piscina Municipal Can Felipa
Pallars, 277.
Tel: 93 308 6047.
Two indoor pools in a stylishly renovated old factory – now a community centre – in Poble Nou. Easy to reach by metro.

Piscina Municipal Montjuïc
Avinguda Miramar, 31.
Tel: 93 443 0046.
Two pools with a view. The Olympic diving events took place here, against the dramatic backdrop of the city.

HORSE RIDING

Hípica Sant Cugat
Finca La Palleria, Avinguda Corts Catalanes, Sant Cugat.
Tel: 93 674 8385.
Bus from Sant Cugat to Cerdanyola will drop you off. Excursions from one hour to the whole day in the Collserola hills.

SKIING

During the season many cheap weekend excursions are available from Barcelona to the Pyrenean resorts, some of which can be reached by train (check out www.lamolina.com). Most travel agencies have information on these.

TENNIS

ClubVall Parc
Carretera. de l'Arrabassada, 97
Tel: 93 212 6789.
Courts open: 8am–midnight. Quite expensive.

WATER SPORTS

Agencia de Viajes Tuareg
Consell de Cent, 378.
For a complete change from sightseeing, hire a deluxe yacht, with or without a captain. They also offer organised boat trips near and far.

Base Nautica de la Mar Bella
Espigó del Ferrocarril
Platja de Bogatell, Avinguda Litoral
Tel. 93 221 0432.
All types of boats for hire by qualified sailors. Sailing courses for the inexperienced. Windsurf hire.

Spectator Sports

Check the weekly entertainment guides or the sports magazines, *Sport* and *El Mundo Deportivo*, for a full calendar. The daily papers also have good sports coverage.

Most local fiestas have various sporting activities as part of their programme, notably the Barcelona fiesta of La Mercé at the end of September.

American Football
The **Barcelona Dragons** play in the Olympic stadium during the summer season. The ticket booth is in Plaça Universitat or buy tickets from Servicaixa machines.

Basketball
Basketball is gaining as ardent a following as football. The "Barça" basketball team is part of the football club and matches are played in the Palau Blaugrana, next to Nou Camp, tel: 93 496 3600.

Motor Racing
A new racing track, Catalunya Circuit, was opened in 1991 about 20 km (12 miles) from Barcelona, in Montmeló. For information tel: 93 571 9700.

Tennis
The Conde de Godó trophy is an annual event at the Real Club de Tenis Barcelona, Bosch i Gimpera, 5, tel: 93 203 7852.

Football

Football is close to a religion in Barcelona. When the favourite local team "Barça" is playing you will know all about it: firstly from the traffic jams to get to the match or to the television; secondly because the town goes silent; and thirdly thanks to the explosion of fireworks, car horns and bugles following a victory.

Fútbol Club Barcelona, Arístides Maillol, tel: 93 496 3600. The stadium, Nou Camp, is one of the largest stadiums in the world, and has a museum that can be visited.

Language

Catalan

Castilian (Spanish) and Catalan are both official languages in Catalonia. In the wake of the repression of Catalan under Franco, when its use in public was forbidden, it is undergoing a resurgence encouraged by the administration, with the aim of fully implementing it in every aspect of daily life. It is often the only language used in public signs, street names, maps, leaflets and cultural information.

Catalan is a Romance language; with a knowledge of French and Spanish you should find it possible to read a little. It is spoken in Catalonia, Valencia, the Balearic Islands, Andorra, the Catalan region of Southern France and L'Alguer, a town in Sardinia.

In the rural regions outside Barcelona you may come across Catalans who cannot speak Castilian, but in the city even the most ardent Catalanista should readily respond if you communicate in Castilian, especially knowing you are a foreigner. Also, many people you meet in bars, restaurants and on public transport will be from other parts of Spain and so will be primarily Castilian speakers.

Spanish

Spanish is also a Romance language, derived from the Latin spoken by the Romans who conquered the Iberian peninsula more than 2,000 years ago. The Moors who settled in the peninsula centuries later contributed a great number of new words. Following the discovery of America, Spaniards took their language with them to the four corners of the globe. Today, Spanish is spoken by 250 million people in north, south and central America and parts of Africa.

Unlike English, Spanish is a phonetic language: words are pronounced exactly as they are spelt, which is why it is somewhat harder for Spaniards to learn English than vice versa (although Spanish distinguishes between the two genders, masculine and feminine, and the subjunctive verb form is an endless source of headaches for students). English is widely spoken in most tourist areas, but even if you speak no Spanish at all, it is worth trying to master a few simple words and phrases.

As a general rule, the accent falls on the second-to-last syllable, unless it is otherwise marked with an accent (´) or the word ends in d, l, r or z. Vowels in Spanish are always pronounced the same way. The double ll is pronounced like the y in "yes", the double rr is rolled, as in Scots. The h is silent in Spanish, whereas j (and g when it precedes

Get by in Catalan

If you want to win a Catalan's heart, here are a few expressions in the local language:
Good morning *Bon dia*
Good afternoon/evening *Bona tarda*
Good night *Bona nit*
How are you? *Com està vostè?*
Very well thank you, and you? *Molt bé, gràcies i vostè?*
Goodbye, see you again *Adéu, a reveure*
See you later *Fins després*
See you tomorrow *Fins demà*
What's your name? *Com us diu?*
My name is... *Em dic...*
Pleased to meet you *Molt de gust*
Do you have any rooms? *Per favor tenen habitacions lliures?*
I'd like an external/internal/ double room *Voldria una habitació exterior/interior/doble*
...for one/two persons *...per a una persona/dues persones*
I want a room with a bath *Vull una habitació amb bany*
I have a room reserved in the name of... *Tinc reservada una habitació a nom de...*
How much is it? *Quin és el preu?*
It's expensive *Es car*
Could I see the room? *Podria veure l'habitació?*
At what time do you serve ...? *A quina hora es pot ...?*
Breakfast/lunch/dinner *esmorzar/dinar/sopar*
How do you say that in Catalan? *Com es diu això en català?*

Speak a little more slowly, please *Parleu una mica més a poc, si us plau*
How do I get to...? *Per a anar a...?*
Is it very far/close? *Es lluny/a prop?*
Where's the nearest motor mechanic? *On és el pròxim taller de reparació?*
Can I change this traveller's cheque? *Pot canviar-me aquest xec de viatge?*
Where can I find a dentist? *On puc trobar un dentista?*
This tooth is hurting *Em fa mal aquesta dent*
Don't take it out. If possible give me something for it until I get home *No me l'extregui. Si és possible doni'm un remei fins que torni a casa*
Please call a doctor *Cridi un metge, per favor*
Where does it hurt? *On li fa mal?*
I have a bad cold *Estic molt refredat*
I want to make a phone call to... *Vull telefonar a...*
It's engaged *La línea está ocupada*
I am... I'd like to speak to Mr... *Sóc... voldria parlar amb el senyor...*
What time will he be back? *A quina hora tornarà?*
Tell him to call me at this number *Digui-li que truqui al número...*
I'll be in town until Saturday *Seré a la ciutat fins dissabte*

an e or i) is pronounced like a guttural h (as if you were clearing your throat).

When addressing someone you are not familiar with, use the more formal "usted". The informal "tu" is reserved for relatives and friends.

Spanish Words and Phrases

yes *sí*
no *no*
please *por favor*
thank you (very much) *(muchas) gracias*
you're welcome *de nada*
excuse me *perdóneme*
OK *bién/vale*
Hello *Hola*
How are you? *¿Cómo está usted?*
How much is it? *¿Cuánto es?*
What is your name? *¿Cómo se llama usted?*
My name is... *Yo me llamo...*
Do you speak English? *¿Habla inglés?*
I am British/American *Yo soy británico(a)/norteamericano(a) (for women)*
I don't understand *No comprendo*
Please speak more slowly *Hable más despacio, por favor*
Can you help me? *¿Me puede ayudar?*
I am looking for... *Estoy buscando...*
Where is...? *¿Dónde está...?*
I'm sorry *Lo siento*
I don't know *No lo se*
No problem *No hay problema*
Have a good day *Que tenga un buen día, or Vaya con Dios*
That's it *Ese es*
Here it is *Aquí está*
There it is *Allí está*
Let's go *Vámonos*
See you tomorrow *Hasta mañana*
See you soon *Hasta pronto*
goodbye *adiós*
Show me the word in the book *Muéstreme la palabra en el libro*
At what time? *¿A qué hora?*
When? *¿Cuándo?*
What time is it? *¿Qué hora es?*

Further Reading

Good Companions

Translated Catalan works of literature are few; they are difficult to find in Barcelona and are probably more available in languages other than English.

Barcelona, Robert Hughes, Harvill Press, 2001. Describes the city's development in relation to the rest of Catalonia, Spain and Europe. Good on Gaudí and modernism.

Barcelona: A Guide to Recent Architecture, Suzanna Strum, Ellipsis London Ltd, 2001. A look at some of the city's stunning buildings.

Catalan Cuisine, Colman Andrews, Grub Street, 1997. Describes the unique aspects of Catalan cooking.

Eating Out in Barcelona and Catalunya, Craig Allen and Robert Budwig, Rosendale Press, 1994. History of Catalan food and guide to Barcelona restaurants.

Forbidden Territory, Juan Goytisolo, Quartet Books, 1989. Autobiography by one of Spain's most important writers.

Homage to Catalonia, George Orwell. Penguin, 1989. Famous account of the author's experiences in the Spanish Civil War.

Homage to Barcelona, Colm Toíbín, Simon & Schuster, 1990

The City of Marvels (La Ciudad de los Prodigios), Eduardo Mendoza Seix Barral (Spanish), 1999, Collins (English). A novel set in Barcelona.

Barcelonas, Manuel Vázquez Montalbán, Verso, 1990. Chatty book covering culture, design, history and some of the city's personalities.

Other Insight Guides

The 190-title Insight Guides series includes eight books on Spain and its islands, all combining the exciting pictures and incisive text associated with this series.

Insight Guides

Insight Guide: Spain is an award-winning title in the series, containing top photography and providing complete background reading to the country.

Insight Guide: Madrid provides an insider's view of a city with a history full of colourful characters. The writers and photographers show you how to make the most of this dynamic destination, where life is lived to the full.

Insight Guide: Northern Spain provides comprehensive coverage of this alluring region, ranging from the bright lights of Bilbao to the breathtaking scenery of the Picos de Europa.

Insight Pocket Guides

Madrid and *Barcelona* are both covered in the complementary 120-title Insight Pocket Guide series. These books, which are specifically written for short-stay visitors, provide a series of carefully timed itineraries designed to help you get the most out of a short visit. Other titles in this series include *Bilbao and Northwest Spain*, *Costa Brava*, *Costa Blanca* and *Costa del Sol*.

Insight Compact Guides

Compact Guide: Barcelona, one of the titles in Apa Publications' third series of books, is the ultimate "portable encyclopedia" to the city. Up-to-date and packed with facts and photographs, it is the ideal easy-reference book to keep in your pocket or handbag.

ART & PHOTO CREDITS

Picture Spreads

Index